The Book of the
Yorkshire Terrier

The Book of the Yorkshire Terrier

Joan McDonald Brearley

Dedication

to
William H. A. Carr

with affection and gratitude for his belief in me, for his introduction to Dr. Herbert Axelrod, for his
encouragement and support, and all the joys of a
friendship that I have treasured for more than two decades

and to
Terrie and Tara of Tolestar

my first two Yorkshire Terriers that
endeared the breed to me forever.

Front Cover: Ch. Dot's Top Banana, owned by Dorothy Gaunt of West Covina, California. Photography by Missy Yuhl of North Hollywood, California.

Back Cover: Ms. Dinah-Mite of Lamplighter and daughter, Gucci Girl of Lamplighter, owned by
Barbara Beissel of Minneapolis, Minnesota.

Title Page: Irish Champion Gleno Playboy, owned by the Wildweir Kennels (Mrs. Leslie Gordon,
Jr., and Miss Janet Bennett), Glenview, Illinois.

ISBN 0-87666-940-2

Distributed in the UNITED STATES by T.F.H. Publications, Inc., 211 West Sylvania Avenue,
Neptune City, NJ 07753; in CANADA by H & L Pet Supplies Inc., 27 Kingston Crescent, Kitch-
ener, Ontario N2B 2T6; Rolf C. Hagen Ltd., 3225 Sartelon Street, Montreal 382 Quebec; in
ENGLAND by T.F.H. Publications Limited, 4 Kier Park, Ascot, Berkshire SL5 7DS; in
AUSTRALIA AND THE SOUTH PACIFIC by T.F.H. (Australia) Pty. Ltd., Box 149, Brookvale 2100
N.S.W., Australia; in NEW ZEALAND by Ross Haines & Son, Ltd., 18 Monmouth Street, Grey
Lynn, Auckland 2 New Zealand; in SINGAPORE AND MALAYSIA by MPH Distributors Pte.,
71-77 Stamford Road, Singapore 0617; in the PHILIPPINES by Bio-Research, 5 Lippay Street,
San Lorenzo Village, Makati, Rizal; in SOUTH AFRICA by Multipet Pty. Ltd., 30 Turners Avenue,
Durban 4001. Published by T.F.H. Publications Inc., Ltd., the British Crown Colony of Hong
Kong

Contents

Preface

It is not the purpose of this book to name each and every Yorkshire Terrier, breeder, owner, or exhibitor that ever lived, nor is it to chronicle a complete history of the breed since its beginning. There are other books which have striven to accomplish this and there are enough other things to be said about the breed without resorting to any such repetition. Neither is it the intention of this book to educate or instruct those of us that have been in the breed, for these many years. We have learned through experience the gentle art of doing our best to improve and perpetuate the Yorkshire Terrier.

It *is* the purpose of this book to reach those who are drawn to the breed as it exists today, and who wish to know the highlights of its history and background in the dog world. Our Yorkies have become so popular, and so admired, that anything new that is said or written about them can be of value if it adds to our knowledge regarding their care and place in our lives.

We would like to think that this book is another entry in our Yorkshire Terrier mutual admiration society and that all who read it and enjoy the little dogs represented will regard it as the meaningful tribute to our wonderful breed the author meant it to be.

Author Joan Brearley introduces one of her puppies to the show ring at a Match Show in the 1960s.

Acknowledgments

The author is grateful to many people for their aid in the publication of this book, dedicated as a lasting tribute to our magnificent breed. I owe a special thanks to my veterinarian of many years' standing, Dr. Robert R. Shomer, V.M.D.; to Fay Gold for her generous offering of back issues of her *Yorkshire Terrier Quarterly* magazine and other papers for research purposes; to Muriel Hunt, former editor of *Yorkie Tales*, for advance publicity and information garnered from her magazine; and to all of those owners, breeders, and exhibitors who so willingly submitted their photographs and memorabilia so that their little dogs could be part of this permanent record of the breed.

Joan McDonald Brearley
Sea Bright, New Jersey

Ch. Sahadi Scarlet O'Hara, bred by author Joan Brearley and owned and shown to her championship by Virginia Bull of Blairstown, New Jersey.

About the Author

Joan Brearley is the first to admit that animals in general—and dogs in particular—are a most important part of her life. Since childhood there has been a steady stream of dogs, cats, birds, fish, rabbits, snakes, alligators, etc., for her own personal menagerie. Over the years she has owned over thirty breeds of pure-bred dogs as well as countless mixtures, since the door was never closed to a needy or homeless animal.

A graduate of the American Academy of Dramatic Arts, where she studied acting and directing, Joan started her career as an actress, dancer, and writer for movie magazines. She studied ballet at the Agnes DeMille Studios in Carnegie Hall and was with an Oriental dance company which performed at the Carnegie Recital Hall. She studied journalism at Columbia University and has written for radio, television, and magazines, and she was a copywriter for some of the major New York City advertising agencies working on the accounts of Metro-Goldwyn-Mayer Studios, Burlington Mills, Cosmopolitan magazine, White Owl Cigars, and World Telegram & Sun newspapers.

While a television producer-director for a major network Joan worked on "Nick Carter, Master Detective"; "Did Justice Triumph"; and news and special feature programs. Joan has written, cast, directed, produced and, on occasion, starred in television commercials. She has written special material for such personalities as Dick Van Dyke, Amy Vanderbilt, William B. Williams, Gene Rayburn, Bill Stern, Herman Hickman, and many other prominent people in the entertainment world. She has appeared as a guest on several of the nation's most popular talk shows, including Mike Douglas, Joe Franklin, Cleveland Amory, David Susskind, and the Today Show, to name just a few. Joan was selected for inclusion in the *Directory of the Foremost Women in Communications* in 1969, and the book *Two Thousand Women of Achievement* in 1971.

Her accomplishments in the dog fancy include breeding and exhibiting top show dogs, being a writer and columnist of various magazines, and author of over thirty books on dogs and cats. For five years she was Executive Vice-President of the Popular Dogs Publishing Company and editor of *Popular Dogs* magazine, the national prestige publication for the fancy at the time.

Her editorials on the status and welfare of animals have been reproduced as educational pamphlets by dog clubs and organizations in many countries of the world.

Joan is just as active in the cat fancy, and in almost as many capacities. The same year her Afghan Hound Champion Sahadi Shikari won the Ken-L-Ration Award as Top Hound of the Year, one of her Siamese cats won the comparable honor in the cat fancy. She has owned and/or bred almost all breeds of cats. Many of her cats and dogs are Best in Show winners and have appeared in magazines and on television. For several years she was editor of the Cat Fanciers Association Annual Yearbook, and her book *All About Himalayan Cats* was published in 1976.

In addition to breeding and showing dogs since 1955, Joan has been active as a member and on the Board of Directors of the Kennel Club of Northern New Jersey, the Afghan Hound Club of America, the Stewards Club of America, and The Dog Fanciers Club. She has been an American Kennel Club judge of several breeds since 1961. She has appeared as a guest speaker at many dog clubs and humane organizations crusading for humane legislation, and has won several awards and citations for her work in this field. She is one of the best-known and most knowledgeable people in the animal world. Joan is proud of the fact that her Champion Sahadi Shikari was top-winning Afghan Hound in the history of the breed for several years, and remains in the number two position today. No other breeder can claim to have bred a Westminster Group winner in the first homebred litter. She has also bred champion Yorkshire Terriers.

Joan has recently been made a Trustee of the Morris Animal Foundation, does free-lance publicity and public relations work, is a Daughter of the American Revolution and the New York Genealogical Society. In her spare time she exhibits her needlework (for which she has also won prizes), haunts the art and auction galleries, and is a graduate auctioneer with the full title of Colonel.

This impressive list of activities doesn't include all of her accomplishments, since she has never been content to have just one interest at a time, but manages to dovetail several occupations and avocations to make for a fascinating career.

Joan lives with her dogs and cats in a townhouse on the oceanfront in Sea Bright, New Jersey.

Ch. Park Royal Centennial Eagle was bred and owned by Kathleen Park of Hacienda Heights, California.

CHAPTER ONE

Early History

The beauty of the Yorkshire Terrier, captured by artist Virginia Miller.

Many millions of years ago, dinosaurs and other strange-looking creatures roamed the earth. As "recently" as sixty million years ago, a mammal existed which resembled a civet cat and is believed to be the common ancestor of dogs, cats, wolves, and coyotes. This animal was the long-extinct Miacis (pronounced My-a-Kiss).

The Miacis were long-bodied, long-tailed, short-legged beasts that stalked and chased their prey, grasped it in their long, powerful, fanged jaws and gnashed their food with their teeth. Just 15,000,000 years ago the Tomcartus evolved from the earlier Miacis and provided an even truer genetic basis for the more highly intelligent prototype of the domesticated dog.

It is only fifteen to twenty thousand years since the first attempts were made to domesticate these ferocious, tree-climbing animals. Archaeologists have uncovered the skeletal remains of dogs that date back to the age of the cavemen. Apparently dogs co-existed with people as members of families in several ancient civilizations.

There are several schools of thought among scholars and scientists on the exact location of the very first creatures to live together with humans. Some contend that the continent of Africa was the original locale. Ancient remains unearthed near Lake Baika date back to 9000 years B.C. In the 1950s in an excavation in Pelegawra, Iraq, a canine fossil (appropriately labeled the Pelegawra dog) was discovered and is said to date back 14,500 years. Siberian remains are said to go back 20,000 years. The Jaquar Cave Dogs of North America have been dated circa 8400 B.C. Others claim the Chinese wolf to be the ancestor of the dog.

Advocates of the theory on the Chinese wolf point out that a language barrier was responsible for the Chinese wolf not being known or acknowledged in earlier comparisons. Because scientists could not yet translate Chinese writing, they could not study or authenticate the early Oriental findings. The theory is also based on the presence of the overhanging bone found in the jawbone of both the Chinese wolf and the dog. This is believed to be significant in the change from their being strictly carnivorous to creatures that eventually became omnivorous.

DOMESTICATION OF DOGS

The general consensus of opinion among scientists dealing in prehistoric and archaeological studies seems to settle on the likelihood that dogs were being domesticated in many parts of the world at approximately the same period in time. Since dogs were to become so essential to man's very existence, they naturally were absorbed into family life wherever and whenever they were found.

Climate, geography, and other environmental conditions all played a part in the evolution of the dog and, much later, the individual types and sizes and breeds of dogs.

The famous Sir Edwin Landseer's painting of three Scotch Terriers staking out a rodent hole in the fields. These little terriers are said to be a strong influence in the development of the Yorkshire Terrier. Entitled "Ratcatchers" and painted about 1821, the picture identifies the terriers, as Vixen, Brutus, and Boxer.

The three most primitive types originated in three parts of the globe. While all bore certain very exact characteristics, the wolf-type (the Dingo) seemed to evolve in southern Asia, the Pariahs in Asia Minor and Japan, and the Basenjis in Africa.

The Dingo found its way north to Russia and Alaska, across what is now the Bering Strait, into North America. The Pariahs moved far north and developed into the various northern breeds of the Arctic regions. The Basenjis and Greyhounds coursed the desert sands and hunted in the jungles of Africa when they weren't guarding royal palaces in Egypt. As dogs found their way across Europe, they served as guard dogs in the castles, rescue dogs in the Alps, barge dogs

on the canals, and hunting dogs in the forests. The smaller dogs were bred down smaller and smaller still, and became companions and pets for the aristocracy. Kings and queens of the world have always maintained their own personal kennels for their favorite breeds.

DEVELOPMENT OF BREEDS

While cavemen used dogs primarily as hunters to help provide meat (and to be served as meat as well) they also made use of the fur as clothing and sought warmth from the dogs' bodies. Dogs were to become even more functional as time went by, according to the dictates of climates and geographical regions. Definite physical changes were taking place; these eventually would distinguish one dog from another even within the same area. Ears ranged in size from the little flaps that we see on terriers to the large upright ears on the Ibizan Hounds. Noses either flattened greatly as they did with Pekingese or they grew to amazing lengths which we see in the Borzoi. Tails grew to be long and plumey such as those we see on the Siberian Husky or doubled up into a curl such as those on the Pug. Legs grew long and thin for coursing breeds such as the Greyhounds or were bent and short for the digging breeds like the Dachshunds and the Bassetts. Sizes went from one extreme to the other, ranging from the tiniest Chihuahua all the way up to the biggest of all breeds, the Irish Wolfhound. Coat lengths became longer or shorter. The northern breeds developed thick, woolly coats and the dogs that worked in the warm climates grew smooth, short coats.

SENSORY PERCEPTION

As dogs changed in physical appearance, their instincts and sensory perception also developed. In some breeds, the German Shepherd for instance, the sense of smell is said to be twenty million times keener than in his human counterpart, allowing it to pick up and follow the scents of other animals miles in the distance. Dogs' eyes developed to such a degree of sharpness that they could spot moving prey on the horizon far across desert sands. Their hearing became so acute that they were able to pick up the sound of the smallest creatures rustling in the leaves across an open field or in a dense forest.

All things considered, it becomes easy to comprehend why man and dog became such successful partners in the fight for survival—and why their attraction and affection for each other is such a wondrous thing.

Toy Smart is the name of the Yorkshire Terrier in this picture from Cassel's *New Illustrated Book of the Dog.* Painted in 1881 by C. Burton Barber, a court painter to Queen Victoria, this painting is perhaps one of the best known of the earlier Yorkshires.

Early Yorkshire breeder Mrs. H.M. Tufille of Hampton Hill, England, with three of her Yorkies: Morpeth Mousie, Augy, and Morpeth Pearl.

CHAPTER TWO

The Breed in England

International Champion Blue Dolly, photographed at five years of age. Dolly earned her English championship before being imported to the United States.

The Yorkshire Terrier is often referred to as a "man-made" breed inasmuch as the people of Yorkshire, England, combined several different breeds of so-called terriers together before a dog resembling our Yorkies came into being as a breed unto itself. However, even from its earliest beginnings its purpose and destiny was to be the best possible little dog to cover ground in the pursuit of vermin and other small game.

The first person known to have written about them was Dame Juliana Berness, Prioress of the Sopwell Nunnery in Hertfordshire back in the 15th century. In a catalog on sporting dogs, she referred to this type of dog as "terras" or "terrarius" throughout the text of this early volume. The name Terrier eventually evolved and came from the Latin word *terra*, or land, and generally connoted "earth dogs" since they hunted and were said to "follow their quarry to the ground." We know them to be indigenous to England.

Another famous writer on animals from earliest times was Dr. Johannes Caius, founder of Caius College in Cambridge, England, and physician to Queen Elizabeth I. In the sixteenth century, he described these spunky little dogs: "Another sorte that there is which hunteth the

Foxe and the Badger or Greye onely, whom we call Terrars. They creep into the ground, and by that means make afrayde, nype, and bite the fox and badger in such sorte that they eyther teare them in pieces with theyr teeth beying in the bosome of the earth, or else hayle and pull them perforce out of theyr lurking angles, dark dungeons and close caves."

By 1603 these rugged little Terriers, which Dr. Caius also referred to as "beggerly beasts," were further described as being "brought out of the barbarous borders from the uttermost countryes northward," and were highly thought of by King James the First of England.

In 1603, King James ordered six "earth dogges or terrieres" from Argyl to be sent to France as a gift, with orders that they be sent by two separate ships to ensure their safe passage. This act made these so-called "earth dogs" the first to be granted royal patronage.

While these dogs were probably from northernmost Scotland and the forerunners of the Skye Terrier, within half a century or so there is written reference to color distinctions within their ranks; namely, black and tan, tan, or red-brown. There were also references made to straight and

dogs of that period. The painting was used as the frontispiece to Stonehenge's famous book, *Dogs of the British Isles*. In addition to Mr. Fitter's "Dandy," Mr. Pearce's "Venture," and Mr. Radcliff's "Rough," center stage is occupied by Mr. Spink's "Bounce," referred to in the book as a Halifax Blue-Fawn or Yorkshire Terrier. Bounce was the grandsire of the famous Huddersfield Ben.

During the 1880s, the famous British magazine, *Punch*, featured several artists' drawings within their pages depicting little dogs of the Yorkshire Terrier type. *Harper's Weekly* was another nineteenth-century publication which featured animal drawings of toy breeds resembling the Yorkshires. By 1897, Arthur Wardle, famous dog artist, came upon the scene with a painting of several little dogs including two Yorkshires. He later produced Yorkie drawings for the book *Modern Dogs*.

During the 1880s, many prints were circulated featuring Yorkshire Terriers. Perhaps the most famous of these was the drawing for the illustration in Stonehenge's 1878 book, featuring Huddersfield Ben and Katie, another famous bitch of those early days in the breed.

As for establishing the current criteria for the Yorkshire Terrier, it was famous dog-man Vero Shaw who selected Mrs. M.A. Foster's Toy Smart to represent the breed in the famous C. Burton Barbor's painting, along with an Italian Greyhound and a Pug. Toy Smart had won at the Alexandra Palace Show, July 1879, and it was deemed a great honor to appear in the painting by Barbor, who along with the aforementioned Sir Edwin Landseer was regarded as one of the two painters to the court of Queen Victoria. This is perhaps one of the best known of all dog paintings of that era and appeared in Cassel's *New Illustrated Book of the Dog*.

One of the very first paintings depicting a Yorkshire with hair tied up in a topknot appeared about 1900. The painting shows a Yorkie floating on a raft with two young boys, and is entitled *Jack, Fred and Rags Floating on the Pond*. The little bow is bright blue.

QUEEN ELIZABETH'S SEA DOGS

It is said that a little dog strongly resembling the Yorkshire Terrier came to America on the good ship Mayflower. Anyone visiting Plymouth, England, who looks into the history of the entire venture of the sailing of the May-

flower, will learn of Queen Elizabeth's dogs—referred to in that area as Elizabeth's sea dogs. There is also a painting, in the collection of the Viscount De L'Isle, showing the sixty-six-year old Queen dancing the Spanish Panic with Leicester and a room full of musicians and courtiers. Front and center in the painting sits a small dog, tan and blackish-blue with a distinctly Yorkshire Terrier appearance. There is no topknot, but the resemblance is unmistakable.

This may be one of the few great works that features our breed so distinctly, for the Yorkshire took so long to become the breed as we know it today that it did not appear in the earlier works of the great masters.

One of the oldest, though not most famous, of all little dogs appearing in art work that resembles the Yorkshire Terrier, is the 1776 painting of the little Scottish girl in a big hat, and muff, her little dog shivering at her feet. This portrait was painted by a famous British artist and was commissioned by the little girl's father, a Scottish Duke. The dog was colored black and tan, but had a wiry coat. Perhaps the most interesting aspect of the winter scene was that the tail was cropped and the ears were erect: two positive signs that the Yorkshire Terrier was on its way as far back as 1776.

FAMOUS EARLY DOGS

Mr. W. Eastwood was the breeder of Huddersfield Ben, the earliest and perhaps most famous of all early Yorkshire Terriers. Mr. Eastwood, along with Mr. John Richardson of Halifax, held the theory that the Yorkshire was created by breeding a Waterside Terrier (popular during the reign of King William IV) to a Clydesdale or Skye Terrier bitch. (If a worthy specimen of the approximately six-pound rare Waterside Terrier could be found today it would make for an interesting experiment!)

Mr. Eastwood's Huddersfield Ben (KCSB 3612) was whelped in 1865, and before his early demise in 1871 had sired enough get to allow his name to appear in the pedigrees of many of that era's top Yorkshires.

Around the turn of the century, James Watson (in his book called, simply, *Dog Book*) stated that all Yorkshire Terrier pedigrees go back to Swift's dog, Old Crab, and Kershaws Old Kitty. Crab was a Black and Tan Terrier with a long coat, while Kitty was a drop-eared Skye, stolen from Manchester and later owned by Mr. J. Kershaw.

This pedigree dates back to 1850, but fifty out of eighty Broken-haired Scotch and Yorkshire Terriers in the stud book have no pedigrees at all. It is from this Crab and Kitty background that Huddersfield Ben descends. He was registered as being out of Mr. Boscovitch's dog out of Lady. He was winner of many variety class prizes, though records of these actual wins have not been found. Ben was first shown in December 1869 at the Manchester show.

Known as "the Father of Yorkshire Terriers," Ben later was owned by a Mrs. Jonas Foster of Bradford, Yorkshire, who was considered a pioneer in the development of the Yorkshire Terrier, as she exhibited extensively. Mrs. Foster also owned Champion Ted, Walshaws Old Sandy, Inmans Don, and Ramsdowns Bounce—which were all in the pedigree of the great Huddersfield Ben.

It was Ben that led to the popularity of the smaller sized Yorkie, and he was acknowledged to be the greatest stud in the breed during his lifetime. It was considered a great loss to the breed when Ben was killed accidentally in September 1871 at only six-and-a-half years of age. It can only be imagined what his additional contribution to this breed would have been had he lived on.

The body of Huddersfield Ben was given over to a taxidermist after his death, and Ben remained encased in glass for many years. Photographs were taken of Ben; and for a while the remains were in the possession of famous dog man Theo Marples.

In addition there was Ben's son, Mozart, whelped in 1869 out of Frisk, and owned by Miss Alderson. Some of Mozart's well-known get were Little Katie, Bismarc, Mr. J. Hills Sandy, Benson, Bruce, Emperor, and Doctor Spark (that Mr. J. Stell also exhibited at the shows as Charley).

Another one of the first breeders of the Yorkshire Terrier was Mr. Peter Eden. Known for his Pugs and Bulldogs, he was also lauded for publicizing the Yorkshire Terrier—so much so that it led to the erroneous belief that he was the "inventor of the Yorkshire Terrier." He did, indeed, purchase many little dogs from the working men in Yorkshire that were breeding them, including a dog named Albert. Albert was shown from 1863 to 1865 and was said to be a prime example of correct Yorkshire type at that time; however, Mr. Eden's work cannot be compared to the impetus Mrs. Jonas Foster provided for the breed.

Mrs. M.A. Foster's Champion Ted was winner of 265 awards and can be classed, along with Huddersfield Ben, as one of the outstanding early contributors to the breed. Ted was a five-pound marvel, whelped July 20, 1883, and was by Young Royal out of Annie. He reigned supreme during a six-year career in the show rings. Ted was purchased by Mrs. Foster in 1887 when he was just four years old and weighed four-and-a-half pounds.

Ted was advertised in the Kennel Club Gazette for stud service, and apparently he was successful. By 1894, eight out of twenty-eight stud book registrations listed him as sire. Just as Huddersfield Ben was a prepotent sire, Ted was also unsurpassed, and produced many fine specimens. He was himself a direct descendant of Huddersfield Ben.

Mrs. Foster was the first woman to judge at a dog show in England—at the 1889 Leeds show. In 1968, she was cited by her peers in the dog fancy as being the oldest known living breeder of Yorkshire Terriers in all of England.

LADY EDITH WINDHAM-DAWSON

Another of the most famous of all English kennels was that of Lady Edith Windham-Dawson. Her kennel name was Soham, which appears in many of the Yorkshire Terrier pedigrees in show rings all over the world even today. Breeder of many champions and also a dog show judge, her Champion James of Soham helped to make Yorkshire Terrier history several decades ago.

Her Champion Victoria, whelped in 1932, was the best Yorkshire Terrier bitch in England at the time and won eight Championship Certificates, as well as numerous First Cup and Special awards. The sire was Champion Eminent, and she was out of Butys.

Lady Windham's James had a litter sister named Champion Rose Crystal, another top bitch, along with her Champion Rose of the World of Soham shown in 1932, and Champion Thyra of Soham.

Some of her other top dogs were David, Eira, Blue Nina, Gloria and Tiny Dutch. Photographs of these dogs can be found in *Hutchinson's Dog Encyclopedia*, along with Harringay Beauty, bred by Mr. E.H. Clenshaw and later purchased by Lady Edith Windham-Dawson for her Soham line. She was also owner of Huddersfield Ben for a time. After World War II, Lady Windham moved to Ireland, where she continued to exhibit and breed her little Yorkshires.

19

MRS. ANNIE SWAN

Mrs. Annie Swan became a prominent breeder, exhibitor, and Yorkshire authority, as well as a canine columnist for many of the leading dog journals abroad. She later became a judge and had forty-six Yorkshires entered under her when she officiated at the Crystal Palace Show in 1929. She is the author of *The Yorkshire Terrier Handbook*, first published in 1958, and reprinted in 1964 by Nicholson and Watson in England. This wonderful little volume is dedicated to her good friend, Lady Edith Windham-Dawson.

Annie Swan's Invincia kennel name is still known and highly regarded on both sides of the Atlantic. Her Splendour of Invincia won seventeen Championship Certificates, and her Invincible of Invincia won fourteen during their respective ring careers. Another famous Invincia dog was Champion Delite of Invincia, shown in 1939. Annie Swan died, at ninety-six years of age, in 1975.

OTHER PROMINENT BREEDERS

When recalling other noteworthy breeders, the names of Mesdames Walton and Beard immediately come to mind. They were owners of Ashton Queen, the bitch that won more prizes than any other living Yorkshire Terrier during its lifetime.

Pictured in a win under judge Teddy Hayes is Ch. Blue Velvet of Soham, imported from Ireland by Mrs. Leslie Gordon and Miss Janet Bennett of Glenview, Illinois. Whelped in 1954, his breeder was Lady Edith Windham. His sire was English and Irish Ch. Twinkle Star of Clu-Mor ex Regine of Soham. He was the sire of one champion and his show record also included seventeen Toy Groups, thirty Group Placings, and fifty Bests of Breed.

Mr. George Hollas of Halifax and Tom Hooton were two other important breeders, as were C.H. Mitchell of Bolton, Mr. J. Shufflebotham of Macclesfield, and Mr. J. Brearley with his Matchless prefix. (The author has done her best to trace the connection to this Brearley with her late husband's genealogy, but at the time this book went to press had not been successful.)

Other outstanding breeder-exhibitors were Mr. H. Lemon, Mr. H. Walton, W. Scolleys, Mr. Dick Marshall, Mr. W. Wood, Mr. C.H. Marlin, Mr. T.J. Cooper, Mr. J. Hardman, and Mr. E. Hayes.

We also see among the names of early supporters of the breed Mr. C. Coates and his dog Burmantoft Little Swell, a dog well known for his luxurious coat. There were T. Moody and his Blossom kennel name, Mr. J. Wood, Mr. J. Bragg, Mr. J. Duwan, Mr. J. Clark, Mr. T. Foster, Mr. F.R. Foster (both senior and junior), and Dave Batty—known for his Smart Boy dog that enjoyed an illustrious show career.

Other pioneers were J.W. Rowley and his son-in-law J. Dunman, who served as Secretary of the Yorkshire Terrier Club in London for a while. Mr. Hague and Mr. J. Sidney were two others. Mr. Sidney rated his own Sneinton Amythyst so highly that it was placed along with Huddersfield Ben and Ted on the pages of his four-volume edition of *The Kennel Encyclopedia*, published in 1911.

The Sneinton prefix owned by the Wiltain Shows was a top winner that year with Champion Sneinton Orchid and Champion Sneinton Turquoise, both of *unregistered* parents. Dogs of the Sneinton prefix were big that year, winning almost everything to be won from the classes at shows including Crufts, the Crystal Palace, and the shows held by the Welsh Kennel Club.

Other breeders of stature during the years before the first World War were the Greenwoods of Halifax with their Pellon kennel name; the judge Mr. Austin Hollingworth; Mr. Harrison of Hyde; Mrs. Ethel Munday, author of *The Popular Yorkshire Terrier* in the United States in 1963; Miss Vera Munday, who owned and bred the Yadnum dogs; George Thomkins, of the Charleview prefix; Mr. E.J. Hubbard; Mr. J. Jackson; Mr. J. Hardman; and Mrs. R. Green, of Ovendon fame.

Miss Olive Saunders, especially recognized for her Champion Lady Roma, was well known for her many years of devotion to the breed before her health failed. Her old stock went to Lady Edith Windham-Dawson. Mrs. E. Smith of Suprema kennel fame, Mrs. May Wood and her Pookshill kennel name, and Mrs. P.I. Noakes were also prominent during the 1930s.

EARLY ENGLISH EXPORTS

The decade of the forties saw many of the top English and Irish breeders exporting some of their best stock to help establish kennels in America. Among them was Mrs. H. D. Burfield of the Buranthea line. Several top winners were sent to Mrs. Leslie Gordon and Miss Janet Bennett of Wildweir fame in the United States. Mr. A. Hughes sent some of his Coulgorm line, including Coulgorm Gay Lady. Mrs. G. M. Bradley sent several Yorkies to the United States, where they also won championships for their new owners.

We must also acknowledge the contribution to the breed from Mrs. J. A. Russell, Mr. W. M. Hayes, Mrs. M. Riley, Mr. and Mrs. H. Cross, Mrs. V. Seymour, Mrs. M. A. Crookshank, Miss G. Stedman, Mr. and Mrs. F. L. Chandler, Mrs. M. Macquire, Mrs. M. Belton, Mr. and Mrs. H. Griffiths, Miss E. Martin, Mrs. M. Hebson, Mrs. M. Nunn, and Mrs. E. A. Stirk of Stirkeans kennel fame.

Mrs. A. E. Palmer also exported some of her Winpal dogs. For quite some time Mrs. Palmer was associated with Lady Edith Windham-Dawson, and she attributes a great deal of her success to that relationship before going out on her own.

Mrs. L. Briggs of the Temple Vale prefix, Mrs. M. Belton, Mrs. V. Mair, Mr. Whiting, Miss M. Howes, Mr. and Mrs. B. Henry, Mrs. Allcock's Tower Hill dogs, Mr. and Mrs. G. Porter and their Pedirnin name, Mrs. H. Thomasson, Mrs. E. M. London, and Mrs. N. Wilkinson all enjoyed their share of success at this time.

More recently we see the names of Mrs. M. Allen and her Obelisk kennels, Mr. A. Armstrong, Mrs. Lowrie, Miss Lewis Hughes, Miss P. Hepworth, Mrs. D. Beech, Mrs. F. C. Raine, Mrs. I. H. Woods, and Mrs. V. Hargreaves.

The list of breeders and exhibitors of champions in our breed is lengthy, both before and after World War II. Many of the names just cited were the producers of champions, along with many others. They make up a list far too long to contain in a book of this size and nature.

Ch. Lyndoney Kindrum Valentine, an English import owned by Mrs. Leslie Gordon and Janet Bennett. Bred by Alan Burrell, Valentine was whelped in 1968 and had a Toy Group to his credit with additional placings. The sire was Bonnie Wee Willie ex Lyndoney Annabelle.

THE FORMATION OF YORKIE CLUBS

As far back as the turn of the century, Yorkshire Terrier popularity grew steadily and area Yorkshire Terrier clubs began to form with the express purposes of attempting to "standardize" the breed and to promote exhibition. These clubs sponsored entries at the various dog shows, with many offering valuable cups to the winners.

While the clubs for the most part served their purpose of standardization, there was still dissension in the ranks of the breeders on many of the finer points of the breed.

Mr. Fred Poole, a prominent breeder in the North of England, was quoted as saying, "I am quite satisfied with type, as I think a good specimen of today is as near perfection as it is possible to get. My club, the Halifax and District Yorkshire Terrier Club, is the oldest society in existence of its kind, and going very strong, with plenty of members. All the Champion dogs of the past and present owe their origin to Halifax, such as Halifax Marvel, the sire of Champion Merry Monarch and Champion Aston Queen."

On the contrary, another important breeder, Mr. Thomas Hooton, was quoted as saying, "I am not satisfied with the type, generally speaking. I want the size lowered, and the animals shorter in body. My ideal is a four-and-a-half pound weight for dogs, and four pounds for bitches." Mr. Hooten continued, "There has, however, been a great improvement in the last few years. I do not set much store on the value of points as laid down, but would give more for size, shape, and activity." And though the controversy raged on, both men were willing to be quoted by Herbert Compton in his book *The Twentieth Century Dog*, published in 1904.

THE START OF THE COLOR CONTROVERSY

We must also take note that in the same book the first rumblings of a controversy on correct color in the breed was heard. Mr. F. Randall, a well-known breeder in the South of England, was quoted as saying, "In my opinion the type of Yorkshire Terrier now shown in London and the South cannot be improved. I consider the *dark*, steel-blue (not silver) a great improvement on the pale-coloured dogs which. . .are easier to breed than the darker ones."

Eighty years later the color question still ignites tempers and perplexes breeders who are more inclined toward personal preferences for their breeding programs. So, while color is seen as a current problem and has not changed from "way back then," most everything else in the breed has been altered by the rigors of time and the extent of the Yorkshire's popularity.

CHANGING TIMES

In the 1920s, Darley Matheson wrote in his book, *Terriers*, the following appraisal of the Yorkshire Terrier in England at that time:

"Although the Yorkshire Terrier has always maintained a certain amount of public support, it has never been one of those varieties creating a craze, as in the case of the Pekingese, Pomeranian, Alsatian Wolf Dog, etc."

We must remember that during the 1920s Yorkie registrations in England were still very low, numbering in the vicinity of 350 to under 500. In addition to Mr. Poole's Halifax and the District Yorkshire Terrier Club, there were also the Bradford Yorkshire Terrier Club, the Oldham Yorkshire Terrier Society, and the Yorkshire Terrier Club, all encouraging the advance of the breed. Entries at the shows were usually under twenty dogs per show, with perhaps a dozen or fewer championship shows at which Yorkies appeared. While these were the years that the famous Champion Invincible of Invincia was being shown, as few as five Yorkshire Terriers were recognized for championships in 1928.

MODERN BRITISH EXPORTS

As the 1960s progressed and the 1970s loomed ahead, the British exports to the United States—indeed, to the entire world—still saw the Yorkshire Terrier at the top of the list.

In 1967, there were 1,213 Yorkshire Terriers exported to several foreign countries, with the majority of them arriving in the United States. In 1968, there were 1,743 Yorkies exported; in 1969, there were 2,361. Again it was the number one breed exported to countries all over the world.

In 1970, as Britain began a new decade with almost 12,000 dogs exported, the Yorkie continued to be the top breed sent abroad. In that year, 2,265 Yorkshires left Britain. By the middle of the 1970s, Britain boasted exports of almost 15,000 dogs, with 2,805 of those being Yorkshires. In a year that saw 15,147 Yorkshire Terrier registrations, the breed replaced the Alsatian as having registered the most dogs, a position the Alsatian had held since 1965. The breed continued to escalate into the 1980s with no sign of decline—a clear indication of the Yorkshire Terrier's enormous appeal.

By 1980, the Yorkshire Terrier headed the list of canine exports with several thousand leaving Britain for foreign shores. By 1982, the breed ranked number eleven in the United States, with over 25,000 registrations for the year 1981.

Blairsville Seal of Approval, an English Import whelped in August 1979, owned by Terence Childs and Joseph Champagne of the Barnhill Kennels in Woodbury, Connecticut. Bred by Frances Boyd, sired by Ch. Blairsville Royal Seal.

THE YORKSHIRE TERRIER CLUB IN ENGLAND

The Yorkshire Terrier Club in England, founded in 1898, has seen the breed increase in tremendous numbers since that beginning. While the club held but one show a year in those early days, they now have three shows each season, with the major event held in London. The Open show and the Members Limited show are held in Essex, where the greatest collection of Yorkshires may be found. Usually a social event is held each year in London, with the club's blue and gold colors in evidence as the theme.

The club also holds a program for the training of judges, since the popularity of the breed has necessitated the need for more judges at the shows. The judge for the club's Championship show is selected at an annual general meeting with the members casting votes for their favorite adjudicator.

The first standard for the breed was drawn up in 1898, based on a 100-point system. That standard held until January of 1950, when a new standard was adopted with emphasis still being on formation and terrier appearance, color of hair on the body, and richness of tan on the head and body.

CRUFTS DOG SHOW

Sometimes referred to as "the greatest show on earth," with all apologies to P. T. Barnum, the Crufts Dog Show was first held in 1891 at the Agricultural Hall in Islington. Apart from the war years (when most all dog shows on both sides of the Atlantic were affected) and one civil disaster, Crufts has continued to the present date with only one change of ownership. Originally called the Crufts Great International Show, it is held every February, either just before or just after the February date of the Westminster Kennel Club in New York City. While the selection of a February Westminster date depends largely on the availability of the Madison Square Garden facilities, the February date for Crufts is determined by the February closing of the game season, since the show originally featured gun dogs and sporting dogs. It was attended by dogs from many nations until the quarantine for foreign dogs prevented entries from other countries. However, it remains the largest dog show in the world, with entries currently near the ten thousand mark.

LADIES DAY

In 1972, a Yorkshire Terrier bitch was winner of the Toy Group at Crufts and Best in Show All-breeds in the Birmingham Show's entry of 7,800. English Champion Deebee's BeeBee was also Best in Show at the Yorkshire Terrier Club of England over an entry of 250 dogs. She is also a multiple Group winner and was undefeated as a champion.

After her phenomenal success in the show ring, she was imported to the United States by new owner Mr. Stanley Lipman of Kings Point, Long Island, New York, and was handled for him by Richard Bauer on the East Coast and by Frank T. Sabella on the West Coast.

Just two years later, at the 1974 Crufts, another little lady brought new honor to the breed by winning Reserve Best in Show. Her name was Champion Blairsville Most Royale, and her owner, breeder, and handler was Mr. Brian Lister. A gift for Mrs. Lister at Christmas in 1963 got the Listers started in the breed, and at the time of this win they had bred six champions at their Blairsville Kennels, including the top winning Yorkie for 1972, Champion Blairsville Samantha. Most Royale was the biggest winning Yorkie of all time in Great Britain. She was Supreme Best in Show at the Belfast Championship Show and Reserve Best in Show at Richmond before her triumph at Crufts. At her last four shows before Crufts, she was unbeaten as a Toy. Mrs. D. Beech was the judge for the breed, and Mrs. De Casembroot was the Best in Show judge. Most Royale was retired from the ring and into motherhood.

THE KENNEL CLUB STANDARD FOR THE YORKSHIRE TERRIER

General appearance: Should be that of a long-coated toy terrier, the coat hanging quite straight and evenly down each side, a parting extending from the nose to the end of the tail. The animal should be very compact and neat, the carriage being very upright and conveying an 'important' air. The general outline should convey the impression of a vigorous and well-proportioned body.

Head and skull: Head should be rather small and flat, not too prominent or round in the skull, nor too long in the muzzle, with a perfect black nose. The fall on the head to be long, of a rich golden tan, deeper in colour at the sides of the head about the ear roots, and on the muzzle where it should be very long. On no account must the tan on the head extend on to the neck, nor must there be any sooty or dark hair intermingled with any of the tan.

Eyes: Medium, dark and sparkling, having a sharp intelligent expression, and placed so as to look directly forward. They should not be prominent and the edge of the eyelids should be of a dark colour.

Ears: Small V-shaped, and carried erect or semi-erect, and not far apart, covered with short hair, colour to be of a very deep rich tan.

Mouth: Perfectly even, with teeth as sound as possible. An animal having lost any teeth through accident not to be faulted providing the jaws are even.

Forequarters: Legs quite straight, well covered with hair of a rich golden tan a few shades lighter at the ends than at the roots, not extending higher on the forelegs than the elbow.

Body: Very compact with a good loin. Level on the top of the back.

Hindquarters: Legs quite straight, well covered with hair of a rich golden tan, a few shades lighter at the ends than at the roots, not extending higher on the hind legs than the stifle.

Feet: As round as possible; the toe-nails black.

Tail: Cut to medium length; with plenty of hair, darker blue in colour than the rest of the body, especially at the end of the tail, and carried a little higher than the level of the back.

Coat: The hair on the body moderately long and perfectly straight (not wavy), glossy like silk, and of a fine silky texture.

Colour: A dark steel blue (not silver blue), extending from the occiput (or back of skull) to the root of tail, and on no account mingled with fawn, bronze or dark hairs. The hair on the chest a rich bright tan. All tan hair should be darker at the roots than in the middle, shading to a still lighter tan at the tips.

Weight and size: Weight up to 7 pounds.

Note: Male animals should have two apparently normal testicles fully descended into the scrotum.

American Canadian Ch. Topsy of Tolestar, imported from England in the 1960s by David and Nancy Lerner, later owned by Ann Seranne.

A top winner in the early 1950s, the English import Ch. Little Sir Model was the first Yorkie to win an all-breed Best in Show (in 1952). His record was 7 Bests in Show, 31 Toy Group Firsts, 23 Group Placings and 63 Bests of Breed. Whelped in 1948, "Rags" was bred by Mrs. M. Smart and sired by English Champion Ben's Blue Pride, the first Yorkie to earn an English title after World War Two. His dam was Allenby Queen. Owned and shown by Mrs. Leslie Gordon and Miss Janet Bennett.

WESTMINSTER KENNEL CLUB
BEST
YORKSHIRE TERRIER
IN THE SHOW

SHAFER

The winner at Westminster in 1962 was English import Ch. Topsy of Tolestar. Nancy Lerner handled. Shafer photo.

CHAPTER THREE

The Yorkshire Terrier Comes to America

Around 1957, famous dog photographer Joan Ludwig snapped this eight-month old puppy owned by Kay Finch, the lady responsible for firmly establishing the breed in the United States.

It is said that a few Yorkshire Terriers were seen in the United States around 1880, with type being described as not well established among them and weights ranging anywhere between just under three pounds up to thirteen pounds.

The first Yorkshire Terrier to be registered in the United States was a bitch named Belle. She was listed as #3307, recorded as blue and tan in color, and whelped in 1877. Her owner was listed as a Mr. A. E. Godeffroy. This entry was taken from A. N. Rouse's ledger, *The National American Kennel Club Stud Book*, which served as the basis for the registering of purebred dogs when the American Kennel Club opened its stud books after it became organized in 1884.

EARLY RECORDS AND REGISTRATIONS

Before the American Kennel Club became established as *the* organization for the registration of purebred dogs, the American Kennel Club Register kept track of some of the breedings. These were compiled by Ernest Watson, a famous dog man and dog writer during the 1880s. Mr. Watson was influential in the formation of the American Kennel Club originally based in Philadelphia, as well. Since his records did not become a part of the first American Kennel Club records, we must list two early imports of our breed which date back as far as 1882. Numbers 667 and 668 in Volume 1 of 1883 were as follows:

> #667 Jim, blue and tan, dog, whelped September 1882. Breeder Mr. Andrew Ford, Glasgow, Scotland. Owners, Messrs. J. A. Nickerson and R. R. Bushell, P.O. Box 2574, Boston, Massachusetts.

> #668 Rose, blue and tan bitch, whelped November 1882. Breeder, Mr. N. McDonald, Glasgow, Scotland. Owners J. A. Nickerson and T. R. Bushell, P.O. Box 2574, Boston, Massachusetts.

By 1889, the American Kennel Club began publishing its own magazine. The purpose of the magazine was to feature articles of interest to dog owners, and specifically to publish the records of the purebred dogs registered with them and contained in the stud books. The January 1889 issue of the *American Kennel Gazette* carried the following information:

Gyp, b. Joseph Bell's, by Tony — owners Lady, September 18, 1887.

Lady, b. Joseph Bell's, sire and dam, and date of birth unknown.

Nelly, b. Joseph Bell's, by Tony — owners Lady, September, 1888.

The October 1890 issue of the *American Kennel Gazette* reported the first champion of record, a dog named Bradford Harry. The complete entry read as follows:

Bradford Harry (13,124)
P. H. Coombs, Bangor, Maine. Breeder, W. Beal, England. Whelped May 16, 1885; blue and tan; by Bruce, out of Lady, by Tyler, out of Lady; Tyler, by Huddersfield Ben, out of Kitty; Bruce, by Sandy, out of Patterson's Minnie; Sandy, by Bateman's Sandy, out of Venus.
Bench Shows, 1st, Newcastle, 2nd, Darlington, 1887; 1st and Special, Boston, 1888; 1st and Special, New Bedford, New York and Lynn; 1st, Troy; equal 1st, Boston, 1889.

In the aforementioned January 1889 issue of the *American Kennel Gazette* there also appeared what seems to be the first written critique of a judging of Yorkshire Terriers at a Westminster Kennel Club show. Judge D. Baillie wrote of his Yorkshire Terrier assignment at this thirteenth annual Madison Square Garden event as follows:

"Yorkshire Terriers. Open dogs; A very strong class. Bradford Harry beats Teddy (second) in color of head and texture of coat. Teddy has a wonderfully long coat for an old dog. Jim (third) is a very nice dog, but not so good in color as the winners. Open bitches were not so strong in quality as the dogs, but Jess (first) stood out well from the others. Guenn (second), Silver (third), were much lighter in color."

In 1885 in Providence, Rhode Island, a First Annual Dog Show was held at Drew's Dime Museum. Judge Thomas Alrich was the judge for the five-day show which lasted from May 18 to 23, and there were five Yorkshire Terriers entered. Their numbers in the catalogue were 47 through 51, and three out of the five were for sale. The class was #17 and for the best entry a Silver Berry Set in Case was offered. For the second best, the catalogue merely stated "Cup."

Number 47 was named Daisey, while the rest of the entry read: "blue and tan, 1 year, Dot, Stubb. $25. Coddling & Boutelle, 805 Eddy Street, Providence."

Entries 48 and 49 were also listed under Coddling and Boutelle, 805 Eddy Street. Number 48 was Dixie, listed as "silver, 4 years, imported. $25." Apparently the fact that she was imported had no affect on her value. Number 49 was "Tiney, silver, 2 years, imported bitch, Wheeler's dog. Not for sale."

And knowing how important coat color is in the breed today, how does the description of Number 50 set for a selling point? "Ben, blue and gray, 15 months, imported. Not for sale. Robert Welch." Number 51 was listed as "Teddy, blue and tan, 2½ years. $35. Thomas Smith, 31 Welden Street, Providence."

We modern advocates of the breed can only hope the Silver Berry Set did not go to the blue and gray Yorkshire Terrier!

In the 1880s the list of owners, breeders, and exhibitors of Yorkshire Terriers included Peter Cassidy (one of the earliest on the scene), Mr. and Mrs. Henry Kisteman, Frank Thompson, Thomas Kallager, Miss Bessie French, breeder and dog writer P. H. Coombs, S. Van Dyke, John Marriott, Mrs. Fred Senn, John Enright, Joseph Bell, J. A. Brown, Mrs. W. A. Haines, and Edwin Plato. It was also during this time that Fred W. Sierp of San Francisco was establishing the breed on the West Coast.

In the 1890s Dr. N. Ellis Oliver became interested in Yorkshire Terriers, as did Hugh McAuley, John L. Lincoln, Jr., Frank Mohan, Mrs. H. H. Teschemacher, L. Cullen, Mrs. C. W. Bishop, D. H. Everett, Mrs. E. B. Grace, Mrs. C. H. Morrel, Mr. W. P. Feeny, Mrs. C. H. Bloomer, and W. R. Kay.

By the turn of the century, many additional kennels appeared. Mrs. Raymond Mallock became active with stock based on Mrs. Senn's breeding stock, as did John Howard Taylor and Mr. and Mrs. Thomas Murphy. While Mrs. Senn's Bessie was the Murphys' first foundation bitch, Mr. and Mrs. Murphy imported several dogs carrying the famous Halifax prefix from Charles Adams in England.

Mrs. Senn's dogs were behind many other kennels during this period, namely those of G. A. Muenchinger, Samuel Baxter, Michael Jennings, Thomas Meade, and Mr. and Mrs. Arthur Mills.

An 1880 drawing by famous cartoonist Thomas Nast features a little Yorkshire Terrier front and center for the speech of Senator Thurman. This cartoon is well known not only for its political message, but also for the grand array of dogs depicted much as they looked at that period in time.

In the United States perhaps the most famous, and surely one of the earliest, paintings to include a Yorkie is the 1880 cartoon rendered by cartoonist Thomas Nast, illustrating Senator Thurman's speech on April 24 at Columbus, Ohio, against a poster proclaiming "The whole country is going to the dogs." He is surrounded by a bevy of mixed breeds, but here once again a little dog resembling the Yorkshire Terrier sits front and center at the Senator's feet, offering rapt attention to the tirade.

INTO THE TWENTIETH CENTURY

While the show at Drew's Dime Museum was held in Providence with five entries, the 1903 Rhode Island Kennel Club's fifth annual bench show had only one entry for judge James Mortimer. It was a dog named Nelly, bred by Albert Kabbery, and whelped in March, 1901. The amazing difference between the two shows, however, is that while the show at Drew's Museum listed Yorkies for sale at twenty-five and thirty-five dollars, Nelly was priced at $1,500. We can only wonder if the difference in price had anything at all to do with quality or was merely owner Milner's illusions of grandeur about his little Yorkie.

By 1904, when famous dog man Charles Hopton judged the Newport Dog Show in September of that year, prices seemed to have returned to somewhat normal figures. Prices listed in the eleven entries ranged from one hundred to two hundred dollars.

Two other items made the Newport show memorable. Entry 482, owned by Mrs. F. Senn and named Halifax Baden, noted: "Date of birth and breeder unknown. By Halifax Ben — Pink." Secondly, the show boasted of ten dollars in gold as a Best of Breed prize offered by Mrs. Edward Spencer. We can only speculate on whether it was won by perhaps "Bumpsey," or "Queen of the Fairies," or James J. Sharkey's entry, "Little Wonder."

THE STEDMAN – SYMONDS ALLIANCE

Four of the first Yorkshire Terriers to arrive in the United States were brought by famous dog man George Stedman Thomas around the turn of the century. Thomas' brother-in-law, Richard Toon (another great dog man) had sold the four Yorkies to Mr. Charles N. Symonds, president of a bank in Salem, Massachusetts, and Mr. Thomas was elected to bring them to America aboard the *Lake Huron*. Mr. Symonds was so pleased with Mr. Thomas that he added on a room to his kennel on Dearborn Street and hired him as his kennel manager.

Later Mr. Thomas bought himself a large place of his own in the town of Hamilton, where he and his wife bred and exhibited dogs. His first dog show was the Westminster Kennel Club Show in 1890. He was not to miss a Westminster event after that first one until 1917. During this time he won more first prizes and prize money than anyone else in the ring at that time. This feat was, however, equaled by his wife, who won more prizes from 1901 to 1915 than any other lady exhibitor. Although many of her wins were with Yorkshires, it is Mr. Thomas who must be credited with introducing the Yorkshire Terrier in the show ring in America during those early days around the turn of the century.

While prices in the United Kingdom ranged from one hundred dollars and up for Yorkshires, by the turn of the century the demand for these little dogs could be seen through some of the prices people were willing to pay for those that caught their eye. No better evidence for this is the $1,250 paid by Mrs. J. K. Emmet, wife of the famous American actor, for "Conqueror." The publicity that this sale attracted did the breed a lot of good. It will be remembered also that it was her husband, J. K. Emmet, who paid $5,000 for his Saint Bernard champion, Plinlimmon, which he used to play the dog's part in the production of *Hans the Boatman* in the early 1900s.

Mrs. Emmet's little Conqueror was thought to be highly desirable because of his coat which reached twenty-four inches in length. His weight was also desirable at the time—Conqueror weighed about five-and-one-half pounds.

GOLDIE STONE

Goldie Vivian Fothergill met and married Charles Stone in 1910. They both came from a circus background, and were successfully performing a high-wire act until Goldie was injured and made her decision to retire. Both Goldie and her husband loved dogs, and a Poodle had traveled with Goldie since 1907. She had seen a Yorkie in a mindreading act on the same bill with her, and from the wings had watched the little dog perform. She then and there made up her mind to get a Yorkie during her retirement years. The accident allowed Goldie to establish her Petite Kennels in 1929, and by 1930 she had purchased a proven bitch named May Blossom and a stud dog named Byngo Boy from Mrs. Henry Riddick.

Goldie's Byngo Boy was a champion by 1935, and a Harringay bitch, Madam-Be-You, which she had purchased from Mr. and Mrs. Henry T. Shannon, was added to her kennel.

May Blossom was bred to Byngo Boy's father, International Champion Bonds Byngo, and Goldie kept a bitch from that litter. She was bred to another Canadian stud, International Champion Haslingden Dandy Dinty. Goldie kept this entire litter since it encompassed the desirable Pellon strain from England. This carefully selected foundation stock was accountable for the seventeen champions she bred during the next quarter of a century—quite an accomplishment when you consider that from 1885 (when the first American champion won its title)

through 1917, only forty-five Yorkies made their championships.

The greatest triumph, perhaps, came on October 31, 1954, when her Champion Petite Magnificent Prince won Best in Show at the Delaware, Ohio, Kennel Club show under judge Selwyn Harris after Marie Meyer gave it the Toy Group. It was the first homebred Yorkshire Terrier in the United States to go all the way to the top award. (The very first Yorkie to win a Best in Show was an import, Champion Little Sir Model, in 1951; but Prince was the first homebred, and it was a cherished win for Goldie and Charlie Stone.) Almost all of their time and efforts were now devoted to their Yorkshire Terriers and continued to be until 1955, when Charlie's illness forced Goldie to cut down tremendously on her activities in the fancy.

In the 1930s, Goldie's chief success was with a little dog named Champion Petite Wee Wee, whose wins totaled twenty Group Placements and twenty Bests of Breed. He also won the Toy Group fourteen times and was runner-up for the Best in Show award on several of those occasions. In 1936, he was second in Group at the famous Morris and Essex show, and third in Group in 1937 at that same show—a remarkable achievement when you consider entries neared the three thousand mark at those shows. One of his chief attributes was his twenty-and-a-half inch coat, which was of proper texture and the desired "bright blue" color.

It was around this time that Goldie Stone was asked to write an article about the breed in America for Edward C. Ash's *The New Book of the Dog*, published in 1938 by Cassell and Company, London. She wrote as follows:

"I believe that I am correct in saying that imported Ch. Robinhood was no doubt the greatest winner along at that time, imported by John Shipp from England. He was sired by Mr. Lemon's Ch. Boy Blue out of Haworth Bessie. Next in line would be the Canadian and American Ch. Haslingden's Dandy Dinty imported by Andrew Patterson, and the Canadian and American Ch. Bond's Byngo, imported by Mrs. H. Riddock; these two dogs were the finest in the show ring and the greatest winners from 1929 to 1931.

"From 1931 on, I can say with assurance that our greatest show winners and champions were American bred Yorkshires.

The pioneer in the breed in the United States, Goldie Stone, pictured in a 1964 photograph with Aileen Martello's Miss Minnow. In 1983, when this book was being written, Goldie Stone was over ninety and completely blind. Her scrapbooks, show records, and photographs are now in the possession of her friend Aileen Martello, who also cherishes the samples of hair taken from twenty-eight of Goldie's dogs. We can only wonder if Goldie Stone, who was born in Waterloo, Iowa, March, 28, 1891, ever dreamed she would be a legend in her own time!

"In bitches we have Ch. Rochdale Queen of Toys, Ch. Petite Queen of the Fancy, and Ch. Petite Baby Jill. In dogs we have Ch. Byngo Boy's Masher, Ch. Petit Byngo Boy and Ch. Petit Wee Wee.

"Int. Ch. Haslingden's Dandy Dinty sired one champion. She is Ch. Rochdale Queen of the Toys, bred and owned by John Shipp, Providence, R.I. Int. Ch. Bond's Byngo sired three champions. They were Ch. Byngo's Royal Masher, Ch. Olinda Wee Tot, and Ch. Petit Byngo Boy.

"Ch. Petit Byngo Boy has sired three champions up to present date; they are Ch. Petite Queen of the Fancy, Ch. Petite Baby Jill and Ch. Petit Wee Wee.

"Of these champions named, the only ones out in the show ring this year were Ch. Byngo's Royal Masher, Ch. Petite Baby Jill, and Ch. Petit Wee Wee. Last year Ch. Rochdale Queen of the Toys was being shown at a few shows. Also Ch. Byngo's Royal Masher, who was only out at a few this year, being a full brother to my own Ch. Petit Byngo Boy. He is now six years old, a Yorkshire who has made history in the show ring in America.

"I am sure that it can be stated without fear of dispute that none has made the winnings that have been made by Ch. Petit Wee Wee. He has made only seven shows to date, at four he has been Best Toy, and at three, he has stood pat for Best in Show all breeds, under three different judges, and at each time he stayed with the finalists until the very last. This in America is really something for a breeder to feel proud of since it takes a mighty good one to go even to the top in the Toy Group over here.

"At Terre Haute, Indiana, June 14, he met in group competition and defeated that wonderful imported Pekingese, Sand Boi of Iwadu, imported from Mrs. Foster Burgess in England, by the Ceylon Court Kennels at Lake Geneva, Wisconsin. He has also defeated other imports in his group competition.

"The Standard is the same as used in England for this breed. We have no Yorkshire Terrier Club over here, and the dogs I have specially named for you are the only champions that are in show form equal to the English Yorkies in coat."

So wrote Goldie Stone in 1935 about the position of our breed in the United States.

Goldie Stone was so well thought of and admired as the pioneer breeder of Yorkshires in America that on April 21, 1974, at the Yorkshire Terrier Club of America supported show held in conjunction with the Central Ohio Kennel Club, Goldie Stone was honored for her more than half a century in the breed. Goldie was present to give the top prize to the winner of Best of Breed, and received a few honors herself. Dear friend Kay Finch had created a gold-leaf sculpture of a Yorkie, which was given to Goldie to commemorate this special day, and television and newspaper coverage was given to the event by local Columbus media. The show catalogue, which contained page after page of tributes and congratulations to Goldie for her contributions to the breed, is a collector's item for anyone interested in the breed.

Artist Kay Finch pictured at work on one of her life-sized models of a Yorkie at her famous studio in Corona del Mar, California.

Thanks to the impetus and suggestions of Kay Finch, another of the early pioneers in the breed in America, and to the hardworking members of the Central Ohio Kennel Club in Goldie's home town of Columbus, Goldie Stone could enjoy her homage while she was still able to get to a show and see her favorite breed performing in the ring, as well as to appreciate the adulation of all her grateful admirers.

Her last little Yorkie, fifteen-year-old Tommy, passed away in 1971. Goldie's failing eyesight prevented her from taking on another dog, but she takes consolation from being near the little cemetery in the backyard of her Columbus home that is the resting place for so many of her little Yorkshires.

This is Ch. Amberlyn's Patent Pending, bred and owned by Lynne Layman Kassidy of West Covina, California. The sire was Ch. Gait Moor Up N Down ex Dot's North Wind. Photo by Missy Yuhl.

Ch. Windsor Gayelyn Maid Marion, owned by Mr. and Mrs. Ralph Hager, was handled by Kathleen Kolbert to this win under judge James Nickerson.

Ch. Trivar's Dueling Banjo is owned by Mr. and Mrs. Andrew T. Seay of Bethesda, Maryland. Whelped in 1976, Banjo is being handled here by Johnny Robinson to a 1978 win under judge William Bergum. Earl Graham photo.

Ch. Bonny's Arielle, bred by Sonya and Mary Lees, is pictured winning under judge Michelle Billings. Pamela Thyssen handled for owners Elda and Nathan Tropper of Los Angeles, California. The sire was Bonny's Mister R ex Twinkie's Buffie Blu. Photo by Missy Yuhl, 1977.

Ondine's Shady Lady wins under judge Frank Oberstar at the 1981 Albany Kennel Club show, handled by Debbie Kirk for owners Claire and Lisa Pollitzer, Ondine Yorkies, Irvington, New Jersey. The sire was Ondine's Coquette Sugar N Spice ex Ch. Windsor Gayelyn Dilettante.

Carlens Blue Blazer and Christwards Mayflower take Best Brace in Show for Helen Stern.

Ch. Carnaby Joyall Maria, owned by Allison J. Dixon and handled for her by Terence Childs, was sired by Best in Show Ch. Carnaby Traditional Rock ex Ch. Carnaby Timpany. Maria is pictured here winning under judge Morris Howard.

BEST OF BREED
WESTBURY
KENNEL ASSOC INC
KLEIN SEPT 1980

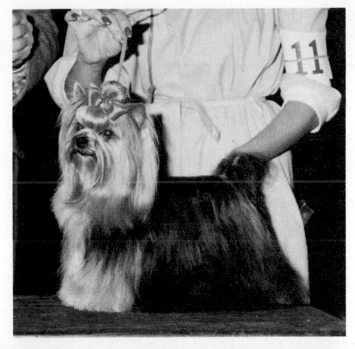

Ch. Gintique's Funny Ronni is pictured while still on the way to her championship. The sire was Ch. Andora's El Bandido ex Gintique's Funny Lady. Owned by Virginia Miller of Mentor, Ohio.

Another Group win for Helen Stern's homebred Ch. Carlens Johnny Walker. Handling to this win under judge Joseph Rowe is Terence Childs.

A darling Yorkie from the home of Charlene Ginn of Kennett Square, Pennsylvania.

Flair and Cricket, eight years and two years respectively, were obedience trained by owner Alyce Eskew of Clarksburg, West Virginia. They were both bred by the KaDoll Kennels.

Joy Madden's Yorkie and her pal, a Himalayan cat, share a chair in their back yard at Bradenton, Florida.

Ch. Gayelyn Gilded Lilly, Ch. Windsor Gayelyn Gilded Lilly, and Ch. Ozmilion Playboy were photographically captured in this charming setting by C.N. Shook of the Cedar Wood Studio.

Ch. Gayla's Melodylane Blue Jeans, bred and owed by D. Wilkinson and S. Keucher. The sire was Ch. Loveland's Good Buddy ex Beauvoir Skip To My Lu.

Dick and Bronya Johnston's beautiful Ch. Phirno Emerald Earl is pictured in full coat.

Ch. Gaytonglen's Fun N Frolic is pictured winning points toward championship under judge Merrill Cohen for owner Gloria Bloch.

Ch. Trivar's Fiddlesticks is waiting her turn in the show ring with owner and handler Alan Harper of Alexandria, Virginia.

Opposite:
Yorkholm's Holiday Doll at seventeen months of age is going
Best of Winners on the way to her championship. The sire was
Ch. Danby's Belziehill Teazel ex Princess Heidi of Yorkholm.
Judge Mrs. Daniell-Jenkins awards this win to Doll.

BEST OF WINNERS

WYOMING VALLEY
KENNEL CLUB
MAY 1981

KLEIN

45

Ch. Robtell Jentre Trump Card is co-owned by Ruth Jenkins and Paul Katzakian.

Ch. Trivar's Hunky Dori is owned by Mike Lytle and Jim Arellano of Los Angeles, California. Missy Yuhl photo.

Ch. Mistyhill Prince George wins at a 1981 show for breeder-owners Colonel and Mrs. John L. Nichols of Asheville, North Carolina.

Ch. Vassar Square Cheesecake is pictured winning for owner Terri Shumsky of Ventnor, New Jersey.

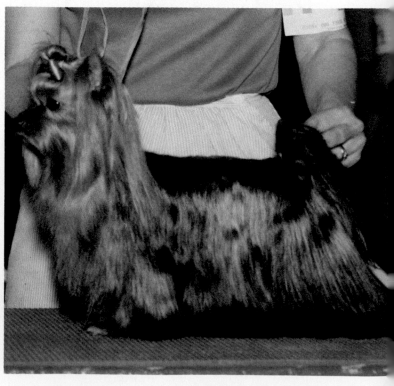

Ch. Hampshire Canyonade finishes for her championship at the November 1981 Delaware Valley Yorkshire Terrier Club Specialty under judge Ann Rogers Clark. Canyonade is co-owned by Bonnie Jean James (her handler) and Mary Ressler of Oak Ridge, New Jersey.

Multiple Group winner Ch. Windsor Gayelyn Hallelujah, bred and owned by Kathleen Kolbert of Oxford, Connecticut. This 1977 win was under breeder-judge Morris Howard.

GOLDIE STONE'S CONTEMPORARIES

While Goldie Stone was to be prominent in the breed for some fifty years, she had many contemporaries in the breed during the 1920s—and many of them had begun their kennel activities earlier; namely, the Rochdale kennels of Mr. and Mrs. John Shipp in Rhode Island, and the Hunslet Kennels of Mrs. Emanuel Battersby, which was founded as far back as 1907. Mention also must be made of Anna Radcliffe, who was an active breeder from 1914 through 1926, and of William Thompson, who began in 1913 and continued until 1942. Mrs. W. A. Beck was another who began in 1907 and later sold a dog to Goldie Stone, in 1933. E. Proctor was active in Colorado, Mrs. Julia McGoldbrick in California, and Mrs. August Kohlmeyer in Chicago.

Andrew Patterson began in 1920 and exhibited into the 1930s. There were Mrs. Michael Jennings, Mr. and Mrs. Peter Menges, Mr. and Mrs. James Dwyer, Anna Dreer, Mr. and Mrs. George Peabody, the Douro Kennels, F. L. Parnham, Mrs. Anna Bell, Mrs. M. W. Baldwin, Gilbert E. Morton, Mr. William Cummings, and Mrs. Senn, whose Senn Senn Kennels continued to flourish.

In the pre-twenties, E. Proctor had his Columbine Kennels in Colorado, as did Nicholas Sharkey in New Jersey, Mr. Henry Black in Ohio, Mrs. Harold Riddock in Detroit, and the Henry Shannons in Illinois. Great strides were made in the breed by Mrs. Orrae Billing, and the Bobbie B dogs of Samuel Baxter. Mrs. Fred Rich had been familiar with the breed since the turn of the century and became active in 1926. In 1966, at the age of 89, Mrs. Rich appeared in the show ring with one of her little dogs for the last time.

Other major contributors were Charles Rutherford, and Mrs. Denver Harmon.

THE THIRTIES

While Goldie Stone was the undisputed pioneer and leader in the breed from her start in the late 1920s all through the 1930s and beyond, there were other active Yorkshire breeders and Yorkies were beginning to appear on both coasts and here and there across the country.

By 1933, a Yorkie scored in the Toy Group at the prestigious Westminster Kennel Club show at Madison Square Garden. Judge Enno Meyer gave Fourth Place in the Toy Group to a Yorkie named Earl Byng. In 1934, Judge Glebe gave a Group Third to Champion Haslingden Dandy Dinty. Both dogs were owned by A. Patterson.

It seemed that Yorkies were on their way to top wins when it was noted that a Yorkshire placed in the Toy Group for the next three years. In 1935, it was Champion Rochdale Queen of the Toys owned by John Shipp. Judge F. W. Simmons gave the Queen a Third Place rosette. Champion Bobbie B. III, owned by Samuel Baxter, placed in the Toy Group in both 1936 and 1937, with Third and Fourth Place consecutive wins under judges W. F. Ford and W. Z. Breed.

No Yorkshire made the grade in 1938, but in 1939 a bit of history was recorded with the First Place Toy Group win by Champion Miss Wynsum under judge Lewis Worden. Miss Wynsum was owned by Arthur Mills, and that was "sum win"!

Mrs. L. E. Copeland became active in 1933 and Edna Apetz started her Wee Sweetie Kennels in 1935. Lily Harris came on the scene in 1937 and so did Mrs. Blanche Dunbar, who remained active until the 1960s. Dongan Kennels were active from 1934 until the mid-1940s.

Millbarry

Unquestionably the most prominent kennel in the 1930s was that of Mary and Arthur Mills, who adopted the Millbarry Kennel prefix and maintained their interest in the breed through the 1950s. Their three English imports, brought back from a trip made there in 1938, were to make breed history during the decade of the 1930s. Champion Fritty (later owned by Mary Carlisle) was one. Champion Miss Wynsum made breed history as winner of the Toy Group at Westminster in 1938, as did Champion Suprema by establishing himself as a top stud dog at that time.

The Millbarry dogs continued to do well, and by the middle of the 1950s, when the Mills ceased breeding, they had owned or bred twelve champions.

THE FORTIES

During the 1930s—much less during the decade of the 1940s—many kennels began breeding and exhibiting Yorkshire Terriers. One need only review some of the show catalogues from this period to see just how the breed was gaining in popularity. It would be virtually impossible to name all of them, or to give credit to all the win-

Oaksaber Hiawatha Eagle, handled by Barbara Bedsted for owner Marcia Knudsen of Hiawatha Valley Yorkies, Lake City, Minnesota. This win for Teddy was under judge Richard Hensel at a 1981 show.

ners. We shall endeavor to deal with some of the major contributors to the breed, however, since some very important major advances were made during this time, especially after the end of World War II.

Two Yorkshire Terriers distinguished themselves during the 1940s by placing in the Group at the Westminster shows. In 1944, Millbarry's Sho-Sho took First in the Group under judge Rozalind Layte. In 1948, Champion Little Boy Blue of Yorktown, owned by Mrs. Bedford, was Group Third under judge H. L. Mapes.

Along with their popularity, the quality of Yorkshire Terriers was noticeably improving and they were winning friends and influencing dog fanciers all over the country.

One of the stalwarts in the breed was a woman greatly respected and still active today. Her name is Aileen Markley Martello.

Aileen Markley Martello

Author of *The Yorkshire Terrier; Origin, History and Complete Care* (Exposition Press, 1971), Aileen Markley Martello has been raising Yorkshire Terriers since the 1940s in Lancaster, California.

This well-known authority on the breed was born in Columbus, Ohio, and her column on the breed has been running in *Dog World* magazine for many years. She is a charter member and past president of the Yorkshire Terrier Club of America and has also held the offices of secretary, treasurer, and member of the board of directors of the Club.

It was also Aileen Martello who was entrusted with the memorabilia of Goldie Stone's kennel. Mrs. Martello was also a personal friend of Mrs. Edith A. Stirk of the Stirkean Yorkies in England. For many years after their first meeting in 1956 at the Chicago International show, these ladies exchanged letters and tapes. On visits to England Ms. Martello was the guest of Mrs. Stirk, and she has brought back from England many of her dogs. This enabled her to carry on the Stirkean line which Mrs. Stirk had worked so hard to create and perpetuate.

Myrtle Durgin

It was in 1940 that Myrtle Durgin started her Yorkshire kennel in St. Paul, Minnesota. Mrs. Durgin was one of the original charter members of the Yorkshire Terrier Club of America, and she served as regional director for her area. She was also a founder of the Land O'Lakes Kennel Club.

Mrs. Durgin bred or owned over twenty champions during her years in the breed, and took special pleasure in exhibiting her little dogs in the Brace classes. She won several Best Brace in Show awards. Her dogs also produced more than thirty other champions.

In 1982, after Mrs. Durgin's death, her friend Mrs. Marcia A. Knudsen took over the operation of her kennel.

Mrs. Stanley Ferguson

In 1941, Mrs. Stanley E. Ferguson got involved in the breed, and owned one of Myrtle Durgin's dogs. Champion Minikin Baby Blue, sired by Minikin Dazzle (a son of Mrs. Durgin's Champion Durgin's Mickey), was her first champion, finishing in 1947.

Starting in 1947, Mrs. Ferguson began importing dogs. It was Mrs. Ferguson who in 1951 imported the legendary Champion Star Twilight of Clu-Mor, which she later sold to the Wildweir Kennels—and the rest of that story is now history. His litter sister, also imported at the same time, Champion Clu-Mor Nina, went on to win five Toy Groups for Mrs. Ferguson. In 1955, Mrs. Ferguson imported from Lady Edith Windham-Dawson five puppies and another breed star, Champion Blue Velvet of Soham, destined to become a Best in Show winner and also sold to the Wildweir Kennels.

Mrs. Ferguson remained active in the breed until the end of the 1950s.

While Mrs. Ferguson was active in Wisconsin, and Mrs. Durgin was breeding and showing in Minnesota, the hub of activity at that time seemed to center around the California breeders, such as Mrs. Pearl Johnson, Mrs. Stella Sally Myers, and Ruby Erickson.

Trudg-Inn Kennels

In 1946, Theron and Bette Trudgian started their line with Fantasy of Crown Crest, bred by Kay Finch. She became the top winning bitch for 1950, a title she held through 1953. In 1951, they imported a bitch from Canada, Champion Abon Hassan's Lady Iris, winner of twelve Toy Groups. The Trudgians owned or bred thirteen champions, and Bette also served as president of the Yorkshire Terrier Club of America in 1968.

Kay Finch and Crown Crest

Kay Finch's name also ranks among the avant-garde of the breed in the United States. Her Champion Pretty Please of Crown Crest was undefeated in her sex in the 1947-1948 show season. Sired by English and American Champion Suprema ex Peggee of Belvedere, this little bitch's show career included twenty Bests of Breed, a Group First, and twelve Group Placings. Her popularity and showmanship in the ring, along with her lovely gold and blue coat, won many fanciers to the breed.

Since her first Yorkshire in 1941 (Yorkshire Puddin and Peggee of Belvedere), other winners have included Champion Crown Crest Tinker Toy, Crown Crest Forever Amber, Champion Wee Willie, Pixie Prince of Crown Crest, and Crown Crest Tidbit—among others. She owned or bred nine Yorkies during her years in the breed.

Kay Finch still maintains her deep interest in the breed more than three decades later. She travels all over the world to officiate as a judge at dog shows and continues to glorify the breed through her sculpture and art work which is world-renowned. Her most recent work is a life-size model of Champion Clarkwyn's Jubilee Eagle.

Ch. Clu Mor Nina, owned by Mrs. Stanley E. Ferguson of Lake Geneva, Wisconsin, shown here winning the Toy Group at the 1952 Wisconsin Kennel Club show.

Famous artist, breeder, and judge Kay Finch did this life-sized bronze of Ruth Jenkins' American and Canadian Ch. Clarkwyn Jubilee Eagle.

Ch. Kel Lyn's Amoretta, bred by Mrs. Betty Arch and owned by Eddy Nicholson, is pictured winning Best in Sweepstakes at the 1980 Yorkshire Terrier Club of America Specialty in Burlingame, California. Kathleen Kolbert judged.

CHAPTER FOUR

Yorkshire Terrier Popularity in America

Trophy Table at the Tyrone Hills Kennels of Ed and Gert Molik in Fenton, Michigan.

Enthusiasm for the Yorkshire Terrier was running high in California at the beginning of the 1950s. It became evident that a breed club was necessary and desired. While the Yorkie was now said to be popular all over the country, the hub of activity was in California, and Kay Finch of the Crown Crest Kennels was being urged to form such a club. This she did, and became its first president, going on to serve four terms.

On August 8, 1951, on stationery which had her own Yorkie drawings decorating the letterhead, she sent out the following letter:

"Dear Friend:

I am anxious for you to be a charter member and help organize the new Yorkshire Terrier Club of America.

A group of friends asked me to serve as organizing President, and naturally, I am highly honored and will do the very best I can to help start this project to success.

Your help and influence are essential in getting the Club off to a good start so that Yorkshire Terrier owners will have more recognition and a strong representation through the American Kennel Club. In Unity there is strength!

Most of the well-known breeders are enthusiastic about our long awaited organization and I believe we will have one of the finest and most representative toy breed clubs in this country. The Club is now making up its charter and charter memberships will close October 1, 1951.

Application blanks are enclosed. Please fill out and return to Mrs. Trudgian as soon as possible so you can go down in history as a charter member and one of the organizers of America's first Yorkie club.

Any donation, large or small, to help us financially, will certainly be appreciated. We will need your support and I'm sure it will be to everyone's best interest.

Hoping you will be one of us! With Kindest personal regards."

It was signed by Kay Finch and sent out to every known Yorkie breeder or exhibitor. It drew sixty-seven charter members!

On the stationery, the National Officers were listed (in addition to President Kay Finch) as Bette Trudgian, Secretary-Treasurer; Joan Gordon, Publicity Director; Lee Lundberg, Publicity Secretary; Stella Sally Myers, Obedience Chairman; and Pearl Johnson, Show Secretary.

The Board of Governors consisted of Alpha Collins, Blanche Dunbar, Lily A. Harris, and Bertha Rice. Regional officers were Myrtle Durgin, Joan Gordon, Ruby Erickson, and Lemoyne Eastwood. Honorary Advisors were Harry Draper, of Canada, and Goldie V. Stone. The first meeting was held at Kay Finch's home at Corona del Mar, California, on October 27, 1951.

On Sunday, July 20, 1952, the club held its first sanctioned A Match in Griffith Park in Los Angeles. Fifty-one Yorkies attended for judging by Violet Boucher, and obedience classes also were held. The winner was a little dog named Golden Globe, owned by Mrs. L. S. Gordon who had made the 2000 mile trip from Illinois.

September 18, 1954, marked the first official Specialty Show, held in Santa Monica along with the Beverly Riviera all-breed show. Seventy-four entries by fifty-seven Yorkshires turned out for judge Dan Shuttleworth, followed by the now-famous Yorkie Square Dance group; movie stars awarded the trophies. Champion Star Twilight of Clu-Mor was Best of Breed and went on to Second in the Group.

Ch. Wildweir Jellybean is going Best of Winners on the way to his championship under judge Bette Trudgian at a Yorkshire Terrier Club of America Specialty show. Co-owners are breeders Mrs. Leslie S. Gordon, Jr., and Miss Janet Bennett, the latter handling.

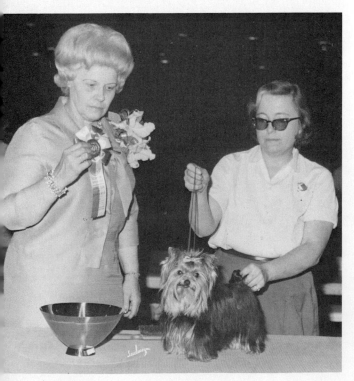

American and Bermudian Ch. Carlens Jack Daniels and Fago Marygold Micah win Best Brace in Show at the 1981 Yorkshire Terrier Club of America Specialty show, owner-handled by Helen Stern of Brooklyn, New York.

AKC ACCEPTANCE OF THE YORKSHIRE TERRIER CLUB

In 1958, the Yorkshire Terrier Club of America was accepted as a member club by the American Kennel Club, and shortly thereafter incorporated in the state of California. By 1966, the club had written a revision of the English standard for the breed, which was accepted by the American Kennel Club.

THE FIRST OBEDIENCE TRIAL

At the February 8, 1981, Specialty Show, the Yorkshire Terrier Club of America held its first Obedience Trial at the Biltmore Hotel on

Madison Avenue in New York City. There was an entry of seventy-six Yorkies in the Sweepstakes, eighty-three Yorkshire dogs, one hundred thirty-one bitches, twenty-eight in Best of Breed competition, two Veterans, two Brood Bitches, seven Stud Dogs, two Braces, four in Junior Showmanship Competition, and thirty-six for Obedience judge Merrill Cohen. Mrs. Dorothy Truitt was the Sweepstakes judge, Mrs. Edith Nash Hellerman and Mr. Tom Stevenson judged the show, and Miss E. Jacqueline Hager handled Junior Showmanship Competition.

Over the years, the club grew and many regional clubs have sprung up all over the country, including Hawaii and Puerto Rico, all taking their lead from the parent organization.

CODE OF ETHICS

While many breed clubs do not advocate a Code of Ethics for their members, realizing it is almost impossible to enforce, still others produce a code and expect their members to adhere to its rules, even if only as a guideline.

These signed documents usually appear on the backs of application blanks for membership in the clubs, and such is the case with the Yorkshire Terrier Club of America. Membership in the club is applied for by securing a membership application from a member in good standing in the club. After signing and filling out the application, it must be sponsored by two additional members who know the applicant personally. Membership applications must then be approved by the Board and printed in the newsletter for members to approve or to object.

CLUB INNOVATIONS

In 1978, the parent club, with an eye toward helping judges do a better job of passing on the breed, formed a committee of breeder-judges and breeder-exhibitors to assist in the judges' interpretations of the standard. A questionnaire was sent out to those listed as qualified by the American Kennel Club to judge Yorkies, with each part of the Yorkie anatomy listed and room to comment on whether or not the standard should be revised and, if so, to clarify how to do so.

Photographed at the 1962 Yorkshire Terrier Club of America Specialty show in New York City, these dogs represent entries from the Pequa Kennels at this show and Westminster.

Ch. Hampshire Pollyanna takes the Winners Bitch ribbon at the 1977 Yorkshire Terrier Club Specialty held in Austin, Texas. The judge was Edd Bivin. Bonnie Jean James handled and co-owns Pollyanna with Mary Ressler of Oak Ridge, New Jersey.

The paper further stated that replies would be held confidential and need not be signed or returned with the sender's return address. The letter was signed by Betty Dullinger, secretary, with requests that the forms be returned before March 1, 1978. Findings of the questionnaires or comments were not available when this book went to press, but the effort put forth by the club is a clear indication of an intense desire to advance the breed and to educate judges as well as the public on all the finer points of our breed.

TWENTY-FIFTH ANNIVERSARY OF THE CLUB

While all Yorkshire Terrier Specialties have been "special" in their own way, the 1976 Twenty-Fifth Anniversary Show was "extra special."

The show was held in the Terrace Ball Room of the Statler-Hilton Hotel in New York City on Sunday, February 8. As usual, it was on the day before the Westminster Kennel Club Show. Nelson Radcliffe judged for the record entry of 168 and in so doing fulfilled his very first Yorkshire Terrier assignment. Mrs. Nell Fietinghoff flew in from California to judge the Sweepstakes. Show Chairman Ann Seranne fairly outdid herself in making the large ring accessible

and beautiful, and the trophy table was a delight to see. There were specially made ceramic place markers denoting First through Fourth placement. An antique silver-leaf Yorkie, designed by Kay Finch, was the "piece de resistance."

The Specialty hospitality included tributes to past presidents of the YTCA at a cocktail party following the judging, and the club's first president, Kay Finch, spoke of the early days of the club and its formation. Both judges and president Robert Eckhardt spoke briefly before turning the program over to Johnny Robinson, the master of ceremonies for the evening.

Best of Breed winner at this show of shows was Champion Mayfair Barban Loup De Mer, co-owned by Ann Seranne and Barbara Wolferman.

EMPIRE YORKSHIRE TERRIER CLUB

In 1965, Ann Seranne was instrumental in forming Yorkshire Terrier Clubs in the metropolitan New York area. First, the Yorkshire Terrier Club—East, and then the Empire Yorkshire Terrier Club, Inc. James Genteel was president, and Ann was secretary. Many names that are familiar today were instrumental in this club: Fay Gold, Helen Stern, Virginia Bull, Joan Brearley, and celebrity Joey Faye.

Ch. Hampshire China Doll, Winners Bitch at a 1969 Yorkshire Terrier Club of America Specialty in Pasadena, California. The judge was Edd Bivin. Doll is co-owned by Mary Ressler and Bonnie Jean James, the latter handling.

Ch. Sundown's New Kid in Town, bred by K. Smith and owned by Suzanne M. Jones of New York Mills, New York. Whelped in 1976, the sire was American and Canadian Ch. Windsor Gayelyn Strut N Stuff ex Legagawanns Doll in Blue Jeans. The "Kid" is pictured with handler Terence Childs winning Best of Winners on the way to his championship at the 1980 National Specialty in New York.

The club held many fun shows on the second Thursday of each month and had dinner meetings as well as AKC-sanctioned matches; it published a Newsletter edited by Beryl Hesketh.

YORKSHIRE TERRIER CLUB OF GREATER NEW YORK

In 1973, a Yorkshire Terrier Club was formed covering—as the name implies—the Greater New York area. A charter meeting was held in March of that year and before it celebrated its first anniversary, the club had a membership of twenty-six. They held their first Fun Match that same year with Bonita Hewes, President of the Delaware Valley Yorkshire Terrier Club judging an entry of twenty-five. Within one year the membership had grown, two more Fun Matches had been judged by Morris Howard and Johnny Robinson, and a third by Betty Dullinger.

Before the club was three years old, an All-Toy Breed Seminar was staged at the Coliseum Holiday Inn in New York City, with the AKC Delegate Johnny Robinson from the Yorkshire Terrier Club of America delivering the keynote address. Movie and TV star Gretchen Wyler was special guest, with the club being praised for their foresight and energy in producing such a worthy event of this size.

YORKSHIRE TERRIER CLUB OF HAWAII

October 1969 was the beginning of the Yorkshire Terrier Club of Hawaii. Joe Tacker, judge from the mainland, officiated at their first Plan B match held in Thomas Square in Central Honolulu. The entry was fifteen and considered to be good, in view of the still relatively small population on the Islands, and that two other Yorkshires were home awaiting litters.

Best Puppy at this match was Joyce B. Palmer's Lilipuna Mini Wahini. Best of Opposite award went to her Bleana Junior. Best of Breed went to June M. Fischer's bitch Minnipoo's Blue Tiffany. Tiffany is a Toy Group winner also.

The Yorkshire Terrier Club of Hawaii is one of several breed clubs on the Islands working toward American Kennel Club Specialty Show approval. Hawaiian fanciers have only two opportunities a year to enter an AKC point show, so naturally Specialty Shows are to be desired in the future.

Major and Mrs. Fred Ritterspach and Roland Adameck are two other breeders of Yorkshires in our fiftieth state. Mr. Adameck for a time served as Islands correspondent for the *Yorkshire Terrier Quarterly* magazine, and is owner of the Lilipuna Kennels. He has maintained the breed in Hawaii since the 1960s.

OTHER YORKSHIRE CLUBS

As the Yorkshire Terrier breed became more and more popular, individual breed clubs began mushrooming all over the country. For a complete list that includes names of present secretaries (which may change during periodic elections), we suggest you write to the American Kennel Club at 51 Madison Avenue, New York, New York 10010.

Needless to say, it is advisable for everyone owning a Yorkie to belong to one or more of the breed clubs, as well as an all-breed club. The meetings and the club bulletins are an ideal way to keep up with what is happening in the dog fancy, as well as to benefit from the experience of others with whom you will come in contact.

Telephone directories, dog columnists in your local newspaper, or local humane societies may also be able to put you in touch with a dog club in or around your neighborhood.

A Best Team win at the 1960 Westminster Kennel Club show went to the four little Yorkies owned and shown by the Wildweir Kennels. The team included Ch. Wildweir Cock of the Walk, Ch. The Duchess of Clu-Mor, Ch. Rose Petal of Clu-Mor, and Ch. Sorreldene Charley Boy. Evelyn Shafer photograph.

THE BREED STANDARD
(APPROVED IN 1966)

General Appearance: That of a long-haired toy terrier whose blue and tan coat is parted on the face and from the base of the skull to the end of the tail and hangs evenly and quite straight down each side of body. The body is neat, compact and well proportioned. The dog's high head carriage and confident manner should give the appearance of vigor and self-importance.

Head: Small and rather flat on top, **the skull** not too prominent or round, **the muzzle** not too long, with **the bite** neither undershot nor overshot and teeth sound. Either scissors bite or level bite is acceptable. **The nose** is black. **Eyes** are medium in size and not too prominent; dark in color and sparkling with a sharp, intelligent expression. Eye rims are dark. **Ears** are small, V-shaped, carried erect and set not too far apart.

Body: Well proportioned and very compact. The back is rather short, the back line level, with height at shoulder the same as at the rump.

Legs and Feet: **Forelegs** should be straight, elbows neither in nor out. **Hind legs** straight when viewed from behind, but stifles are moderately bent when viewed from the sides. **Feet** are round with black toenails. Dewclaws, if any, are generally removed from the hind legs. Dewclaws on the forelegs may be removed.

Tail: Docked to a medium length and carried slightly higher than the level of the back.

Coat: Quality, texture and quantity of coat are of prime importance. Hair is glossy, fine and silky in texture. Coat on the body is moderately long and perfectly straight (not wavy). It may be trimmed to floor length to give ease of movement and a neater appearance, if desired. The fall on the head is long, tied with one bow in center of head or parted in the middle and tied with two bows. Hair on muzzle is very long. Hair should be trimmed short on tips of ears and may be trimmed on feet to give them a neat appearance.

Colors: Puppies are born black and tan and are normally darker in body color, showing an intermingling of black hair in the tan until they are matured. Color of hair on body and richness of tan on head and legs are of prime importance in *adult dogs*, to which the following color requirements apply:

BLUE: Is a dark steel-blue, not a silver-blue and not mingled with fawn, bronzy or black hairs.

TAN: All tan hair is darker at the roots than in the middle, shading to still lighter tan at the tips.

There should be no sooty or black hair intermingled with any of the tan.

Color on Body: The blue extends over the body from back of neck to root of tail. Hair on tail is a darker blue, especially at end of tail.

Headfall: A rich golden tan, deeper in color at sides of head, at ear roots and on the muzzle, with ears a deep rich tan. Tan color should not extend down on back of neck.

Chest and Legs: A bright, rich tan, not extending above the elbow on the forelegs nor above the stifle on the hind legs.

Weight: Must not exceed seven pounds.

YORKSHIRE TERRIER STRUCTURE

The following drawing, courtesy of Jeanne Grimsby and the *Yorkshire Terrier Quarterly*, provides a view of the ideal Yorkie structure.

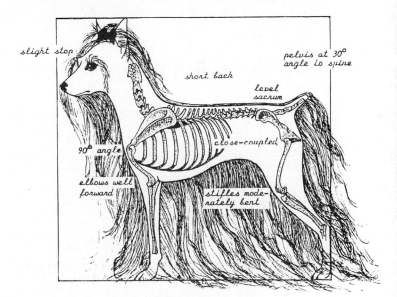

YORKSHIRE TERRIER COAT
AND COLOR

There is no easier way to spark a heated discussion among Yorkie owners than to become involved in an interpretation of the standard and, specifically, the meaning of the color blue. We emphasize the wording used in the actual standard, which is blue and then steel blue.

The definition of steel blue as found in some dictionaries may be quoted as reading, in part, as "a dark, somewhat bluish gray." Once again we note there is no reference to the color black. It is hard to understand, then, why we see a predominance of black and tan Yorkshires—even in the show ring—when the standard so clearly emphasizes blue and steel blue.

A litter of seven, all hand-raised by the Silverwinds Kennels of Elissa Taddie in West Chester, Pennsylvania.

True, Yorkie puppies are said to be born black and tan. Is that even truly black, or is it dark steel blue? There are those who will argue this point as well. We do know that the color fades as the puppies grow, and we are left to declare just what color our Yorkies are. Trying to compare the steel blue with other breeds which are said to be blue is equally questionable, and seemingly does not even apply to our discussions.

Hope springs eternal in our minds when the coat first starts to "break," and diligent searching begins for dark hairs among the gold portions of the body.

Perhaps the confusion began when Mr. F. Randall, a prominent breeder in the south of England at the turn of the century, was quoted as saying, "I consider the *dark*, steel-blue (not silver) a great improvement on the pale-coloured dogs which. . .are easier to breed than the darker ones." Other opinions seem to stem more from a desire to establish the color of the dogs they themselves were breeding than for a regard to the proper interpretation of a standard.

Annie Swan, in her book on the breed, stated: "A dark steel blue is the correct shade as laid down by the Yorkshire Terrier clubs, the colour resembling a surface of highly polished steel when viewed in a subdued light, and it should be as even as possible."

While today's emphasis is definitely on trying to establish a true definition of color, it also should be remembered that the standard applies to an entire dog. Color is very important, but not to the exclusion of all else or the breed will suffer for it. Toy breeds need structure and soundness and all-around good health before all else. Color is something to strive for, and should perhaps be clarified in our standard.

A litter of beautiful puppies, sired by Ch. Eden Valley Circuit Breaker ex American, Mexican and International Ch. Gemaneaux Holly Go Lightly. Breeder is Anita Wray of Houston, Texas.

Three-month-old puppies from Wildweir Kennels in Glenview, Illinois.

For those just getting into the Yorkshire breed, this can be a very puzzling aspect in selecting their first dog—especially for newcomers seeking to buy the best possible breeding stock. If in doubt, it would be wise to take additional time consulting with many breeders and exhibitors and learning as much as possible about color definitions. Do not make hasty decisions.

We are all agreed on the texture of the Yorkshire coat. It is silky, as long as possible, and definitely beautiful!

THE ILLUSTRATED STANDARD

In 1979, the Yorkshire Terrier Club of America under the auspices of Education Chairman Anne H. Goldman, published a valuable booklet entitled *The Illustrated Discussion of the Yorkshire Terrier*. Delightfully illustrated by Lusa LaGuire, the booklet was intended to further clarify the standard for our breed, with the breeder being particularly influenced by its presentation and slightly exaggerated faults to indicate the rights from the wrongs.

This booklet is available through the parent club for a nominal fee, and it is strongly suggested that all interested in the correct breeding and anatomy of the Yorkshire obtain and study a copy. Name and address of the club secretary may be obtained by requesting same from the American Kennel Club, 51 Madison Avenue, New York, New York 10010.

The key to the major purpose of this book can be noted in the preface where the closing remark suggests that it be used for the evaluation of puppies, and also that it is the hope of the Yorkshire Terrier Club of America that breeders will recognize themselves as being the guardians of our breed.

American and Canadian Ch. Starfire Titan of Encore and her little brother, Ch. Starfire Titan pictured at 4½ months of age. Owned by Anne Herzberg Goldman of Santa Monica, California, these darling puppies were sired by Starfire's great American and Mexican Ch. Wildweir Keepsake.

THE FABULOUS FIFTIES

There was a tremendous surge of popularity in the breed during the decade of the 1950s, and the breed made some remarkable strides in the show ring. These were recorded and became history with the advent of the Phillips System ratings which began in 1956. However, the "fabulous fifties" belong to and were dominated by the Wildweir Kennels.

Wildweir

Miss Janet Bennett and her sister, Mrs. Joan Gordon, began what is perhaps the greatest success story ever told in our breed. It is difficult to know where to begin when relating their dedication to the breed, their uninterrupted line of great dogs which they either imported or bred over the years, and their marvelous presentation of their dogs in the show rings. There is no one, in *any* breed, that can deny their fame.

When they imported Champion Little Sir Model in 1950, they were on their way. In addition to Model's illustrious show career, he was the sire of Wildweir Cover Girl, the dam of five champions. But perhaps Model's greatest claim to fame was that he was to become the first Yorkshire Terrier to win an all-breed Best in Show, in 1952. His total record was seven Bests in Show, thirty-one Toy Group Firsts, twenty-three Group Placings, and sixty-three Bests of Breed.

Model was imported from Ben Williamson in England. From him was also imported Champion Golden Fame, later to be the winner of the first Sanctioned Match of the Yorkshire Terrier Club of America in 1952.

Mention must be made here of Champion Golden Flame's chief contribution, pointed out so deservedly in *The Complete Yorkshire Terrier* written by Mrs. Gordon and Miss Bennett.

Ringside in 1954 at the Westminster Kennel Club were Mrs. Leslie Gordon Jr., with Kelsbro Blue-Tan Jenny Wren, and her sister Janet Bennett, with English Ch. Jessica of Westridge. Their dedication to the breed covers more than three decades.

Ch. Star Twilight of Clu-Mor is pictured winning the 1956 Yorkshire Terrier Club of America Specialty show under the late judge Colonel Ed McQuown. Famous dog columnist Alice Scott presented the trophy. This Irish import, whelped in 1950 and bred by Miss Maudloton, was the sire of 15 champions and had a total show record of 26 Bests in Show, 4 Specialty Bests in Show, 81 Toy Groups, 22 Group Placings, and 103 Bests of Breed. His sire was English-Irish Ch. Twinkle Star of Clu-Mor ex My Pretty Maid. Owned and shown by Mrs. Leslie Gordon and Miss Janet Bennett, Wildweir Kennels, Glenview, Illinois.

Through three of his get (namely, Champion Blue Symon, Bea's Finale, and Wildweir Periwinkle) Golden Fame is found in the background of pedigrees of more American Best in Show winners than any other dog.

The Wildweir Kennels English and American Champion Blue Dolly, imported from A. H. Coates in England, became the first bitch to win a Toy Group for Wildweir.

The next "star" on the Wildweir horizon was Champion Star Twilight of Clu-Mor, which they campaigned from 1953 through 1958. This Irish import was the sire of fifteen champions that racked up a grand total of twenty-five Bests in Show, four Specialty Bests, eight-one Toy Groups, twenty-two Group Placings, and one hundred three Bests of Breed. One of the Specialty "Bests" included the first Yorkshire Terrier Club of America Specialty Show. Star Twilight was truly the star of the fifties, topping his career by Westminster Toy Group wins in 1954 and 1955 and a Group Second in 1956.

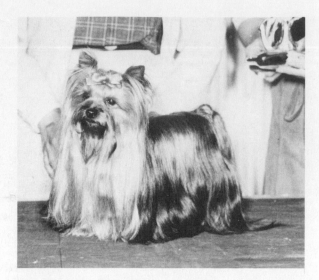

Ch. Proud Girl of Clu-Mor was the first Yorkshire bitch to win a Best in Show. This Irish import was owned and handled by Mrs. Leslie Gordon and Miss Janet Bennett during her 1963-1964 show ring career. In addition to a Best in Show, Proud Girl won 22 Toy Groups, 19 Group Placings and 49 Bests of Breed. Born in 1960, she was bred by Misses Maud and Florence Coton.

Ch. Wildweir Contrail, shown during the 1972-1974 show seasons, was the winner of three Bests in Show and a Specialty. She also had 13 Toy Groups to her credit. Whelped in 1969, she was the dam of Best in Show winner Ch. Wildweir Counterpart. Her sire was Irish and American Ch. Continuation of Gleno ex Wildweir Whimsey. Bred, owned, and handled by Mrs. Leslie Gordon and Janet Bennett.

While Star Twilight was gathering his record wins, another Irish import owned by the Wildweir Kennels was moving up in the ranks. Champion Blue Velvet of Soham began his show ring career in 1957, and by the end of 1959 had won a Best in Show and seventeen Toy Groups. Thirty Group Placings and fifty Bests of Breed were included before his retirement. He was also the sire of one champion. Originally imported by Mrs. Stanley Ferguson and sold to Wildweir as a four-month-old puppy, he went on to become the Number Six Toy Dog in the 1957 Phillips System, and won Fourth Place in the Toy Group at Westminster in 1957.

Champion Proud Girl of Clu-Mor was shown during the 1963-1964 show seasons. Imported from Ireland in 1963, she was to become the first Yorkshire Terrier bitch to win Best in Show. Her total record in addition to the Best in Show was twenty-two Toy Groups, nineteen Group Placements, and forty-nine Bests of Breed.

English import Champion Gloamin Christmas Cracker was shown in 1958-1959, and won three Bests in Show, one Specialty, eleven Toy Groups, twelve Group Placings, and twenty-eight Bests of Breed.

Other Wildweir winners at this time included English and American Champion Buranthea's Doutelle in 1959, Champion Yorkfold Chocolate Boy (imported in 1962), and Champion Royal Picador, who won a Specialty show and fourteen Toy Groups. He was also the sire of two champions.

In 1968, Wildweir Kennels imported Irish and later American Champion Continuation of Gleno from Eugene Weir. He became the winner of five Bests in Show, two Specialties, twenty-eight Toy Group Firsts, thirty-seven Group placings, and seventy-four Bests of Breed. He was also the sire of a Best in Show winner, Champion Wildweir Contrail, who won three Bests in Show, one Specialty, and thirteen Toy Groups. She was the dam of a Best in Show winner, Champion Wildweir Counterpart.

Later Group-winning imports for Wildweir were Irish and American Champion Wedgewood's Frivolity, Champion Coulgorm Gay Lady, and Champion Lyndoney Kindrum Valentine.

While the Wildweir Kennels clearly dominated the winners' rings during the 1950s, the decade of the 1960s was to bring them their greatest glory. This came in the form of a beautiful little dog named Champion Wildweir Pomp N'Circumstance. Whelped May 1, 1959, he was sired by Champion Wildweir Cock of the Walk out of Capri Venus, and was a double grandson of Champion Star Twilight of Clu-Mor. Pompy was the sire of ninety-five champions: ninety-three American, one Mexican and one Colombian. Among them were four Best in Show winners and fourteen Group winners, including those that went on to Best in Show. Pompy was also the great-great grandsire of Champion Wildweir Bumper Sticker, sire of five champions and twelve Bests in Show, nine Specialties, sixty-two Toy Groups, eight-seven Group Placings, and one hundred fifty-one Bests of Breed. He was also the great-great grandsire of Champion CeDe Higgens, the Westminster Kennel Club Best in Show winner in 1978.

Pompy twice tied for Top Stud Dog honors, in all-breed competition, in 1965 and 1966. In 1966, his son, Champion Wildweir Fair N'Square, out of Champion Rose Petal of Clu-Mor, was campaigned; by 1968 he had won three Bests in Show, two Specialty Bests, twenty-five Toy Groups, thirty-seven Group Placings, and seventy Bests of Breed. He became the sire of eighteen champions.

Fair N'Square was a half-brother to Champion Wildweir Moonrose, who was shown in 1964 and 1965, and was the dam of a champion Group winner. Moonrose won three Bests in

Show, two Specialties, twenty-six Toy Groups, thirty Group Placings, and no less than fifty-nine Bests of Breed. Her sire was another Wildweir import, Champion Prince Moon of Clu-Mor, and she was whelped in August 1961.

At the beginning of the 1980s, Wildweir was still producing and exhibiting top quality Yorkshire Terriers. Some of these included Champion Wildweir Royal Credit, Champion Wildweir Small Print, and Champion Wildweir Household Finance. The sire of Household Finance was Gleno Credit Card out of Wildweir Haired Houseperson, the latter being one of the author's all-time favorite names for a dog!

As we continue into the 1980s and beyond, we must recall that by the 1980s, Wildweir had bred or owned in excess of 170 champions—surely a record that will stand for many more years, as their continued success can only add to this impressive accomplishment. Truly a record of which to be proud.

In 1976, Joan B. Gordon and Janet E. Bennett produced a book entitled, *The Complete Yorkshire Terrier*, a remarkable volume of Yorkshire Terrier records and information that further proves their dedication to this breed. They also became dog show judges for the same reason.

A beautiful camera study of Ch. Wildweir Pomp N' Circumstance, sire of 95 champions. This little Yorkie was bred, owned, and shown by Mrs. Leslie Gordon, Jr., and Miss Janet Bennett.

Ch. Wildweir Fair N' Square, sire of 18 champions, was a leading show star in the 1960s. His record included 3 all-breed Bests in Show, 25 Groups, 37 Group Placings, and 70 Bests of Breed. This fine little dog was the winner of Yorkshire Terrier Club of America Specialties in 1967 and 1968 and also was listed as one of the top fifty Toy dogs in 1967. Bred, owned, and shown by Mrs. Leslie Gordon, Jr., and Miss Janet E. Bennett.

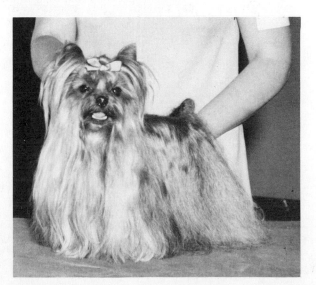

Windfall

Gloria Knight Bloch, owner of the Windfall Kennels, first came to America in 1951. After her marriage to Ray Bloch, known to Saluki fanciers, Gloria purchased her first Yorkshire Terrier. Sired by the well-known Champion Tzumiaos Millionaire of Gaytonglen, Happy Lady Babette became her first champion and the foundation bitch of her kennel.

Born in Ireland, a resident of England and later of Kansas City, Kansas, Gloria inherited a love of animals from her father, who bred Irish Terriers. During the war, Gloria's father went to great lengths to protect their dogs from the ravages of war by secreting them in the bomb shelters during air raids.

Once Gloria got into the breed in this country, her list of champions grew. As owner-handler, Gloria finished Champion Jofre's Ruff & Reddy, Champion Windfall's Blockbuster, and Champion Gaytonglen's Fun N Frolic, to name a few.

In addition to a career as an executive secretary with one of America's top electronics companies, Gloria's spare time has been spent as editor and publisher of the Yorkshire Terrier Club of America newsletter and serving in the Owner Handler's Association, Indian River Dog Training Club, and the Gold Coast Yorkshire Terrier Club.

Gloria Knight-Bloch with Turyanne's Golden Rocket, Ch. Gaytonglen's Fun N Frolic, and Plantation's Windfall.

Ch. Happy Lady Babette is pictured winning at a 1977 show on the way to her championship. Owner is Gloria Bloch of Palm Bay, Florida. The sire was Ch. Tzumaio's Millionaire of Gaytonglen, an English import.

Goldenblue

1952 saw the beginning of the Goldenblue Kennels of Muriel Kreig in Anaheim, California. Active in both the breed and obedience rings, Mrs. Kreig also served as Yorkshire Terrier Club of America president in 1958.

Mrs. Kreig's Champion Green's Chipsal Blu Twink was the Best of Breed winner from Puppy class at just eight months of age at one of the Yorkshire Terrier Club of America's Specialty shows held in San Francisco several years ago. He is still believed to be the youngest Specialty winner in the breed. Twink's mother was the first Yorkshire Terrier to be whelped in Alaska, and was appropriately named Green's Pioneer Girl of Alaska by her breeder, Melba Green. The sire was Mrs. Green's Yorkfold Chipmonk.

Mrs. Kreig was instrumental in the formation of the squaredancing Yorkshire Terrier group. Her interest has been in obedience from the earliest days, and it will be recalled that her Ginger Lei won the C.D. title in just three straight shows, and was Best Brace in show at the 1957 Beverly-Riviera show in California that year, along with her daughter Champion Kathy Dorn.

Maybelle Neuguth

It is not difficult to imagine the further success Maybelle Neuguth would have enjoyed with her Maybelle Yorkshires had not a tragedy ended her life several years ago. Maybelle was a completely dedicated dog person, deeply devoted to her Yorkies and her Poodles.

Perhaps her most remembered dog was Champion Wildweir E Major of Maybelle. A prepotent stud, he produced many fine puppies, but the dog which gave Maybelle her start was Wildweir Liberty Belle, C.D. Others included Champion Wildweir Hot Fudge and Ballerina.

Three of Maybelle Neuguth's puppies, circa 1950s. Her kennels were located in Asbury Park, New Jersey.

Wildweir Liberty Belle, owned by Maybelle Neuguth.

Maybelle frequently showed her own dogs, but also on occasion had a handler to show them to their wins. It was hard to say if Maybelle received more enjoyment by being in the ring or by being on the sidelines watching Richard Bauer put them through their paces.

A tragic fire in 1970 at her daughter's home in Pennsylvania, where Maybelle was baby-sitting for her four grandchildren along with her son-in-law's mother, put a sudden end to Maybelle's life. In keeping with her humane beliefs, Maybelle chose to save all the children, the mother-in-law, and some of the dogs before collapsing on the lawn with severe burns. She died at the hospital the next day. Those of us who knew Maybelle, and those who saw her with her dogs at the shows, will always remember her—and especially this final courageous act.

Pequa

Myrtle Young and her little Pequa Yorkshires were started in 1957 in New Jersey and later moved to California. Two Irish imports, litter sisters, were her first champions. Purchased from and bred by Mrs. M. K. McFadden, their names were Champion Tully Tincel and Tully Trinket. At Myrtle's kennel, Tincel became the dam of two champions.

Ch. Willow of Pagham and daughter Ch. Pequa Small Rachel, owned by the Pequa Kennels and photographed winning at a 1962 show.

Another import, Champion Caprice of Pagham, became her top stud dog and was the sire of twelve champions. Champion Pequa Mustang, co-owned by Myrtle and Joe Glaser of Poodle fame, was the sire of two champions and was a Best in Show winner with four Toy Groups and several Group placements to his credit.

Among the twenty-one or more champions owned or bred by Myrtle, Champion Pequa Amigo was another top dog. Mrs. Young also imported the English, and later American, Champion Don Carlos of Progresso. He was to sire five champions bearing the Pequa name, including the Group winning Champion Pequa de Lovely.

Myrtle Young wins Best Brace in Show at the Albany Kennel Club in 1960. Her Ch. Future of Pagham and Caprice were also Second Best in Toy Group and Best Yorkie Brace at the Westminster Kennel Club show in 1961.

Two of Myrtle Young's Yorkies, photographed about 1960 by famous dog photographer Tauskey.

Windamere

It all began at the 1956 Chicago International show. Jim Nickerson and his partner, Bud Priser, went to the show with the intent of buying a Miniature Pinscher. However, once Yorkshire Champion Star Twilight of Clu Mor caught their eye, there was no denying that this was to be the breed for them.

Their first purchase was Minkin Lovely Lady Bridget, bred by Ethel Ferguson of the Minkin Yorkie kennels. It took Jim and Bud eight years to establish the "Windamere type" within their breeding program and to present in the show ring what they felt was what a Yorkshire Terrier should be. This not only took a great amount of time, but led to their importation of some thirty-three Yorkies over a fifteen-year span.

When Jim became a judge of Yorkshires in 1972, Windamere stopped showing, and by 1979 had also ceased breeding. Perhaps their most famous English import was the beautiful International Champion Progress of Progreso, who arrived in 1962.

Over forty champions were owned or bred at Windamere before the untimely death of Bud Priser in 1971. It was their Champion Windamere Minnipoo that produced Champion Windamere Blue Tiffany, the little lass that was destined to become Hawaii's first homebred Yorkie to win a championship in that state.

Merrill Cohen

Merrill Cohen began his interest in Yorkshire Terriers with stock purchased from the Wild-weir Kennels. Mr. Cohen and his daughter both showed their little dogs in the show ring as well as the obedience ring.

Mr. Cohen is also an obedience and conformation judge of Yorkshires, and in 1976 established what is perhaps a "first" in the fancy. He was invited to judge Open B class as well as Best in Show at the Newtown Kennel Club show in Newtown, Connecticut. It is believed that no other judge has officiated in both these capacities on the same day at the same show.

Helen and Merrill Cohen also have the distinction of finishing one of only fourteen Utility Degree Yorkshires up to that time. Their little Mar-del's Terrence won C.D., C.D.X., and U.D. titles under their guidance.

Merrill Cohen handles Ch. Wildweir Prim N Proper to a Toy Group win under judge Edith Nash Hellerman.

Best in Show for Ch. Progress of Progesso, handled by Julayne K. Puckett for owners Messrs. Priser and J.A. Nickerson. The judge was the late Heywood Hartley.

Ch. The Vale Tinymite, imported and owned by Nancy and David Lerner of Port Chester, New York.

Nancy and David Lerner

Nancy and David Lerner will be remembered for their Renrel Kennels and their handling of several little Yorkies in the show ring bearing the Tolestar prefix. Nancy and David were most active in the 1960s when they imported Topsy, Terrie, and Tara of Tolestar, among others from that line. Nancy showed Tzumiao's Lil Apollo as well.

Topsy enjoyed the best part of her life with Ann Seranne and the Mayfair Kennels, but it was Nancy Lerner that piloted Topsy to her Best of Breed Win at the Westminster Kennel Club show. The Lerners also purchased the imported American and Canadian Champion The Vale Tiny Mite in 1957.

The author is happy to say that Nancy finished the championship of Terrie of Tolestar, who

became the stud dog at my Sahadi Kennels. I also purchased Tara of Tolestar from the Lerners. These two little Yorkies of mine produced Champion Sahadi Scarlet O'Hara, owned and finished by Virginia Bull, that was from the author's Gone With the Wind litter.

Nancy and David Lerner were an engaging young couple, but did not stay active in the breed, or the fancy, for very long. But for the little time they were in it, Ann Seranne and I both are grateful for our Tolestar dogs and what we learned from them in those early days in the breed.

Danby Belziehill

1958 was the year Muriel Hornbrook founded her Danby Belziehill Kennels in Ithaca, New York. She imported, in whelp, Belzie Hill Lindy Loo from the Belziehill Kennels of Thomas Morrison in Lanarks, Scotland. Her Belziehills Dondi became the sire of sixteen champions, and her Steiff Toy was her first Toy Group winner. Ann Seranne and Barbara Wolferman owned two of her other Group winners, Champion Danby Belziehill Amanda and Danby Belziehill Raindrop.

Danby's Belziehill Tigre, handled by Wendell Sammet for owner Mildred Hornbrook, at the 1965 Rockland County Kennel Club show. Judge was Miss Virginia Sivori.

Bertha Smith's Ch. St. Aubrey Tzumiao's Lil Apollo won at the 1961 Gloucester County Kennel Club show. Nancy Lerner handled for the owner. Evelyn Shafer photo.

Muriel later imported Daisy of Liberty Hill, bred by W. Provan of Scotland, that when bred to her Dondi produced nine champions. In all, Muriel Hornbrook produced twenty-two champions.

The amputation of both legs has prevented Muriel Hornbrook from continuing to breed her little Yorkies, but her interest is still keen in the breed and she manages to keep in touch with those of the fancy through her friends.

Fago

Fay Gold has been active in Yorkies since 1958 and active as a member of the Yorkshire Terrier Club of America since 1963, serving as a director in 1972.

Fay kept her Champion Galaxy's Orion, C.D., from her second homebred litter, and "Louie" finished both his championship and his

Companion Dog titles under Fay's guidance. While Fay has shown other Yorkies, her chief interest is in obedience work. She was chairperson for the 1981 Yorkshire Terrier Club of America Specialty Show, Obedience Chairperson for the Yorkshire Terrier Club of America from 1964 to 1967, and received the Blue Horn and Medal Award for her work, as well as the President's Award in 1970.

Fay has been a staunch advocate of educating the fancy in genetic studies over the years, and has had many papers on the subject published under her name. These include "The Miracle of the Nucleus" in a 1977 Gaines Research Progress Report. She also runs a Yorkshire Terrier Information Service, which should be especially popular with novices in the breed.

Ch. Galaxy's Orion, C.D., the foundation stud of the Fago Kennels of Fay Gold, New York, New York.

Fago Moon Goddess's Gamin, was bred, owned, and handled by Fay Gold.

Fay can probably be best remembered for her worthy editorship of the *Yorkshire Terrier Quarterly*, a magazine she conceived, published, and dedicated to the breed. The magazine was issued from 1968 through 1976, and contained many articles and beautiful drawings of interest to all.

She is also a part-time actress in New York City and has appeared in many television commercials and soap operas, as well as dramatic programs. However, there is no denying that her first love is Yorkies!

Fay Gold and puppies from a litter sired by Ch. C.W. Harper ex Fago's Miraculous Mona. They are Fago's Mona's Marigold, Ch. Carlen s Kahlua Mist, and Fago Mona's Madcap.

Starfire

The Starfire Yorkshire Terriers of Anne Herzberg Goldman in Santa Monica stemmed from a 1959 Christmas walk along Wilshire Boulevard in Beverly Hills, California. Her daughter Liz spotted a Yorkie strutting along as if he owned the world. That night Liz announced to her family what she wanted for her Christmas present. Laviner Little Eva, or "Missy," was the answer to her request. But Missy was only the beginning. Since 1960 some forty Yorkshire Terriers have won their titles for Starfire.

One of Starfire's early Yorkies, American and Mexican Champion Wildweir Keepsake,

The great International Champion Wildweir Keepsake, photographed at 24 months of age by famed dog photographer Joan Ludwig. Keepsake has earned the letters P.C. after his name to indicate he earned the Mexican novice obedience degree, Perro Companero.

became the top-producing son of the famous Champion Wildweir Pomp N' Circumstance, who was the top-producing toy dog of all time and the sire of ninety-five champions. Keepsake sired thirty-one champions.

"Tuffy" (as Keepsake was known) had a mind of his own, and it was Kay Finch who advised Anne to take him to obedience classes, because he was too good a dog not to be shown in conformation classes and to get his championship title. By the end of the ten-week course, Tuffy graduated first in his class with a score of 199½. Through all the succeeding years, that first place obedience trophy remains the one Anne covets the most. Tuffy went on to win his Mexican championship and also his Perro Companero, the Mexican Novice Obedience Degree.

Tuffy's most famous daughter was Anne's Champion Starfire Gold Bangle who became the top-winning Western Yorkie in 1968 and the only Yorkshire Terrier ever to be a *Kennel Review* Best Western Toy Dog nominee. Bangle was also obedience trained before starting her show ring career.

Anne's Champion Starfire For Keeps was Best Senior Puppy and Grand Sweepstakes Winner at a Yorkshire Terrier Club of America Specialty Show held in Atlantic City under breeder-judge Margaret Spilling. At the same show, Starfire For Keeps was also chosen Winners Bitch by breeder-judge Mrs. Wendy Whiteley.

Two sons of American and Mexican Champion Wildweir Keepsake, P.C., also made names for themselves. American, Canadian, and Mexi-

Starfire For Keeps, when just 11½ months of age, the Yorkshire Terrier Club of America Specialty show in Atlantic City.

Mrs. Anne Herzberg Goldman takes the Best Brace in Show award at the 1965 Del Monte Kennel Club show with a half-brother and sister pair sired by Ch. Wildweir Pomp N Circumstance. Mr. Tom Stevenson presents the trophy for judge Cyrus Richel.

can Champion Starfire Mitey Model sired six champions, and was owned by Mrs. Margery C. May. American and Mexican Champion Starfire Titan sired the Group and multi-Best in Show winner, American and Mexican Champion Camelot's Little Pixie, owned by Lee and Richard Sakal.

One of Keepsake's last sons, Champion Starfire Design By Keepsake, was chosen by breeder-judge Jim Nickerson at his Winners Dog at a National Yorkshire Terrier Club of America Specialty held in San Francisco, and is the sire of three champions to date.

Anne Goldman not only is devoted to her Yorkshires, but also is active in the parent club.

Ch. Starfire Design By Keepsake is owned, bred, and shown by Mrs. Anne Herzberg Goldman.

Clarkwyn

Mrs. John A. Clark became interested in Yorkshire Terriers in the late 1950s. In 1960, she purchased American and Canadian Champion Toy Clown of Rusklyn. Clown was an English import and became the foundation of her Clarkwyn Kennels. He became her top winner and was a top producer for the Clarkwyn line.

Yorkies from Ila Clark's line have won many Bests in Show, Toy Groups, and more than a dozen Yorkshire Terrier Specialty Shows, including seven National Specialties.

Perhaps her best known dog is American and Canadian Champion Clarkwyn's Jubilee Eagle, who became the foundation dog for Ruth Jenkins' Jentre Kennels in California.

The late radio announcer Don Wilson presents a trophy to Ch. Ru Gene's King Corkyson, owned by Ruth and Gene Fields. Photo by Joan Ludwig.

With over forty champions to his credit, including eight in 1981, Ruth Jenkins' American and Canadian Ch. Clarkwyn Jubilee Eagle is one of the top-producing studs for 1979, 1980, and 1981. He is pictured here with Pat Tripp.

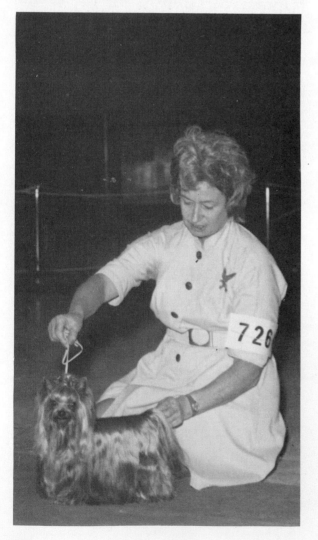

Other Kennels From the Fifties

While the hub of activity continued to be in California during this decade, there were other prominent kennels throughout the United States. Mrs. Mildred Townsend's Clonmel Kennels were in Kansas; Mrs. Felix Drake operated her Drax Kennels in Hialeah, Florida; Marjorie Lane was active in the Baltimore area; Mrs. Jane Johnson owned Pop-n-Jay Kennels in Texas; and Lynn Devan was owner of the Devanvale Kennels in Michigan. Mrs. Iola Dowd's Patoot Kennels were also based in Michigan.

On the East Coast, Mr. and Mrs. George Houston had their Judlu Kennel on Long Island in 1953. Madeline Hoffman imported French, Belgian, Luxembourg Champion W'Monarch of Assam, which soon became an American champion.

In California, Stella and Allan Davis had their Ramon Kennels. There were also Mary and Lee Schaller with the Marlee prefix; Mrs. Charles Anderson; the Fran-Dell Kennels of Frances Davis; Mr. and Mrs. George Hermel; the Kirnel Kennels of Nell and Kirill Flietinghoff; Frank and Marjorie Kitson; Mabel Ennis and her Enrose name; and Louise Jeremy's Yorkshires. The Ru Gene Kennels of Ruth and Gene Fields began in 1951 and produced thirteen champions. Mrs. Fields was also Yorkshire Terrier Club of America president in 1961, 1962, and 1963.

Ch. Pateets Mary Etta, owned by Iola Suhr of Escondido, California, wins the Toy Group at the 1955 Heart of the Plains Kennel Club show under judge Isidore Schoenberg.

Ch. Drax Little Craftsman, owned by Felix and Winifred Drake, wins the Toy Group and a 5-point major at his first show in Havana, Cuba. Judging was Maxwell Riddle; handling was Winifred Drake. The dog was just 10½ months of age at this 1956 show.

Ch. Wildweir Brass Hat, photographed by Evelyn M. Shafer, about 1955.

Ch. Windfall's Blockbuster, owned by Gloria Knight-Bloch.

One of Maybelle Neuguth's lovely Yorkshire Terriers.

In the 1950s was Aerial of Winpat, owned by Mrs. F.P. Fox.

Ch. Valleyend Wistful, owned by Ruth Cooper and pictured winning at the 1957 Progressive Dog Club show.

Ann Seranne, one of America's leading and most famous cookbook authors, takes time out from her chores to say hello to two of the Mayfair Yorkie House puppies. Barbara Wolferman, Ann's partner in the kennel, and the puppies want to know "what's cooking!"

FROM ONE DECADE TO THE NEXT

By the end of the 1950s, Yorkshire Terriers were climbing in popularity as evidenced by increases in kennel club registrations and show entries. Many kennels, such as Starfire, Renrel, and (of course) Wildweir, were continuing to surge ahead; many more were to burst on the scene in the next decade.

THE SENSATIONAL SIXTIES

The 1960s were sensational for many reasons, but especially because of the formation of the Mayfair Kennels with its dynamic and dedicated owner, Ann Seranne.

Already a successful author of cookbooks, an editor of a top gourmet food magazine, and owner of a public relations and food consultant agency, Ann turned her efforts and enthusiasm to the breed she loved the most: the Yorkshire Terrier.

Mayfair

Ann Seranne purchased her first Yorkie from Nancy and David Lerner in 1960. This was Champion Renrel Wee Puddn' of Yorkshire, sired by their famous import, Champion The Vale Tiny Mite.

In 1962 Ann purchased another import from the Lerners, American and Canadian Champion Topsy of Tolestar, bred by Ethel Tole. In Topsy, already campaigned by the Lerners, including a Best of Breed at Westminster in 1962, Miss Seranne saw her value as a brood bitch and wanted her as foundation stock for her newly formed Mayfair Kennels. Her instincts were correct. Topsy produced their first big winner in Champion Dandy Diamond of Mayfair, as well as Champion Dondy Duke of Mayfair owned by Ann Summa. Their sire was Kelpie's Belziehill Dondi, a top-producing stud in his own right, owned by Mildred Hornbrook. Dandy Diamond won fourteen Group Placings and was in the Top Ten Yorkie listings for 1966 in the Phillips System. In turn his son, American and Canadian Champion Mayfair's Oddfella, was to be the next big winner for Mayfair.

In 1966, Barbara Wolferman became a partner with Ann Seranne, and the kennel was moved to a mountain bluff in Newton, New Jersey. Just as the Wildweir sisters were to become world famous in the breed, the Mayfair "partners" were to attain new heights as the list of champions and show wins began to accumulate.

In 1967, American and Canadian Champion Gaytonglen Teddy of Mayfair arrived. Teddy brought the Progresso bloodline to Mayfair through his sire, Champion Progress of Progresso. After winning his championship title in 1969, he went on to win four Bests in Show, twenty-six Toy Groups, and fifty-five Group Placings. He also won two parent club Specialties, in 1970 and 1973, and sired over twenty champions. Teddy is the sire of another Best in Show winner for Mayfair, Champion Mayfair Barban Loup de Mer. Teddy is also all-time top-winning American male in the history of the breed.

Ch. Gaytonglen Teddy of Mayfair, a Best in Show winner and multiple Group winner as well, was also the sire of many champions. Handled by Wendell Sammet for Ann Seranne and Barbara Wolferman.

During the 1980s, the Yorkshires are shown under the Mayfair-Barban name, which combines the kennel representation of both women, and which represents over fifty champions in the breed. Barbara Wolferman, who was active in the theatrical world before joining Ann Seranne at Mayfair, had her first Yorkshire in the early 1950s. While Wendell Sammett is usually the professional handler for the Mayfair-Barban Yorkies, once in a great while Barbara appears in the ring with them. Both women are at ringside to enjoy the "fruits of their labor" and to discuss the joys of owning Yorkies with other exhibitors.

Ann Seranne has always been active in the various Yorkshire clubs over the years, has served as show chairman for the parent club specialties in New York City on occasion, and is now judging at dog shows across the country. Ann has also written many important articles on the breed for the various breed publications. It was a wonderful day for Yorkshire Terriers when Ann Seranne and Barbara Wolferman fell in love with our breed!

They celebrate a quarter of a century of dedication and a successful breeding program in 1985.

Mayfair Yorkie House kennel manager Peter D'Arria, Jr. with three of his young charges. All future champions, they became Mayfair Barban Yogi, Yo-Hoo, and Yummy.

Ch. Mayfair Barban Loup-de-Mer Poses with some of his ribbons and trophies. Co-owned by and bred at Mayfair Yorkie House.

Sahadi

The author's Sahadi Kennels were breeding miniature and toy Poodles when the charm of the Yorkshire Terrier took over. Ann Seranne and I became interested in the Tolestar lines being shown by Nancy and David Lerner, and I purchased Champion Terrie of Tolestar and Tara of Tolestar for my Sahadi Kennels.

Terrie weighed a little over two pounds and was personality plus. In 1962 and during 1963, he was used at stud for Wildweir Orange Girl, owned by Mrs. Walp. During the years before his untimely death in 1965, he was also used for Murray Hill, Tzumiao, and Judlu lines, and produced several puppies out of my Tara of Tolestar. Terrie was sired by Pride of the Manor out of Michaela of Tolestar.

Perhaps the most famous of these puppies was Champion Sahadi Scarlet O'Hara from the Gone With the Wind litter, and owned by Alan and Virginia Bull. Scarlet joined the Bulls' Durrisdeer Kennel, where among her kennel mates were Bouvier des Flandres. There she managed to rule the roost. Scarlet finished for her championship with three majors, and started her ring career by winning the Toy Group at the Ladies Kennel Club A Match in May 1965.

Terrie was also used for photographic works, by famous animal photographer Mary Ellen Browning, during his lifetime as being a true representative of the breed.

Rhett Butler from the Gone With The Wind litter was sold to a Playboy bunny, with a warning that he was not to be used in any photo layouts in that magazine!

Tara's sire was Coulgorm Charles out of Madaleina of Tolestar.

Durrisdeer Maximillian, owned by Virginia Clemens and bred by Virginia Bull. Timmie is a son of Ch. Sahadi Scarlet O'Hara.

Heskethane

It was early in the 1960s that Beryl Hesketh moved from California to Connecticut along with her Yorkshire Terriers. Beryl, who is English, has been associated with Yorkies on three different continents. In the early days, Beryl's husband (a geologist and exploration manager for an oil company) was sent from England to Venezuela. Beryl and her Yorkies were the new only inhabitants of a jungle area, where a jaguar and a wild pig joined forces with her.

Sahadi Roberta, owned by Virginia Bull of Blairstown, New Jersey. "Pebbles" was bred by the author, Joan Brearley.

In 1960, when Beryl and her husband arrived in America with seventeen Yorkies, she began breeding and showing in earnest. Laddie was the name of her first champion here, and the stud force at her kennel. Laddie also had a C.D. degree. A bitch named Amanda of Heskethane was the first homebred champion, but now Heskethane Yorkies can be found in homes and kennels all over the world.

Early in the 1960s Beryl purchased Tilda of Tolestar from Bertha Smith. She also had two puppies out of Tilda's dam. Tango of Tolestar was one, which gave her two first and two second generation Tolestar Yorkshires. Tilda was later sold to Ann Seranne to further expand her Tolestar lines.

In the 1980s, Beryl's record of champions finished in the show ring is impressive, and continues to grow. Some of her top winners were Champion Heskethane Quick March, Heskethane Dandy-Lion, Heskethane Warrior, and Champion Wee Geordie of Heskethane. Her current base of operations is a new kennel in Gardiner, New York.

The well-known Florence van Wyck and two of her Yorkshire Terriers, Heskethane the Magician (also known as Merlin) and his nephew Heskethane the Pendragon, (also known as Dragon). Florence van Wyck resides in Gardiner, New York.

Florence van Wyck

1961 was the year that Florence van Wyck became enamored of Yorkshire Terriers, and she has been devoted ever since. At present she is the owner of two little Heskethane Yorkies: Merlin, and his nephew Dragon.

Florence has been a career woman all of her life. For eighteen years she was an editor of *Architectural Record,* a professional magazine for architects and engineers, after receiving her A.B. degree at Randolph-Macon Women's College and her A.M. from Harvard-Radcliffe. She formerly was a columnist for *Yachting* magazine, and the late *Yorkshire Terrier Quarterly* during its run. Since June 1977, she has been a columnist for *Yorkie Tales,* reporting on the fancy on all fronts with the help, of course, of Merlin and Dragon. She is currently working with Merlin on a volume of verses entitled, appropriately enough, *Merlin's Musings.* This new effort is based on the success of an earlier volume co-authored with her first Yorkie, Ranchit de Plata Pina, known as Mister. This little book was entitled *A Dog's Garden of Verses,* and was published in 1971.

Leprechaun Kennels

Leprechaun is the kennel name for the Yorkshires bred, owned, and shown by Betty R. Dullinger of Halifax, Massachusetts. Betty has been active in the breed for many years, holding office within the specialty clubs for the breed as well as breeding and showing her own dogs.

One of her first stud dogs was Champion Mr. Wonderful. After his retirement there were his son and grandson, American and Canadian Champion Antiqua's T.N.T. of Leprechaun, C.D., and his great-great grandson.

Also at Leprechaun were Champion Leprechaun's Alexander, who also earned his American, Canadian, and Bermudian Companion Dog obedience degrees. There also were Champion Leprechaun's Dungaree Doll, and American and Canadian Champion Leprechaun's Fancy.

Betty Dullinger is now also a judge of Yorkshire Terriers.

Carlen

Helen Stern, whose Carlen Kennels are in Brooklyn, New York, is unquestionably one of the breed's staunchest supporters. Helen constantly campaigns her little Yorkshires in the ring, especially in the Brace classes where she is a consistent winner. Her daughter is responsible for Helen's introduction to the breed. In 1960, she gave Helen a puppy that was later to become

Helen Stern's Ch. Carlen's Johnny Walker, handled by Terence Childs to this Best of Breed win under judge Kathleen Kolbert, was placed from the classes over Specials and went on to Group Second. He was undefeated in the breed for the first two months of his "specials" career.

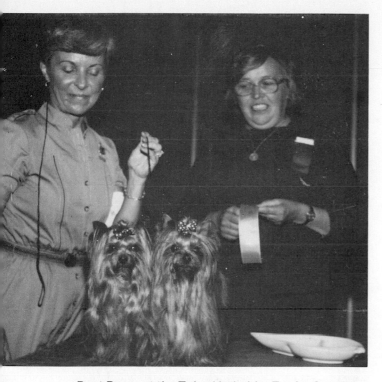

Best Brace at the Tulsa Yorkshire Terrier Specialty show in 1981 was Ch. Oakshire's Mollie Brown and her son, Oakshire's Mr. Waldmeister. This win was under noted breeder-judge Betty Dullinger. Shirlee Sly handled and is co-owner with Francis Sly, both of Overland Park, Kansas.

Champion Kanga's Stinger of Carlen. From this little dog, Helen's kennel grew and is still going strong over two decades later.

Helen travels far and wide with her dogs, and many of them are seen competing for their championships at the Bermuda shows each year. She has produced many champions bearing her kennel name, and won a Best in Show with her Champion Carlen's Johnny Walker. In the 1982 charts for top-winning Yorkies, Johnny Walker was listed as Number One.

Trivar

An impressive array of top-winning Yorkies have been produced at the Trivar Kennels in Maryland. Partners Johnny Robinson and Morris Howard began campaigning winners in 1960, and as of this writing have passed the forty mark in champions.

Their first Group winner was an import, Champion Fashion Wise of Astolat, in 1963. Though their foundation bitch, Champion Bambi Lass, was related to the Pequa Kennels' Pagham lines, it was her daughter, Trivar's Contessa, to which they can attribute their continued

success with the champions that followed. Contessa produced six champions for them, including their Champion Trivar's Tycoon.

In addition to siring many champions, Tycoon was a Best in Show winner in Canada, and won thirty-one Toy Groups plus thirty-five other Group Placings. Tycoon also won the 1972 Yorkshire Terrier Club of Greater St. Louis Specialty. His daughter, Champion Trivar's Golddigger, has won two Bests in Show, ten Groups, and eighteen Group Placements.

In the 1980s, their big winner is Champion Trivar's Cookie Monster, racking up quite a show record and still going strong at the time of this writing. Another winner is Champion Trivar's Suds Sipper. The Trivar dogs are shown and beautifully presented by Johnny Robinson.

Morris Howard is a judge and a former Yorkshire Terrier columnist for *Popular Dogs* magazine. He is also the author of the book *Your Yorkshire Terrier*.

Winner of four all-breed Bests in Show, Ch. Trivar's Gold Digger is pictured winning one of them in 1974 for owners Johnny Robinson and Morris Howard. Ashbey photo.

Windsor-Gayelyn

In 1962, Marilyn Koenig and Barbara Welch founded the Gayelyn Kennels, based on the Stirkean line. Beryl Hesketh had imported Stirkean Bright Star, and then sold it to Gayelyn for their foundation stock. The following year her Champion Heskethane Rob of Lilactime was added. He was another import bred by the Lilactime Kennels. He became the foundation stud for Gayelyn. In 1968 Mrs. Welch died, and Marilyn Koenig carried on until 1969 when she went into partnership with Kathleen Kolbert and formed the Windsor-Gayelyn Kennels based in Connecticut.

Miss Kolbert formed the Windsor Kennels in 1963 with the purchase of Champion Windamere Dolly Dewdrop. Since the partnership, a long succession of champions has been produced. These include American and Canadian Champion Windsor-Gayelyn Robin, a Group Winner and Best Opposite Sex at the 1972 Yorkshire Terrier Club of St. Louis Specialty Show.

Others were Champion Gayelyn Prim N'Proper, Champion Windsor-Gayelyn Silk N'Saffron, and Champion Gayelyn Troubador. Champion Ozmillion Playboy was imported in 1972 to further extend their stud force.

Ch. Windsor Gayelyn Fire Cracker, bred by Kathleen B. Kolbert and Marilyn J. Koenig of Oxford, Connecticut. Fire Cracker is the dam of Ch. Windsor Gayelyn Sky Rocket.

Ch. Windsor Gayelyn Gilded Lilly is pictured winning on the way to her championship. Bred by Kathleen Kolbert and Marilyn Koenig, she is owned by Ms. Koenig.

Radnor Yorkies

Bonita B. Hewes, better known as Bonnie, is another perfect example of a dedicated breeder who does well campaigning her own dogs and who can hold her own against the best of the professional handlers.

Quiet and unassuming, Bonnie's Radnor Yorkies are charmers that do a great deal of winning. Perhaps her best known dog was her Champion Mars Radnor. This little dog finished with all major wins, and as a Special he won eleven Bests of Breed and two Group Placings.

Mars was at stud at Bonnie's kennel in Elverson, Pennsylvania, and is behind many of the lovely little Yorkies with which she is winning at the shows today.

Fred Wolpert and Frojo

Based primarily on his Champion Frojo's Blue Buttons of Maybelle and Mayfair-Barban breeding, Fred Wolpert has been showing and breeding Yorkshire Terriers since 1967. Since then the Wolperts have bred or owned twelve champions, with their Blue Buttons being the dam of four of them. Blue Buttons was sired by Champion Wildweir E. Major of Maybelle out of Kella don Shanadora.

Champion Blue Buttons was Top Yorkshire Terrier Dam in 1971, with three champions to her credit. A fourth finished in 1972.

Ch. Windsor Gayelyn Robin, bred by Barbara Welch and Marilyn Koenig, owned and shown by Kathleen B. Kolbert. This win was under the late judge and famous dog man, Percy Roberts.

Commander and Mrs. John Leonard's Star Sapphire winning at a 1969 foreign dog show.

Devanvale

Champion Yorkfold Jackanapes, Champion Yorkfold Gold Choice, and Champion Yorkfold Little Pixie of Theale were the foundation dogs of Lynne M. Devan's Devanvale Kennels in Birmingham, Michigan, in the 1960s.

Jackanapes, or "Jaimie" as he was better known, was consistently producing quality puppies for her lines, was a producer of champion get, a Group winner and was Best Male Yorkshire at the 1965 Westminster and Chicago International dog shows.

Ch. Devanvale Jack's Son took Best of Breed and Group Third at a 1965 Sturgis Kennel Club show. Owned by Lynne Devan of Birmingham, Michigan.

Dorchester

Commander and Mrs. John Leonard have their Dorchester Kennels in Berkeley, California, and have the great distinction of owning the only two American-bred Yorkshire Terriers that have won International Champion titles. They are International, American, Canadian, Mexican Champion Stirkean's Tiny Tim of Kingsmere, and International, American, Canadian, and Mexican Champion Arribo of Arriso.

This handsome couple travels extensively with their little dogs.

A breed double-header. Best of breed was Ch. Dorchester's Merry Monarch and Best of Opposite Sex was Ch. Dorchester's My Kind of Love. Owners are Commander and Mrs. John Leonard of Berkeley, California.

A beautiful photograph of one of Mel Davis's Yorkies from the camera of Ben Burwell.

Mel Davis

Mel Davis has been active in Yorkshires all during the 1960s. His two great Yorkshire Champions were Champion Tabordale Pepperpot, or "Mickey" as he was better known, and Champion Gayelen's Darn Toot'n. Tootie was Number Two Yorkshire Terrier in the country in 1967 and Number Five in 1968, according to the Phillips System Top Ten listings.

Mel is the owner of a grooming parlor in New York City, where Yorkies and Poodles—Mel also owned Champion Easter Parade, a Toy Poodle—are groomed to perfection for their show ring careers.

Windshaven

Windshaven Kennels, owned by Nancy Lee Webb, began in 1967 when her brood bitch produced her first litter. Three foundation studs were obtained in 1968, one of which finished for his championship that year. He was Champion Mayfairs Unbelieveable. The other two were finished the following year: Champion Viclar's Heesa Dandy and Champion Yorkfold Wags to Riches. Wags was the sire of Champion Windshaven's Wags Tale, American and Canadian Champion Windshaven's Genie, and American and Bermudian Champion Windshaven's Witches Brew.

Champion Wynsippi's Candid Lass, a foundation bitch obtained late in 1969, was added to the kennel and by 1970 two homebreds were campaigned to their titles. One was Witches Brew and the other was Champion Windshaven's Lilliputian, featured in the Special Toy Issue of *Popular Dogs* magazine in December 1971. Other champions followed in Champion Windshaven's Genie and Champion Windshaven's Incredible. Nancy Lee Webb's kennels were located in Broomall, Pennsylvania.

Wynsippi's Candid Lass, one of the many winners from Nancy Lee Webb's Windshaven Kennels in Broomall, Pennsylvania. Pictured at the 1970 Twin Brooks Kennel Club Show, this was Lass's third major for her championship.

Fancy Pants of Progresso, shown in 1962 and owned by Suzanne Rogers of Bloomfield Hills, Michigan.

Suzanne Rogers

Suzanne Rogers of Bloomfield Hills, Michigan, was active in Yorkies in the early 1960s. Her imports from Mrs. C. Hutchins' Progresso line did some nice winning during the 1962 season.

Her Champion Fancy Pants of Progresso and Champion Paper Doll of Progresso were two memorable winners under the adept handling of Barbara Humphries. Fancy Pants was second in the Group, from the classes, under judge Louis Murr at the 1962 Ft. Wayne show.

Miss Rogers also owns the lovely Champion Windameres M'liss.

Ch. Paper Doll of Progresso, owned by Suzanne Rogers, is pictured winning at the 1962 Badger Kennel Club show under judge Isidore Schoenberg. Frasie photo.

Tinker Town

Betty Sallard Johnston's Tinker Town Yorkies were known all over the world in the 1960s. Betty finished many of her tiny Yorkies, and sold and imported many little dogs to perfect her line. It was her Champion Tinker Town Storming-A-Long that made a hit in Japan and was featured in *Kennel Review's* "Illustrating the Standard of the Breed" series.

Some of her most famous dogs were Tri-International Champion Grand Slam of Lilactime, Tinker Town's Toy Tiger, sire of Canadian Champion Tinker Town's Nic-Nac-A-Progress, Champion Heytesbury Eric of Nordlaw, Champion Patoot's Te-Amo, and Canadian Champion Tzumials Solario.

Betty's kennel was located in Sepulveda, California.

Mazelaine

While perhaps known best for her Mazelaine Boxers, Mrs. Mazie Wagner was active in Yorkshires from as far back as the 1930s when she purchased a bitch from Goldie Stone. During the 1940s one of her Yorkshires, Harringay High Tracy, did some winning in the Toy Groups. In 1961 her Champion Mazelaine's Gold Gambit was sold to Wildweir Kennels.

Other Kennels of the Sixties

Also active during the 1960s were four top-winning operations in Illinois: Kay Radcliffe's Kajimanor, Dotty and Wally Naegele's Northshire, Mrs. Ruth Cooper's Cottleston Kennels, and of course Wildweir. Frances C. Geraghty's Yorkfold dogs were winning with their home base in Ohio, and Doris Craig had her Gaytonglen Yorkies in Virginia. The Darshire Kennels of Harriet and Darrel Karns were located in Tennessee, and Hazel Thrasher's Zelden Kennels were in Kansas City, Missouri. Yorksmith Kennels were in New Jersey, owned by Betty Smith.

In 1964 Mrs. Wendy Ann Whitely emigrated to California with her Wenscoes line. Active in the fancy in England before her arrival in this country, Mrs. Whitely produced thirteen American champions with her name. Two other California kennels active in the mid-sixties were the Topaz Kennels of Margery May and the Lorill Kennels of Janice and William Jordan. Beerex was another prefix in the sixties, and was the kennel name of Beatrice and Rex Kramer.

On the East Coast, Gloria and Stanley Lipman began their Nikko Kennels on Long Island.

Ch. Wildweir Skater's Waltz, owned by Ruth Cooper and photographed for her in the 1960's by famous dog photographer Tauskey.

1960 was the year that Ray Ryan became the first American judge to be asked to officiate at an English Yorkshire Terrier Specialty. Ray Ryan and Ken Thompson were owners of the Raybrook Kennels.

Mrs. L. Dowdy of Texas, V. Gregory of Florida, and P. Trojan were all owners of Top Ten Yorkshires during the decade of the sixties.

Best of Breed at the Westminster Kennel Club show in 1969 was Margery May's "Topaz." Evelyn Shafer photo.

Tatty of Pagham, circa 1960s, bred and owned by the Pagham Kennels.

Ch. Kirnels Yum Yum, one of the top three winning Yorkies in 1963. She is pictured here with handler Mitch Wooten winning the Breed at the Yorkshire Terrier Club of America Specialty show. Bred and owned by Kirill and Nell Flietinghoff of Downey, California, this was Yummie's first show after weaning a litter of puppies.

Crystal of Pagham and some of her trophies. The Pagham Kennels were important to the breed in the 1960s era.

Lamsgrove Sharon of Glomin is pictured winning at the 1961 Susquenango Show under Maxwell Riddle. Owner is Lucy B. Duffy. Stephen Klein photo.

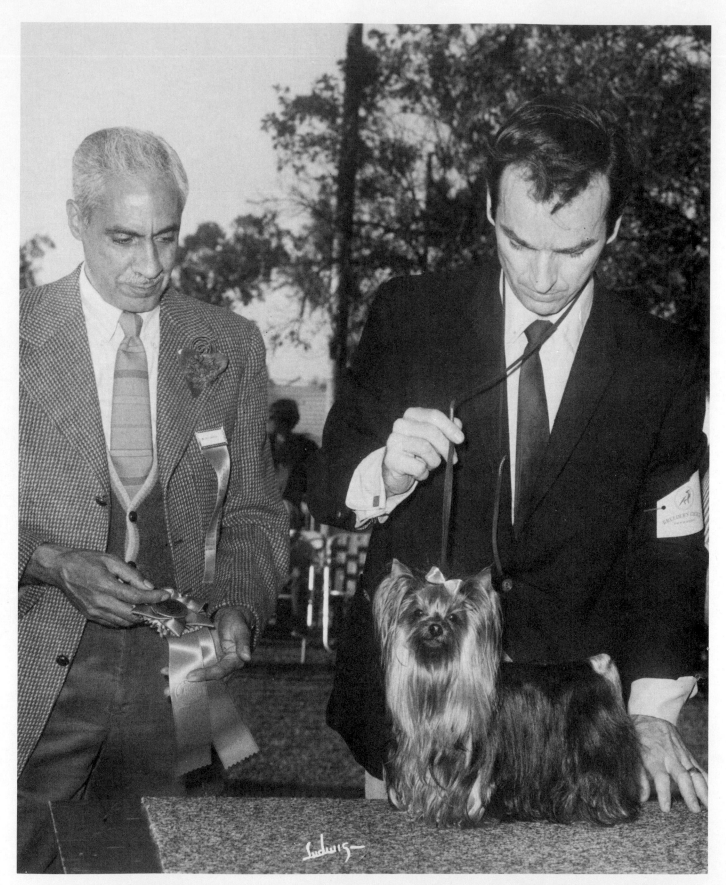

American and Mexican Ch. Camelot's Little Pixie, Americas top-winning Yorkie for 1970, bred and owned by Mrs. Lee Sakal of Orange, California. In just 10 months of showing, Pixie defeated more than 9,000 dogs under 41 different judges and was handled exclusively by Mrs. Sakal's husband, Richard M. Sakal. Pixie is pictured here winning another Group under Mr. Ellsworth Gamble.

English Ch. Don Carlos of Progresso, an import owned by John Young. Don Carlos was the winner in England of eleven Challenge Certificates and three all-breed Bests in Show, and was Best of Breed at the Boston show in 1961 shortly after his arrival in this country.

Beerex's Rakald is pictured winning at a 1969 show in Savannah, Georgia, with Michele Leathers Billings handling. Graham photo.

Lamsgrove Little Fella, owned by Lucy B. Duffy, was a winner at the 1962 Chicago show.

TOY GROUP 1ST.

One of Mrs. Stanley E. Ferguson's Yorkshires, circa 1960s.

Leprechaun's Nik Nak winning at the 1968 Greater Lowell Kennel Club show. Owner was Margot Dwyer, De Cuivre Kennels, Lynbook Farm, Southboro, Massachusetts.

A Christmas sleigh ride for two of Maybelle Neuguth's puppies, photographed by Terence Gili in the 1960s.

Commander John Leonard is pictured winning with a Hi Society Yorkshire Terrier several years ago.

THE NINETEEN-SEVENTIES

Jentre

Ruth S. Jenkins of Lakeside, California, is the owner of the famous Jentre Yorkshire Terriers. Perhaps most famous of her dogs is American and Canadian Champion Clarkwyn Jubilee Eagle, sire of dozens of champions in America, Canada, and England. His get have won Bests in Show and are top producers in their own right.

It was Jubilee Eagle that served as the model for artist Kay Finch when creating her life-size bronze figure honoring famous Goldie Stone, pioneer breeder of Yorkshire Terriers in 1974. Bred by Mrs. John Clark, "Jubie" has made his mark in the breed and continues to produce winners, including the 1980 top producing bitch in the country. He has also been bred to the famous All Breed Best in Show winner at Westminster, Champion CeDe Higgens. Jubie's puppies are

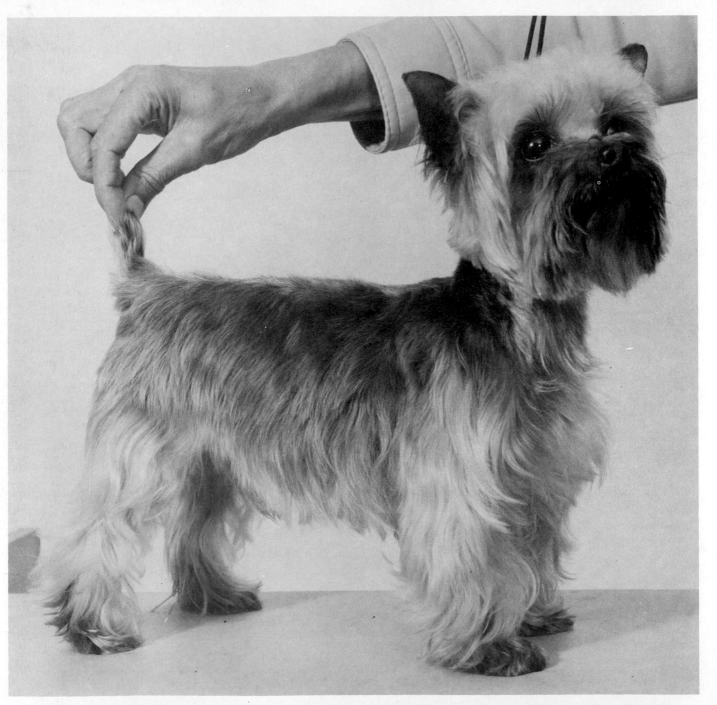

One of the great Yorkies of all time, here trimmed down to show his excellent conformation, is American and Canadian Ch. Clarkwyn Jubilee Eagle, top producer for 1979, 1980, and 1981. Owned by R. Jenkins of Lakeside, California.

top winners and producers in every foreign country to which they have gone to new owners. In 1981 another Best in Show offspring came on the scene with the win of Canadian Champion Bloomsbury Golden Jubilee. This Jubie daughter is owned by Lynn Bishop. Other Best in Show or Specialty Show winners are Champion Cameo's Talk of the Town, Champion Fardust's Fury, and Champion Topaz Verity's Victor.

Fardust

The Fardust Kennels of Dustine F. Bitterlin are located in San Diego, California. Their Champion Clarkwyn Jubilee Eagle's son, American and Mexican Champion Fardust's Fury, was a top winner in the late 1970s. He started his impressive ring career in 1975 at the Yorkshire Terrier Club of America Specialty Show held in San Francisco, where he won the Sweepstakes, Winner's Dog, and Best of Breed. He completed his championship two days later. His Mexican championship was won just as quickly—two shows in two days, followed by another Group and Best in Show. He had won fifty Bests of Breed and many group placings by the time he was retired in 1977.

Fury won the 1978 Stud Dog Award from the Yorkshire Terrier Club of Greater Los Angeles, and was listed in *Yorkie Tales* as being among the Top Producers for 1978. He was featured on the cover of *Yorkie Tales*, May 1979 issue.

Dustine Bitterlin declares Fury a hero since his barking alerted the family in time to escape a fire. He is at stud with his owners, siring quality puppies that are winning in the show rings.

At the time of his passing on July 4, 1982, Fury was the sire of fifteen American champions.

Barbee and the CeDe Higgens Story

It can be said that the pinnacle of success, or at least the ultimate dream, of every Yorkshire breeder is to breed a dog so wonderful and nearly perfect that he could win Best in Show at the Westminster Kennel Club. American and Canadian Champion CeDe Higgens did just that! On Tuesday, February 14, 1978, the little five and three-quarter pound Yorkie from Seattle, Washington, went all the way to the top. Owned by Bill and Barbara Switzer, and handled for them as always by their daughter Marlene, this little darling became everyone's Valentine by achieving the honor of being the only Yorkshire Terrier ever to win "the Garden."

A life-sized bronze statue of Ch. Clarkwyn Jubilee Eagle done by artist and breeder-judge Kay Finch for owner Ruth Jenkins.

The previous Sunday, he had managed to win the National Specialty of the Yorkshire Terrier Club of America over another record entry, and on Monday won the Breed at Westminster, the first step up the ladder to his Best in Show under judge Mrs. Geraldine Hess. That evening he walked away with the Toy Group under the highly respected judge Iris de la Torre Bueno.

Those of us at ringside on that momentous occasion had tears in our eyes as Anne Rogers Clark awarded the top honor—a truly popular win that made Yorkshire Terrier history.

Higgens was purchased as a puppy by William Switzer as an anniversary present for his wife from his breeder, C. D. Lawrence. Mr. Lawrence cautioned that the dog might be too small for a top show prospect, but Higgens went on to win a four-point major at his first show at nine months of age. The Switzers' attractive daughter Marlene took him to handling class; Mrs. Switzer dedicated herself to his grooming routine, while Mr. Switzer planned the show ring career. Truly a family affair! Marlene color-coordinated her ring clothes to match Higgens' trademark—red and white polka dot hair bows. CeDe Higgens and Marlene became an unbeatable team that led to the ultimate success in the ring. We are pleased that Higgens was nominated for the Dog Hall of Fame, and Marlene nominated as a Female Owner-Handler for 1977.

Sired by American and Canadian Champion Clarkwyn Jubilee Eagle out of CeDe Bonnie, Higgens has a great deal of Clarkwyn breeding behind him on both sides, and a good deal of Wildweir also—a fact that owners of those lines can be proud of as well. Perhaps one of the nicest things to know about Higgens is that he is not a "kennel dog," nor does he spend his life in a crate. He is an active member of the family, with a Siamese cat as his favorite playmate at home.

Higgens' sons and daughters, all bearing the Barbee prefix, are winning all over the country at the top shows.

While Higgens' win at the Garden was a highlight in the breed history, we all know that records are made to be broken. However, it will likely be a long time before another great dog will come along who can top this one. Every Yorkshire Terrier lover has to be very proud of CeDe Higgens . . . long may he reign!

Carnaby

Professional handler Terence Childs and his partner are owners of the Carnaby Kennels in Connecticut. All of the Carnaby Yorkshires are handled by Terry himself, though he also is handler for some of the other top-winning Yorkies.

Dr. and Mrs. Robert Neibling with their first two champion Yorkshire Terriers, bred by the Barnhill Kennels in Woodbury, Connecticut. Pictured in the middle is Terence Childs with Champion Carnaby Rock N Roll.

Ch. Carnaby Rondelay, pictured at two years of age winning Best of Breed under judge and breeder Janet Bennett. Rondelay finished for his championship in six shows with four majors. Breeder-owner-handlers are Terence Childs, pictured here, and Joseph Champagne.

Some of their Best in Show and Specialty winners are Champion Carnaby Rock N Roll, Champion Carnaby Jazz Man, Champion Carnaby Rondeley, and Champion Carnaby Tradition Rock.

Group winners, all homebreds carrying the Carnaby prefix, include Champion Jazzman, Trad Jazz (litter brothers), Bit O Brass, Modern Jazz, Tamborine, Piece of the Rock, and Joyall Maria, owned by Allison Dixon.

Montclair

Montclair is the prefix used by Mrs. David L. Ammon for her Yorkshire Terriers. Jay was also known for her breeding of Afghan Hounds during the 1960s, and continues in her belief that "there is no substitute for quality." In 1981 Jay purchased the last Yorkshire Terrier ever to be bred at the Nitetrain Kennels of Mrs. Georgene Sheldon. His name is Montclair Legacy. Jay considers him to be a "legacy" indeed.

Her American and Canadian Champion Montclair Fly-By-Night won the breed from the classes while working toward his championships, and is a son of Champion Clarkwyn Jubilee Eagle.

Jo-Lyle

Sara Jo Woodward began breeding dogs way back in 1956, but it was only in the late 1970s that she got "hooked" on Yorkshire Terriers.

Today she has eight Yorkies including "Poppy," a Champion CeDe Higgens daughter. She is also the owner of Krackerjack, the son of Champion Shado Mountain Sparrow Hawk. Krackerjack is the main stud force at her Jo-Lyle Kennels in Orlando, Florida, where she plans to continue a selective breeding program as well as exhibiting in the show ring.

Susan's Raggedy Andy, C.D., one of Susan Sandlin's obedience trained and titled obedience dogs. This son of Ch. Trivar's Tycoon was photographed by Olan Mills.

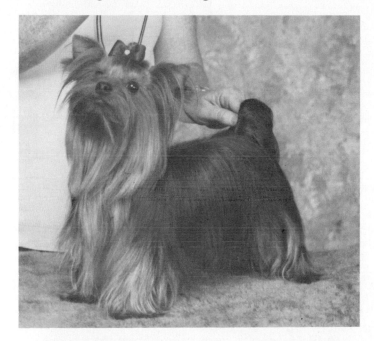

Eden Valley Kracker Jack is owned by Sara Jo Woodward of Orlando, Florida. The sire was American and Canadian Ch. Shadow Mountain Sparrow Hawk ex Beholda Glow.

miniature rooms with little Yorkies actively participating in family life. Many of her pieces have found their way to Switzerland, Austria, South America, Australia, and Japan.

In addition to her Yorkshires, Susan also has included Maltese both in her home and in her art work.

Original designs in silk petit point by Susan M. Sandlin of Arlington, Virginia.

Petit Point

The Petit Point Kennels of Susan M. Sandlin in Arlington, Virginia, must be further identified as The Original Petit Point Yorkshires since there is some confusion with a similar name in another country. However, there is further distinction with this operation. Susan started her petit point (needlework, that is) business in 1963. It was in 1974 that she started showing her Yorkshire Terriers, and quite naturally her Petit Point Yorkshires followed.

Her work has won numerous prizes and can be found in the collections of people all over the world. In addition to her darling little framed pictures of mottos and Yorkshires in animated poses and bright colors, Susan now produces

Ch. Marsan's Carnaby Minuet, bred and owned by Marion Santoro and Terence Childs, winning at a 1975 show. "Minny" was Ms. Santoro's first Champion Yorkie and the foundation bitch at her Marsan Kennels. The sire was Ch. Carnaby Rock N Roll ex Marsan's Fancy Pants.

Ch. Melodylane Ever Lovin', owner-handled by Leo Glynn. Bred by Mary Purvis, the sire was Ch. Melodylane Mini Trail ex Melodylane Golden Slippers.

Bred, owned, and shown by Terence Childs is
Ch. Carnaby Traditional Rock.

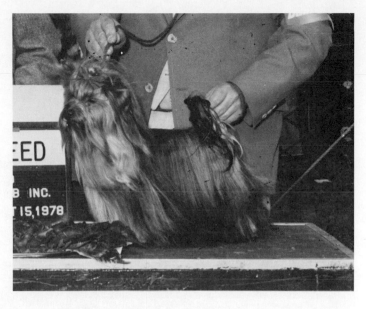

Ch. Carnaby Tamborine, pictured winning at the 1977 Westminster Kennel Club under judge Edna Ackerman,
Shown by Terence Childs, Barnhill Kennels, Woodbury, Connecticut.

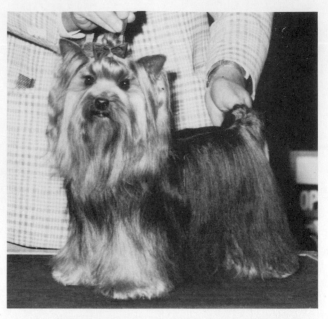

Ch. Windsor Gayelyn Sky Rocket is pictured winning at the 1978 Somerset Hills Kennel Club show on the way to her championship. Bred by Marilyn J. Koenig and Kathleen B. Kolbert.

Ch. Carlens Kahlua Mist, owned by Helen Stern of Brooklyn, New York.

Ch. Trivar's Hanky Panky, pictured winning the Breed at a 1978 show with owner-handler Eugene Hauff, Broomhill Kennels, Anoka, Minnesota. Hanky Panky was sired by Ch. Trivar's Tycoon ex Trivar's Country Girl, and is one of the brood bitches at Broomhill Kennels.

Ch. Kaacey's Devilish Angel of Bon, pictured winning at a show on the way to her championship. Owner is Kaacey Lynn of Margate, Florida.

Ch. Jacolyn Kibet's Honey Bear, owned by Shelby Stevens and Carolyn Servis. Bred by Barbara Perkins, Honey Bear is pictured winning at a recent show on the way to her championship. Sire was Ch. Anderleighs Golden Bear ex Barbara's Celestial Angel.

WINNERS
GREENVILLE
KENNEL CLUB
JULY 1979
PHOTO BY *Graham*

Ch. Nitetrain Painted Lady, a daughter of Ch. Sheldon's Canis Major, is owned by Arlene Mack of Westlake, Ohio. Lady started her show career as a Best in Match winner under judge Ann Seranne in 1979 at the Southeastern Michigan Yorkshire Terrier Specialty Match Show.

Ch. Carnaby Sky Rocket, owned by Bobbie Dodds and handled for her by Terence Childs at the 1979 Bucks County Kennel Club show for a 5-point major under judge William Taylor to achieve the championship for Rocket. His dam, Ch. Carnaby Celebration, was one of the top-producing Yorkies, with a litter of three which attained their titles.

Ch. Melodylane Golden Rule, owned by Joy and Keith Wieland, bred by Mary Purvis. The sire was Ch. Melodylane Candy Man ex Melodylane Sound of Music.

The multiple Group winning Ch. Windsor Gayelyn Adam's Rib II, bred and owned by Kathleen B. Kolbert.

Ch. Jofre's Ruff N Reddy is pictured winning at a 1979 St. Louis Specialty Show on the way to his championship. He is owned by Lillian Fittz.

Ch. Wingate Windsor Gayelyn Hapi was bred, owned, and handled by Suzanne M. Jones to this win under judge Iris Bueno. This Group First, from the classes, completed Hapi's championship. She was whelped in 1978.

THE DECADE OF THE EIGHTIES

The 1980s began with all the enthusiasm and increases in interest and accomplishment that everyone readily expected. The breed was climbing the charts in popularity and managed to hit the Number Eleven spot, just one niche away from the all-breed Top Ten favorites.

Ann Seranne and Barbara Wolferman's Champion Mayfair Barban Verikoko, Champion Trivar's Cookie Monster, and Champion Wildweir Bumpersticker managed to hit the Top Twenty-Five in the Toy Group and show no indications of letting up on their winning streaks.

Two Barbee Kennels dogs, Champion Barbee Denaire Dickens and Champion Barbee Good Time Charlie were among the Top Ten; and Barbee was the only kennel represented with two of their breeding ranking near the top. Pegmate's Man About Town, Champion Penney's Touch of Class, Champion Jen's Chiquita, Champion Amwalk's Tigre De Oro, and Champion Cameo's Jubilee Dickens were also right up there.

It was plain to see that by the start of this new decade it would be impossible to record the names of all the kennels and all the dogs that were participating in breed activities. Names like

Ch. Trivar's Cookie Monster wins the Breed under judge Kathleen Kolbert at the Mohawk Valley Kennel Club, where he went on to Best in Show. Bred by Jean and Thomas Ranch, the Cookie Monster is owned by Morris Howard and Johnny Robinson, Jr., pictured here handling.

Top of the Line, owned by Mr. and Mrs. Eddy Nicholson, and Zerox owned by T. Conner Zerod, and Mr. and Mrs. C. E. Roberts' Rob-Tell Kennels are just a few of those whose advertisements grace the pages of the magazines announcing their accomplishments. Many of those mentioned, as well as many more of those who are supporting our breed, arc pictured elsewhere in this book. For any that might have been overlooked we apologize and declare the omission as nothing more than lack of space, and certainly regret that every last deserving little Yorkie could not have been included!

Petit Point Peach Fuzz, bred and owned by Susan M. Sandlin.

At left and at bottom left is Windsor Gayelyns Ms' Troubles, the daughter of Ch. Windsor Gayelyn Treemonisha, the fourth generation of champion breeding in owner Kathleen Kolbert's line. Directly below is Ch. Taramanor Veraranda owned by Kathleen B. Kolbert and Helen Mellucci, and bred by Helen Mellucci. She is pictured here finishing for her championship, handled by Kathleen Kolbert at a 1980 show.

Ch. Wildweir Household Finance is pictured winning on the way to his championship title at two years of age. Whelped in 1980, "Happy" was by Gleno Credit Card ex Wildweir Haired Houseperson. Bred, owned, and shown by Mrs. Leslie Gordon and Miss Janet Bennett.

Ch. Broomhill's Teen Angel owned and shown by Eugene Hauff of the Broomhill Kennels, Anoka, Minnesota. The sire was Ch. Trivar's Tycoon ex Trivar's Hanky Panky.

Topaz Bran Muffin, bred by Margery May and owned by Elda and Nathan Tropper of Los Angeles, California. This charming photo was taken in 1978.

Kaacey's Small Wonder, a four-pound bitch whelped in 1980, is owned by Kaacey Lynn of Margate, Florida.

Ch. Windsor Gayelyn Hot to Trot, bred by Lois McDonald and co-owned by Joseph Iannone and Agustin Gomez.

Ch. Estugo's Wynsippi Diamond Lil wins the breed at a 1981 show.

Ch. Windsor Gayelyn Tia Maria, owned by Ellen S. Rowland of Newington, Connecticut.

Yorkholms Christopher Robin (above) and Yorkholms Sweet Sheree (below), both owned by Muriel Holman of Livonia, Michigan.

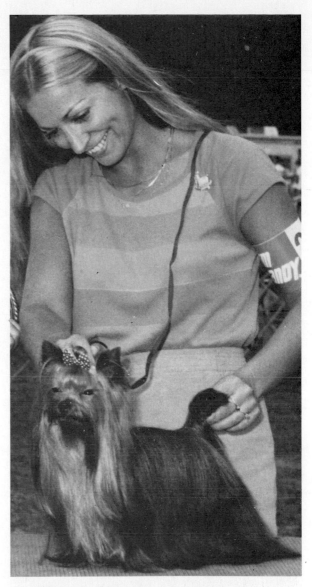

Ch. Wildweir Wish Come True (above), bred by Nancy Donovan and owner-handled by Mary Bratschi; and Ch. Wildweir Small Print (below), bred and owned by Mrs. Leslie S. Gordon, Jr., and Miss Janet E. Bennett.

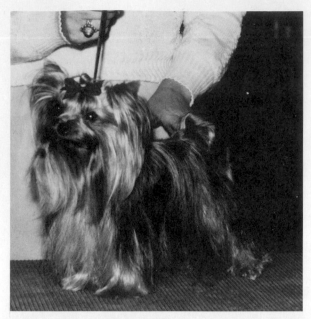

Bred, owned, and handled by Suzanne M. Jones of New York Mills, New York, is Turyanne Wingate Rocky Roads.

Kaacey's Blue Blazer O Shady, owned by Kaacey Lynn of Margate, Florida. Whelped July 1981, Blazer is sired by American and Canadian Ch. Dandi Tu of Jenia's.

Melodylane Moonshine is pictured winning on the way to her championship. She is co-owned by Bruce and Mary Ann Paul and her breeders Freeman and Mary Purvis of Centerville, Iowa.

Ch. Jacolyn Kibet's Golden Girl, bred by Carolyn Servis and owned by her and Shelby Stevens of Fort Lauderdale, Florida.

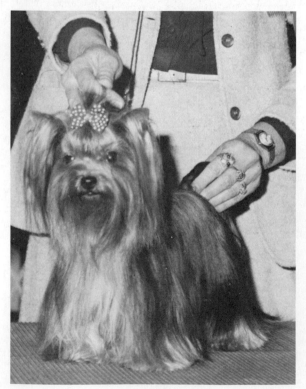

Just what every Yorkie lover wants to find under their Christmas tree—Lor-Dean's Spirit in the Sky fits the bill.

Barbara Scott Goegel, agent for the Pagham Kennels in England a few decades ago, is responsible for this adorable Yorkie picture, photographed for her by Eleanor Rost.

American and Canadian Ch. Marcliff's London Bobby, owned by Drs. W.C. and M.A. Hacking of Uxbridge, Ontario, Canada.

CHAPTER FIVE

Yorkshire Terriers Around the World

Ch. Barbways Marquis MacDuff, Canadian Obedience Trained and Canadian and American Ch. Utility Dog titlist, is winner of 27 High in Trial wins. "Tuffy" is the top-winning obedience Yorkie in the history of the breed and possibly the top-winning obedience Toy dog.

As air travel narrows our world and cuts travel time to a minimum, more and more dogs are covering great distances to attain additional titles. Along with the desirable "Ch." in front of a dog's name, many are carrying the even more desirable "Int. Ch." Most everyone knows that the "Int." stands for International Champion, but few realize what is involved in earning it or how to go about getting one. Far too many people believe that simply winning a championship in another country besides the United States entitles them to call their dogs International Champions. Nothing could be farther from the truth.

THE FCI—WHAT IT IS AND HOW IT WORKS

The International Championship is bestowed on dogs that are exhibited and win according to certain rules and regulations set up by the *Federation Cynologique Internationale*, with headquarters in Brussels, Belgium. Most English-speaking countries **do not** belong to it, but nearly all other countries interested in exhibiting dogs **do**.

The Federation holds an annual show, each year in a different member country, and their kennel club officials play host. Judges are selected from all the member countries, and the shows usually last two or three days. Entries may be in the thousands, and entry fees vary from country to country. Group Division is similar to the American form, but there can be a group held specially for dogs native to that particular country hosting the show.

To win an International Championship, a dog must win a total of four Championship Certificates in at least four countries under at least three different judges within a period of one year.

CANADA

The Yorkshire Terrier has been popular in Canada for almost as long as it has been in the United States. During the 1970s, one of the top winners was Canadian and American Champion Camelots Robin of Yorkboro owned by Mrs. Doreen Hubbard. This charming little multiple Best in Show winner made quite a name for himself in Canada during his show ring career.

The Brecon Kennels near Toronto imported Wildweir Obviously a Lover from the Bennets Kennel. "Luv" was sired by American Champion Wildweir Fairly Obvious by a Champion Wildweir Weekend Warrior daughter. Luv was co-owned with G. Mascarenas. Brecon Kennels also campaigned the homebred champion "*Cassanova*," Champion Brecon's Dark and Dangerous, and Brecon's Cavalier, sire of five champions.

Kelim's Devil in Disguise, photographed at four months of age. Bred and owned by Laurie Mahood of the Kelim Kennels, Richmond, British Columbia.

The Mascarenas line carrying the Blanjo prefix is well known in Yorkshire Terrier circles. They bred Champion Blanjo's Grand Slam, and also Blanjo's Buzz About. Some of the very best bloodlines are bred into their strain.

Mrs. Carol Proctor is the owner of the Caraway Kennels in Ontario. Her list of champions include her Caraway's Blue Denium, Champion Gypsy Gold of Highland, Caraway's Wee Dooley, and Caraway's Rock N Rythm.

Farrkee Yorkies also boast of a champion line in their stock. Champion Farrkee's First Lady was sired by American Champion Clarkwyn Honeyson ex Champion Cedarlee's Tiny Gem of Jubilee. Their line also includes both Wildweir and Northshire lines. Their Champion Northshire's Dapper Dan was a top stud force there.

Also active in the breed during the 1970s were (in alphabetical order): Ms. B. Beatty and Ms. J. Kruch's Cubic Acre Kennels, Mrs. Irene Blanchi and Mr. William Lanes' Blanchilane Ken-

nels, Mrs. J. D. Clark's Vingarde line, Miss Audry Cumming and her B-Elegant name, Ms. Cecily Doerflein, and Ms. Mae Dunlop with her Sneak A Peak Kennels.

Mrs. Frances Evan and Rose Pre Kennels, Horst and Gisela Fischer with Walburga, the Stanley Graves Kingtree line, Drs. W. and M. Hacking with Marcliff, Mrs. H. Harland's Helwina Kennels, Mrs. Lorraine Hayes and Pastoral, and the Highland Yorkies of Mrs. DeForest Simmons were also all active.

We saw the names of Frances Hyndman, Dorothea Montgomery, Mrs. Marion Kirk of Mardonlyn, Ms. Gene Loughheed, and Mrs. Laurie Mahood who owned the top obedience dog Champion Barbways' Marquis Mac Duff, U.D. and American C.D. Mrs. Mahood is active in the show ring as well, in both Canada and the United States.

On the right, Bob Mahood of British Columbia was the winner of his twenty-seventh High in Trial award under judge Ben Taylor. With Can. O.T. Ch. Barbway's Marquis MacDuff, Canadian and American U.D. On the left is Tuffy's great grandson, Kelim's Little Bit of Joy. He finished for his C.D. title the same day at the age of nine months, pictured here with owner-trainer-handler, Regina Whitehorn.

Mr. and Mrs. H. Matsubayashi own the Lemuria line, Mrs. Peggie Norris has the Gwyn Afon Yorkies, and Helen Price owns the Masterpeke Kennels, which also gives us a hint as to another breed in which she is interested! The Harlow Kennels are owned by James and Louise Proctor, Little Twig by Mr. and Mrs. William Ransom, and Kirkstan by Mrs. Barbara Rowell. Marian Stoner owns Breckland, Ronald Thompson owns Abon Hassan, and Elvin and Kathie Townsend are known for their Yorkland Kennels.

The Yorkshire Terrier Club of Canada held its first annual specialty show in August of 1971 in Toronto, judged by Mrs. Yan Paul. There is also a Canadian Yorkshire Terrier Association, Inc., in Ontario.

Virginia Frederic was a founding member and a first vice president of the Yorkshire Terrier Club of Canada, even though her residence was in New York State. She was the owner of American and Canadian Champion Mayfair's A La Mode.

In the early 1980s, there were several top quality dogs heading the list of Canadian winners. Champion Encore's Cherlokee Warrior, owned by R. Hardy, was one. Others were Yorkboro One Step Closer, owned by D. Hubbard; Champion Farrkee's Diamond Jim, owned by S. Farrier; Champion Lavally Super Atom, owned by Mrs. H. Deinfee; and Champion Buttonbrite's Royal Tartan, owned by Mr. and Mrs. G. Salls.

SCOTLAND

In recent decades, many of the fine dogs we see in the rings today on both sides of the Atlantic have been bred from stock throughout the British Isles.

Laura Boyd is one of the older breeders of Yorkshire Terriers in Scotland, dating back to the 1930s when, as a young child, she enjoyed the care and company of her grandmother's Yorkie named Rufus. She and her sister shared the chore of replacing his rag curlers—as well as washing and ironing them—and rubbing black sulphur and olive oil into his coat twice weekly.

Laura Boyd also reports that in those early days the dogs were more black and tan, rather than the desired "steel blue" of today, and many were very small—too small to breed at all, or else they ran the risk of Caesarean section deliveries.

In later years, her Tiny Tim of Girthon was Best Toy at the Hamilton Show near Glasgow. She also showed her Gina, or Glamour Girl of Lan-ber, that usually won her classes or was first

in the breed at the Aberdeen and Kincardine shows in that country.

The grandfather of Laura Boyd's Tiny Tim was the famous Champion Glamour Boy Glingonnes, a Champion at Crufts several years ago.

The Yorkshire Terrier Club of Scotland was formed at More's Hotel in Glasgow, Scotland, on February 23, 1963. Their first meeting was to select officers and to set up a complete list of rules and regulations to meet the approval of The Kennel Club in England, under whose jurisdiction their club was held.

Mrs. M. Riley of Blackpool was invited to be the first judge at the twelve-member club show in November 1963. Two shows were held that year, one of them open, and their first championship status club show was held in April 1969. At their member's show, classes for children's handling are held. In the early days of the club approximately sixty members belonged. Naturally, as the breed grew in popularity, the number of members also increased, along with special activities within the club.

Ch. Soham Pearl. Soham was one of the major Kennel names even during the 1950s and 1960s.

IRELAND

The presence of Yorkshire Terriers in Ireland preceded the founding of the Irish Kennel Club more than half a century ago. Lady Edith Hyndham and a Miss Loton were two of the earliest pioneers in the breed in that country and are responsible for getting the breed off to good start there. From their Soham and Clu-Mor Kennels they did a great deal of exporting to other countries of the world, and their lines can be found behind many of the top winners in other countries. Mrs. Crookshank came along with a top kennel bearing the name Johnstounburn, and has produced top quality dogs. Her Yorkies also were exported to many countries. All three names can be found in important winning pedigrees even today.

While Yorkies always managed to do well in the Toy Groups in dog shows throughout Great Britain, the breed has also come to suffer from some of the effects of over-popularity. It can be hoped that the breed will survive as long as the efforts of breeders such as Maureen Holmes, one of today's dedicated fanciers, are aware of the importance of maintaining the standard and holding to the valuable bloodlines that established the breed in that country.

English Champion Martywyn's Wee Mischief, owned by the Wildweir Kennels, Glenview, Illinois.

GERMANY

Wiesbaden was the location for one of the bigger and better dog shows in Germany in 1973—the Internationale Dog Show held under the auspices of the German Canine Association, with FCI rules. It was organized by the German Dog Lovers Association. The World Championship show that year was held in Dortmund. Germany played host to other World Championship shows in 1935, 1956, and again in 1973 with approximately 5,000 entries. The 1973 show was held at the convention hall, with some of the events being held outdoors. Obedience trials are usually held at separate shows.

In Germany, Yorkshire Terriers belong to the Terrier Clubs and not the Toy Groups. Yorkies are very popular in Germany and prices are high. The smaller dogs are the most highly prized and usually weigh in at four pounds or under.

Showing is rather casual as compared to professional standards in the United States, and the grooming leaves a lot to be desired. Written critiques are given and there is also a Performance Class. The name for a championship title in Germany is Sieger.

FRANCE

The largest and most important dog show in France is held in March in the city of Paris, and is called *Exposition Canine Internationale de Paris*. Translated, of course, it becomes The Paris International Dog Show. It is always held in conjunction with the Agriculture show, so a visitor who wishes to see the Yorkshire Terrier judging will also be in close company with hundreds of rabbits, ducks, chickens, turkeys, and cattle, not to mention the food and wine samples offered from the French provinces.

Anyone desiring to make a French championship must win at this show as well as three other French shows for the title. All dogs have to receive an "Excellent" rating in order to be eligible to compete. There is no selection of a Best in Show dog, and entries are received from almost every European country.

SWEDEN AND OTHER SCANDINAVIAN COUNTRIES

Around 1911, the first Yorkshire Terriers went from England to Sweden where they had been imported by a Mrs. D. Arn. She had two, named Prince and Minnie. A German import, Ilka Holsatia, was next.

This three-month-old puppy, bred by Hugo Ibanez and Stephen Maggard of Charlotte, North Carolina, grew up to be the International Ch. Estugo's Stella Star.

In 1945, Mrs. Runefels imported English Champion Parkview Princeling that lived to the ripe old age of 12. He sired a great number of champions in Sweden before his demise, and was largely responsible for the growing popularity of the breed. Irma Ryden, a staunch advocate of the breed, purchased her first Yorkie from Mrs. Runefel's kennel. Her name was Klarissa Musett Av Sano. A broken leg early in life left her a little lame, but she was used for breeding and produced six champions, one of them a world champion in 1964 that was later sold to Denmark.

In 1960, Irma Ryden also imported, from Mrs. Hutchin in England, Shamrock Star of Progresso that won two Bests in Show.

By 1968, registrations in Sweden had reached over 350. This figure was a twenty-five percent increase over the preceding years. Now, almost two decades later, you can imagine the registration figures.

Judging at shows in Sweden is similar to judging in England. Three certificates are needed for a champion, under several different judges. Exhibitors keep their dogs moving until the judges have placed them, and there are no money prizes. There are obedience classes in Sweden, but as of the 1970s, no Yorkshires have been reported to have taken part in them.

In 1981, a Yorkshire Terrier named International Champion Parcvern Smuggler won the title of Top Dog, all-breeds, in Scandinavia. Smuggler was an import from England and is co-owned by Kari Haave and Per Unden. Smuggler's sire was Champion Chantmarles Stowaway.

During 1981, Smuggler won four Bests in Show and ten Groups in Sweden, but also had top wins in Norway and Finland, all won during a total of sixteen times entered.

Most kennels in Sweden are based on the English imported dogs from the Ozmilion Kennels, owned for the most part by Bernice Unden. Approximately a thousand Yorkies are registered each year by the Swedish Kennel Club. Recently, an American, Ms. Dorothy Naegele, visited Sweden and judged at an all-breed show just north of Stockholm. There was a large entry, with a Finnish dog named Pikkupenni winning the show from the Open class.

Ch. Melodylane Independent Imp, owned by Jacqualine J. Hadfield and handled by Norman Patton for this win under judge Dorothy Naegele. The sire was Ch. Northshire's Mazel Tov Melodylane Patti Marie.

POLAND

Needless to say, dog shows in Communist countries are not well attended by people from the free world.

In 1973, for the tenth anniversary of the International Dog Show, the Polish Kennel Club played host; at the same time, the club commemorated their twenty-fifth anniversary. The Polish Kennel Club is the only one recognized in that country by the FCI, and the show was held at the Fair Grounds that year under FCI rules.

Of the approximately 1500 dogs entered, only twelve of them were Yorkshire Terriers. It was reported that three of these entries represented breeders in Poland, while the rest were pet dog owners.

The lack of enthusiasm can be attributed in part to the fact that few dogs can be imported, not only because of financial restrictions, but also due to stringent rules and regulations concerning the importation of dogs. Even taking dogs in and out of the country poses problems at the borders.

In Poland, Yorkshire Terriers are considered as Working Dogs and not part of the Toy Group.

Further information about the breed in Poland since this 1973 show has not come to our attention.

SOVIET UNION

The Soviet Union acknowledges both local and national champions, and these regional titles can be won many times, although there is usually only one regional show per year. Every few years there is a show called an All National, and the national champion from this show is the top winning dog in the USSR. Dogs are rated excellent, very good, fair, poor, or unacceptable, depending on both performance and conformation.

Russia held its first dog show in 1923, and shows have survived all regimes and political changes, though they are on a smaller scale than in other countries of the world. As elsewhere in the world, a dedicated core of devoted breeders managed to preserve the important bloodlines during the various wars.

If you wish to buy a dog in the Soviet Union, you must do so through a local dog club; the cost will depend on the quality and success of its sire and dam. You must register the dog with the club after receiving the dog's papers, and if you wish to breed it, you must consult the breeding section of the same local club. Dogs which are permitted to be bred must have a show mark of X, or VG (excellent or very good) for dogs, and G (good), for bitches. They must also have an obedience or utility degree.

Dogs are registered with three independent branch organizations under Toy, Hunting, or Service Dog categories, and then also individually by breed. These service dog clubs can be found in all major cities of Russia, and they are the central body overseeing all the activity under the name of the Federation of Service Dog Breeding.

There is no advertising of "puppies for sale," since there is always a demand for puppies and, therefore, the need to advertise does not exist. Russian show dogs are a healthy lot, since veterinary care is free. There is, however, a dog tax of fifteen rubles—about $25 in United States money—on each dog. This tax is considered a fee for dog care such as vaccinations and registration, as well as for what the deputy chief of the veterinary department explains as compensation for the expenditures of dogs' walking and training grounds.

During the researching of this book there was no evidence of activity in the Yorkshire Terrier breed, but there are said to be almost thirty or more clubs for the different breeds of dogs popular there, with memberships totaling almost six thousand.

JAPAN

Yorkshire Terriers had found their way to Japan by 1962. American Champion Ru Genes Prince Ricardo, owned by Mrs. Ryuko Mikuni, was being shown in that country and was featured on the cover of the July 1962 *Inu-Nusaki*, the Japanese Dog World magazine.

There were advertisements featuring Yorkshire Terriers in the same issue on which Mrs. Mikuni's dog was featured on the cover. An ad on page 14, headlined "Jihiin's Best Young Yorkie," showed pictures of two darling little dogs and their names were readable. They were Champion Buranthea's Son O Piccolo, and Champion Buranthea's Sunny Bright. Both their English and Japanese Kennel club registration numbers were included along with their sires and dams. Piccolo was sired by Champion Piccolo Patrico ex Buranthea's Media of Johnstounburn, and Sunny Bright was sired by Champion Buranthea's Smokey's Memory Martynwyns Blue Princess.

We are all well aware of how popular our breed is in Japan today, with probably more breeders and exhibitors than could be listed here. The Japanese Kennel Club is a strong and very active group with many dedicated breeders who, we hope, can reverse the bad publicity connected with some of the earlier importers of dogs to that country.

By the early 1970s, Japan had organized the Japanese Yorkshire Terrier Club with Mr. O. Honda as its president. The shows are judged much like those in England, with the first in both the dog and the bitch classes competing for the Best in Show. Entry fees in the mid-70s were 5000 yen (with 660 yen to a British pound), and there is no prize money—only ribbons or an occasional statuette.

English and American Ch. Buranthea's Angel Bright, pictured with some of her trophy collection.

Japan's Dog of the Year

In 1980, the Dog of the Year in Japan was a Yorkshire Terrier whose full name and titles were FCI, International Champion and Grand Champion Kana of Beautiful Scarlet. It was a particular triumph and accomplishment, since the little Yorkie bitch was the first dog of all breeds in Japan to become an FCI International Champion. Her total record for the year included three times All-Breed Best in Show, three times Reserve Best in Show, Best of Breed at three Yorkie Specialties, Best in Japan once, and Runner-Up Best Dog in Japan once. Her breeder and owner is Miss Yoshiko Tsukamoto. The sire is International Champion Usafir Van Refouka ex Sky Ema of River Onok. She has been retired and will be used for breeding.

Nippon Yorkshire Terrier Club

All of the Specialties held by the Nippon Yorkshire Terrier Club are featured in photographs on the pages of Yorkie Tales. A new honor was bestowed upon a Yorkshire Terrier in Japan at the 1982 FCI Japan Kennel Club, when a Yorkshire was Best in Show. The Japanese-bred Yorkie, Fujimiland Julia, won this world FCI show, and was reported in the December 1982 issue of Dog World magazine.

The Nippon Yorkshire Terrier Club was organized in 1966 by Mr. Yoshiyuki Nukura, who has served as its president. There are more than half a dozen associate clubs located throughout Japan, boasting a combined membership in four figures.

The Nippon club is not affiliated with any other kennel clubs in Japan and it issues its own certified pedigrees for Yorkies registered with its club. Headquarters is located in Tokyo, and the club holds monthly meetings. Their breed publication, called The Yorkie, is issued annually; photographs and pedigrees of all new champions are featured in it. The club holds several specialty shows a year and entries usually top the hundred mark. Classes, divided by sex, are as follows: three to six months, six to nine months, nine to twelve months, twelve to twenty-four months, over twenty-four months, bred by exhibitor, open, novice, and specialty.

While many rules are similar to American and British shows, there are exceptions. The Specialty Class is for champions only, and the day's Best in Show and Best Opposite winners can challenge the Champions for points to become Grand Champion. Once the Yorkies become champions, they cannot compete for Best in Show or Best Opposite Sex in Show. The winner of this Specialty Class gets one point, and Reserve Winner gets one-half point. By accumulating three points, a dog becomes a Grand Champion. Twice a year, in June and December, there is a Grand Champion Class. These Grand Champions compete for the title of Best in Japan.

The 1982 FCI Show

Japan's first year as a member of the FCI saw them playing host to the international group in 1982. To add to the celebration, a Japanese Yorkshire Terrier won Best in Show! The little bitch, named Fujimiland Julia and owned by Chieko Matsunaga of Osaka, took the top win at this most prestigious event. Mr. Toyosaku Kariyabu is president of the Japanese Kennel Club, and is also honorary president of the FCI.

The Japanese Kennel Club was founded in 1948 and boasts 50,000 members. It registers more than 2000 dogs each year, primarily Toy breeds. The club holds its show in the Japanese Trade Center, and many restaurants and concessions are present as well. The aisles are wide and the rings large, since the show is spread out over three floors of the building. More than 100,000 people are said to attend the event, and hospitality lounges are set up for foreign visitors.

AUSTRALIA

Dog shows in Australia are quite extensive and well supported. Unlike the United States where there is just one AKC, each of the seven states of Australia has its own governing body for dogs. Rules, and even the classes at shows, vary from state to state.

Each club holds a certain number of shows a year, in two categories: those that award the Challenge Certificates and are called Championship shows, and those called Parades, which are judged by those training to be judges.

There are few professional trainers, and seldom is prize money offered for wins. They have a point system for championship requirements, but even the distribution of points may vary from state to state.

Recently, the clubs in Australia have been obtaining the services of American judges. These judges are treated royally, and every effort is made to assist them in the rules and regulations at the shows they will be judging. Using Ameri-

English and American Ch. Martywyns Wee Mischief, photographed by famous dog photographer Evelyn Shafer.

can judges has had a very stimulating effect on the number of entries at these shows, as well as on the quality of the dogs themselves.

With shows and exhibitors being so far flung in this vast country, it is hard to report accurately on their popularity or on established kennels. Suffice it to say that by the 1970s, Yorkshire Terriers had accounted for at least one Best in Show, and several Group awards.

By the beginning of the 1980s, entries and registrations in Australian shows were on the decline. Revisions and changes in the government's official laws concerning them took their toll. While things now seem to be evening off, those wishing to exhibit in Australia have a quarantine to discourage them, and will have difficulty in locating breeders, as well.

NEW ZEALAND

Yorkshires are certainly not the number one breed in New Zealand, but they continue to grow in popularity.

It was a Mrs. K. Butler of Otago, New Zealand, who was highly instrumental in getting the breed into the show ring in that country. Few of those which are bred there ever reach the show ring.

Best known of Mrs. Butler's dogs were Champion Maria of Greater Lea and her son, Von Ronkims Wee Blue Atom.

AFRICA

The breed in Africa is scarce. However, Mrs. Stella Parks owned the Ponchertis Kennels in the Transvaal, South Africa. Mrs. Parks came to the United States for the Yorkshire Terrier Club of America Specialty in 1976, celebrating the club's twenty-fifth anniversary.

Pamela Fedder is another Yorkshire Terrier enthusiast in South Africa. Her dogs were imports from the Ozmilion Kennels in England, bred by Mr. Sameja. A Mrs. Dunstan also showed Yorkies in Africa; these were imported from the Progresso Kennels and made their championships. Mrs. Parks imported several Yorkies from a Mr. Stroud's English kennels, and Mrs. Strachan imported Peglea Danny Boy during the 1970s.

Ms. Fedder's imports were based on the Hampark and Stirkean lines. She also imported a little male from California. Bred by Carmen Greenmayer, this was Kavancha's Starbright's Jackie's Big Deal. His sire was American Cham-

122

pion Starbright's Jack in a Box. She also imported Mrs. Dunstan's Kavancha's Polly Flinders of Mountmorris.

There are still few entries at the shows, and it requires a lot of traveling and considerable money to finish a champion in Africa. The Yorkies are shown on red velvet boxes to keep them up off the ground, since most of the shows are outdoors.

Classes include: Junior Puppy, Puppy, Maiden, Novice, Members, South African Bred, Open, and Champions. The Members and Champions classes are referred to as Closed Classes because the dogs entered in those classes cannot be called into the Open Classes, and thus be eligible for a Challenge Certificate. Normally the dogs in these classes would not be competing for certificates because they are already champions. At these African shows, four Challenge Certificates are required in three additional countries under four different judges to make a championship. It is plain to see how difficult championships become when the distance from South Africa to "three other countries" is contemplated!

Any dog entered in the other classes that has been unbeaten can be called into the Open Class after that class has been judged, and may be awarded the Challenge Certificate if the judge wishes to do so. For Best of Breed, all unbeaten dogs and bitches are called in and the judge makes his selection.

Champions may be put in the Open Class, and this is often done. There is controversy over this practice, however, because if the champion is exceptionally good, it can take away a Challenge Certificate from a dog coming up.

In spite of the difficulty in attaining a championship title, Yorkshire Terrier imports in Africa are increasing annually, with the majority of the dogs coming from England and the United States.

BRAZIL

The Yorkshire Terrier Club in Rio de Janeiro, Brazil, was founded in 1978. To give an indication of the popularity of our breed in that country, it is only necessary to recall their Specialty Show success, just two years later in 1980.

There was an entry of fifty-eight dogs for Argentine judge Oswaldo Curi. The week of September 8 through 16 included four international shows with the dogs being eligible for their CACIB's, and two Congresses. The show

Ch. Alexandrina of Soham, an imported Yorkshire Terrier bitch. Owned by Mr. and Mrs. Charles F. Dow of Chestnut Hill, Massachusetts.

officials wore red culottes, red short-sleeved blazers, and white tee-shirts with Yorkies on them. There were flowers and a cake at the head table to celebrate this second anniversary of the club and the success of the show.

There is no Best of Breed award at Specialties in Brazil, just a Best Dog and Best Bitch ribbon. By way of indicating the bloodlines active in the country at this time, we will report the winners of this show.

The Best Dog win went to American Champion Appoline's Hot Fudge, bred by Judy Giddens and owned by Celma Joia. The Best Bitch was Champion Blyth's Busy Bee, bred and owned by Blyth Hollmeyer. Ms. Hollmeyer's Blyths Joseph's Lily also finished her Junior Championship at this show. She is a daughter of American, British, and International Champion Heskethane's Lady's Joseph.

Among the members of this active club are Noia Romero, the director of the second anniversary show; Sandra Mazzoni, treasurer of the club; Celma Joia, president; Marilia Salema, vice president; Suely Perseke, assistant treasurer; and Marilia Macedo, secretary.

The first Yorkies in Brazil were undoubtedly brought there in the 1950s by Blyth Hollmeyer. Countess Beatrice Orssick brought two to Brazil from Mrs. Ethel Munday's kennels in England. While Ms. Hollmeyer's first dogs were from the United States, she imported a few dogs from Mrs. Munday also, followed by others from the Yadnum Kennels and another from America.

Most of the showing in Brazil is done by the owners, with very few professional handlers.

Trail West Frustration, owned by Anabelle de la Cruz of Costa Rica, has two sons in the United States: American and Canadian Ch. Trail West High and Mitey and American and Canadian Ch. Trail West Short-Stop.

COSTA RICA

Anabelle de la Cruz is the major breeder of Yorkshire Terriers in Costa Rica, Central America. Her Trail West Yorkshire Terriers are shown in the United States by her teenage daughter, Sandra, who, with their little Trail West Frustration, graced the cover of the April 1977 issue of *Yorkie Tales*. "Sean" is by Champion Wenscoe's Zipperdee Du Dah out of Champion Jentre's Josephine.

Other Trail West Yorkies include American and Canadian Champion Juana, Jentres Blue Jeans, American and Canadian Champion Trail West High and Mitey, and Champion Jentres Josephine.

Anabelle de la Cruz became interested in Yorkshire Terriers in the mid-seventies with stock based on Clarkwyn, Wenscoe, and Jentre, and two Melodylane bitches. There are few shows in Costa Rica, but Anabelle enjoys showing her little dogs there anyway.

124

PUERTO RICO

Yorkshire Terriers in Puerto Rico went from practically none to "very many" within a decade. By the 1970s, Yorkshire Terriers were very much in evidence and doing well.

Perhaps the leader in popularizing the breed was Trivar's Prince Jervic, which did a lot of winning for Victor Recondo and Jerry Vine, as did their Trivar's Princess Jervic.

Marie and Ed Parker imported Wildweir Fringe Benefit to get themselves started in the breed there, and Marie also served as a columnist for the defunct *Yorkshire Terrier Quarterly* in the 1970s. At their Tristesse Kennels they also had their Champion Windamere Mr. Kricket at stud.

The many Americans from the mainland that vacationed in Puerto Rico with their Yorkshire Terriers during the shows there helped to endear the breed in that country, and Yorkies soon were regarded as the "in" breed there. Their popularity has been growing ever since. Both show and pet quality can now be seen all over the island. Mr. and Mrs. Milton Amill have also bred Yorkies in Puerto Rico.

Since the establishment of the Yorkshire Terrier Club in September of 1970, interest in the breed keeps increasing, with the best news of all to start the decade of the 1980s: that Audrey Walkmaster's little Tigre won a Best in Show under Maxwell Riddle with Dorothy White handling.

A beautiful litter sired by Trail West Frustration out of Beholda Blue Violet, bred in Costa Rica by Anabelle de la Cruz.

Right: Best in Show for Ch. Amwalk's Tigre de Oro at the 1981 Puerto Rican Kennel Club show under judge Maxwell Riddle. Dorothy White handled for owner Audrey Walkmaster of San Juan, Puerto Rico. Ileana Miller, club president, presents the trophy.
Below: A Group First for American and Puerto Rican Ch. Amwalk's Tigre de Oro. Ed Dixon was the judge for this auspicious win. Whelped in 1979, Tigre's sire was Trivar's Little Black Sambo ex Jervic's Rosy Future. Stephen Klein photo.

Left: Puerto Rican Ch. Storybook's Little Bo Peep, whelped in 1980, was bred and is owned by Audrey Walkmaster of San Juan, Puerto Rico. The sire was Trivar's Little Black Sambo ex Jervic's Rosy Future. **Below:** Ch. Wind N Tide Rebel Sea, bred by Mrs. Franz Lewis and owned by Audrey Walkmaster. Whelped in 1979, Rebel was sired by Ch. Mayfair Barban Jamoca ex Oaksaber's Confetti. Dorothy White handled Rebel to this win on the way to his championship.

BEST OF WINNERS
WESTERN RESERVE
KENNEL CLUB
AUGUST 1980

PHOTO BY *Graham*

American and Mexican Ch. Park Royal Centennial
Eagle and his daughter Park Royal All That Glitters
pose prettily for this memorable photograph for
breeder-owner Kathleen Park of Hacienda Heights,
California.

Starfire Bo-Keep, daughter of American and Mexican Ch. Wildweir Keepsake, P.C. Owned, bred, and always
handled by Mrs. Anne Herzberg Goldman of Santa Monica, California.

Maybelle's Belle of the Ball is pictured while waiting to go into the ring at the 1968 Bermuda Kennel Club show. Belle was eleven months of age in this Ed Kelly photograph. Owned by Maybelle F. Neuguth of Media, Pennsylvania.

Genineaux Cambridge Corker is pictured here at seven months of age. Bred by Anita Wray of Houston, Texas, the sire was Eden Valley Matcho Man ex American, Mexican, and International Ch. Gemineaux Holly Golightly.

Ch. Wingate's Windsor Gayelyn Silk is bred, owned, and handled by Suzanne M. Jones, pictured winning at the 1979 Canadian Specialty show under judge Iris Bueno. "Silk" was sired by Ch. Windsor Gayelyn Strut N Stuff ex Windsor Gayelyn Happiness.

America's first and only World Champion, Ch. Dorchester's My Kind of Love, also holds International (FCI) titles in America and Mexico. Sired by the famous English import, Ch. Arriba of Arriso, she is bred, owned, and shown by Commander and Mrs. John Leonard of Berkeley, California.

MEJOR DE LA RAZA

One of America's most titled Yorkies is Ch. Arriba of Arriso, a Westminster Kennel Club show winner and one of few dogs to have attained the International (FCI) titles of champion in the United States, Canada, and Mexico. He is also one of only several Yorkies to win the coveted "Dog World Award of Canine Distinction." Arriba is pictured here winning the Breed and his International Championship in Mexico City under prominent English judge Joe Braddon. Owners are Commander and Mrs. John Leonard of Berkeley, California.

American and Canadian Ch. Tyrone Hills Adorable Alfie, bred and owned by Ed and Gert Molik of Fenton, Michigan; handled by Jim Lehman for this win under judge James Vaughters.

American and Canadian Ch. Kaacey's Dandi Tu of Jenia's, pictured winning under judge Ed Bracey. Dandi has several Breed wins and Group placings for breeder-owner Kaacey Lynn of Margate, Florida.

Ch. Royal Picador, pictured winning under famous dog man Percy Roberts at the 1968 Mattoon Kennel Club show, was imported from Ireland by Mrs. Leslie Gordon and Miss Janet Bennett, Wildweir Kennels, Glenview, Illinois. He was the sire of two champions and had a Specialty Best in Show plus fourteen Toy Groups to his credit. Whelped in 1965, his breeder was Mrs. Beatrice Kelly.

Wind N Tide Commodore is handled here by Jim Hupp for owner Marcia A. Knudsen of the Hiawatha Valley Yorkies in Lake City, Minnesota. Barney's win is under noted Toy judge Frank Oberstar.

Ch. JusbeCus Blue Creek Muffin is pictured winning in Canada under Dr. Lahan as Best of Breed on the way to her championship. Owned by Lori and Gary D. Williams of Shoshone, Idaho.

Ch. Trivar's Tiny de Herrera, owned by Guillermo Herrera of Mexico City, Mexico, is handled here for owner Johnny Robinson to this win under judge Sue Rowe on the way to championship before leaving for a new home in Mexico.

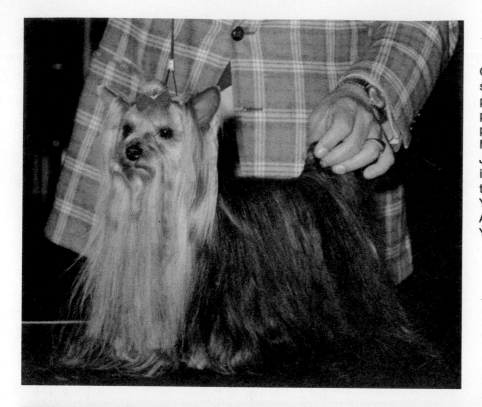

Ch. Trivar's Tycoon is the sire of 52 American champions, 5 Brazilian champions, and 2 German champions. Bred and owned by Morris E. Howard and Johnny A. Robinson, Jr. he is pictured here winning the Veterans Class at the Yorkshire Terrier Club of America Specialty in New York City.

Ch. Trivar's Cookie Monster racks up another top win, this one under judge Dr. Harry Smith. Cookie Monster is owned and bred by Johnny Robinson (handling) and Morris Howard, Trivar Kennels, Potomac, Maryland.

American, Mexican, International Ch. Gemineaux Holly Golightly, owned and bred by Anita Wray of Houston, Texas.

Pictured in show pose is American, Mexican, International Ch. Gemineaux Holly Golightly, owned by Anita Wray of Houston, Texas.

American and Mexican Ch. Park Royal Centennial Eagle is pictured finishing for his Mexican championship at Ensenada, Mexico. Jo Ann Noffsinger handled for owner Kathleen Park, Park Royal Yorkies, Hacienda Heights, California. The judge was Harold Schlintz.

Artist Susan M. Sandlin, the Original Petit Point Yorkies, of Arlington, Virginia, with Petit Point Nutmeg and Canadian Ch. Petit Point Nutshell. Both were sired by Ch. Mayfair Barban Quinnat.

International (FCI), American, Venezuelan, Puerto Rican, and Dominican Republic Ch. Estugo's Stargazer is pictured at sixteen months of age. Photographed by Johnell Kinsey for owners Hugo J. Ibanez and Stephen B. Maggard.

American and Canadian Ch. Wynsippi's Mr. Dinks, bred by Mrs. Virginia Knoche and owned by Richard S. Lawrence of New York City. The handler is Terence Childs.

American and Canadian Ch. Carlens Jack Daniels is pictured winning the breed under judge Geraldine Hess for owner-handler-breeder Helen Stern of Brooklyn, New York.

Canadian Ch. Myork Muffin's Magic was featured on both the March 1981 and May 1982 covers of *Yorkie Tales* magazine. She is owned by Mr. and Mrs. Monroe Hall, House of Yorklea, Orting, Washington.

CHAPTER SIX

Yorkshires in the Limelight

Movie star Connie Stevens and her Yorkshire Terrier both sport sweaters for this informal photo on a Hollywood lot during a film break.

There have been several excellent books published throughout the years dedicated to the Yorkshire Terrier. And there are many more books in print with sections devoted to the breed, or at least with references to Yorkies. There are also countless articles which have been included in various publications on the breed. There is no complete list of them, but for those who wish to pursue breed history further, the main sources of information would be found in the library of the American Kennel Club in New York City.

In the dog fancy, we have seen several magazines come and go. They made valiant attempts to glorify the breed and to inform the public, but most met eventual demise. There is, however, a most worthy publication available today that serves the breed well. Its title is *Yorkie Tales.*

YORKIE TALES

Anyone interested in Yorkshire Terriers, either for show or as pets, should be aware of the *Yorkie Tales* magazine that has become an important part of every fancier's life.

Darrell Smith was the first editor when the magazine put out its first issue in October 1974. *Yorkie Tales* began with a paid circulation of 145, and by 1983 had well over two thousand. The magazine is now sent to Canada, Mexico, Hong Kong, Japan, Australia, South America, Sweden, Germany, Italy, and England.

Yorkie Tales is published monthly and features annual editions on Stud Registers (in May), Bitch Registers (in October), and Puppy Hopefuls (in January). There also is an Honor Roll issue (in August). More recently the magazine has recognized the need for Obedience and Junior Handler coverage, and reports annually on the top producing sires and dams.

Darrell Smith sold *Yorkie Tales* to Muriel Hunt and her husband in March 1978, and Muriel became its editor through the August 1982 issue. Muriel Hunt then sold *Yorkie Tales* to Amberdunes Publications, and the new editor is Barbara Stewart. The magazine will undoubtedly retain the same high quality its readers have come to expect, with bound copies of all issues to be found in the American Kennel Club library.

The first Yorkshire to appear on the cover of *Yorkie Tales* was Wynsum Corporate Wee Sample, bred and owned by Mrs. Robert Truitt, a performance that "Samantha" repeated in October 1975.

Jennifer Rebecca, first place winner in the 1981 *Yorkie Tales* photo contest. The sire was Myra's Little Munchkin ex Myra's Little Prissy. Owner is Gladys Jackson of Charleston, South Carolina.

Our Cover Dogs

As expected, Yorkshire Terriers grace the covers of all our breed publications, but at least once in each decade we are happy to say that they also have been featured on the covers of some of the better all-breed magazines.

In 1959, Maxine Mitchell's Champion Joey Boy of Mitey was on the cover of the November issue of *Kennel Review* magazine.

In May 1960, two little Yorkshires were on the cover of *Pure-Bred Dogs, American Kennel Gazette*; and in December 1971, Nancy Lee Webb's Champion Windshaven's Lilliputian was on the special Toy issue of *Popular Dogs* magazine.

The most recent coverage was the beautiful pastel portrait of a Yorkie on the cover of the *American Kennel Gazette*. The artist was Alisonn Zorba and the dog was "Sir," who spends most of his waking hours on a purple cushion in the office of the editor of that worthy publication. The pastel was photographed for the December 1982 issue by Grant Taylor.

LIFE MAGAZINE CONFIRMS IT

If there was a doubt in anyone's mind about the stir the Yorkshire Terrier was causing in both the show and pet world, *Life* magazine should have dispelled it when in their November 20, 1964, issue they did a four-page spread on the breed. The headline for the article told it all: "Top Dog with a Topknot." The full-page head study of Champion Wildweir Moonrose was a charmer, as was the photograph of the little head of Beryl Hesketh's Feather sticking out of the water in the swimming pool.

The article covered all bases in presenting the breed as a most adorable little dog. It featured a puppy picture, the dogs at play put up in their wrappers, and a lovely photo of Wildweir Proud Girl with her show coat falling over on Mrs. Leslie Gordon's arm as if ready to enter the show ring. The closing photograph for the article featured Moonrose "sitting pretty" among a magnificent collection of her silver trophies. As the caption stated, it is hard to believe that her nickname is "the Witch" because of her bossy ways toward the other dogs at the Wildweir Kennels in Glenview, Illinois.

MODERN YORKSHIRE ART AND ARTISTS

Many reproductions of original paintings, lithographs and prints are currently available through various sources, including a marvelous collection owned by Jeanne Grimsby in Merrick, New York. Jeanne Grimsby, by the way, will be remembered for her "Albums" of famous works on Yorkies, featured in the *Yorkshire Quarterly* several years ago.

In addition to today's truly artistic logos and stationery letterheads, many artists are creating wonderful Yorkshire Terrier artwork.

American and Canadian Ch. Myork Mistress Mae was featured on the front cover of the August 1980 issue of *Yorkie Tales*. Owners are Mr. and Mrs. Monroe Hall of the House of Yorklea, Orting, Washington.

Fay Gold's drawing of her little "Louie," Galaxy's Mr. Louis Orion, C.D. This likeness of Louie was featured on the pages of *The Yorkshire Terrier Quarterly,* which Fay Gold edited and published during the 1960s.

Fine Arts Associates in Muncie, Indiana, produce exquisite one-of-a-kind jeweled ostrich eggs, lined in velvet, with Yorkshire countenances carved into the surface of the eggs. These classic masterpieces sell in the several-hundred-dollar category, but are truly magnificent pieces for the collector. They also feature Bud Priser Yorkshire figurines, life-sized, for those wishing ceramic pieces.

There are also the lovely petit point needlework creations by Susan M. Sandlin of Arlington, Virginia, who also has named her kennel after her needlework pieces. One of her most beautiful must be the poem in oval frame: "All things bright and beautiful, All Creatures great and small, All things wise and wonderful, The Lord God made them all."

Laurelwood Enterprises in Lehigh Valley, Pennsylvania, began issuing a Yorkie plate in 1979 in a limited quantity of 150 at just fifteen dollars each. These truly capture the Yorkie personality.

Above and below are some of the many designs in silk petit point created by Susan M. Sandlin of Arlington, Virginia.

A silk petit point by Susan M. Sandlin, the original Petit Point. This delicate design features 1600 stitches to the square inch.

Three of Susan Sandlin's hand-made miniatures. In a ratio of one inch to one foot, the delicate size of her creations can be judged by comparing with the coin shown with each of them. Susan's miniatures and silk petit point designs are in collections throughout the world.

Jewelry has always been highly desired by those Yorkie lovers who wish to wear their "hearts" on their sleeves. The gold custom-designed Yorkshire Terrier of Madelaine Konner is a thing of beauty to be truly admired. And who hasn't been delighted by the Mari Sam Specialties Ceramic Yorkie wind chimes! Their Yorkie figurines, note paper, and pins are also a delight.

Two Yorkie headstudies from Madelaine Konner's creations. Her artistic Yorkie jewelry is popular with fanciers because of its accurate detail and fine workmanship.

Note paper is very popular. Who among us has ever received written communication from another Yorkie fancier on anything *but* Yorkshire Terrier stationery? Elissa Taddi is among the artists who produce some of the best in this medium (a particular joy to the author since her most famous work is of my own little Champion Sahadi Scarlet O'Hara). Sherle is another note paper artist.

Perhaps the most productive among these artists is the group which make our fine sculptures. Numbered among them are Coryn Monaghan, Elizabeth Brisell, Bill and Tina Misko, Dannyquest Designs (who also produce ceramic windchimes), Dolores Kauffman, Nancy Eiche, Balont Kramlik, and, exclusively from Hawaii, Yorkies by Brad—Bradley Odagiri to be specific.

When mentioning sculptures of Yorkshire Terriers, no list would be complete without mentioning perhaps the most famous of all the Yorkshire Terrier sculptors—Kay Finch. Her

Yorkshires in Advertising

The unique charms of the Yorkshire Terrier have not escaped the eyes of advertising moguls either. We have all enjoyed the appearance of Yorkshire Terriers in advertisements for Starflite luggage, Anglo fabrics, Benson and Hedges cigarettes, countless fashion houses, and even the United States Post Office.

Calendars give you an entire year to enjoy Yorkies in twelve different poses. One of the breed publications produced a special Yorkie calendar, and a Yorkshire Terrier was featured on the cover of the 1979 Purina "Every Dog Has His Day" calendar.

Yorkie Bows

Part of the charm of the darling little Yorkie faces is the brightly colored bows on their top-knots. Various colors, plaids, dots, velvets, and so forth help add to the individuality of the dogs and their owners.

Hilde Kozera of Portland, Oregon, has taken to making them not only for her own brood but professionally as well. They come in all colors with little beads on them and tiny rubber bands already attached. These ready-made bows are easy to attach and guarantee a perfect bow every time. She will take orders on colors and in whatever amount you might desire for your dogs. They are definitely another "art form" of which Yorkie owners may make use.

Charming pen-and-ink drawing of Marian and Michael Allen's Marianettes Tiny Trojan, rendered by artist Nick Leonard.

limited, certified, signed, and often life-size sculptures of our breed are incomparable. They are collector's items of the finest order, mostly in bronze, but also available on commission in other medium.

In correspondence relating to the publication of this book, many charming and characteristic letterheads and kennel cards were received. The Marianette Kennels of Marian and Michael Allen had a particularly interesting one, as did Petit Point, Tyrone Hills, John and Terri Shumsky, the Lamplighter Kennels, Vassar Square, J. Seybold, and Chelsea Nimar, to name just a few.

This lovely painting of a Yorkshire Terrier was done by Ernamary Mullen of Nova Scotia.

Artist Larsen's rendering of five Wildweir Kennels Yorkshire Terriers.

THEATRICAL YORKSHIRES

The appeal of the Yorkshire Terrier has not gone unnoticed in the theater or in the television medium. The long-standing role of a Yorkshire as an office companion of Mrs. Pynchon on the "Lou Grant" series is perhaps the most recent evidence. Gretchen Wyler had her friend Ellen Burke Rawls of New York City furnish her with her Yorkie, Pretoria Lady Patrice, to star as "Flotsam" in the "On Our Own" television series.

In the theater, Susan M. Sandlin's Petit Point Yorkies, Nutmeg and Nutshell, and some of the other Yorkies from her kennel, appeared in Franz Lehar's *The Merry Widow* in Washington, D.C., during a recent run.

Captured in oils by artist Audrey Naughton is Ann Seranne and Barbara Wolferman's Mayfairs Mocha Mousse.

Yorkshires even shared billing on one of the nation's more popular soap operas, along with guest star Zsa Zsa Gabor. In 1981, Allegra appeared on "As The World Turns." She had a gold star on her dressing room door when owner Marilyn Fuhr arrived at the studio, and her hair bows were color coordinated with Zsa Zsa's gowns!

Famous drama coach Lee Strasberg's Yorkshire was named Cherie after Marilyn Monroe's part in the movie *Bus Stop*. Author Fannie Hurst had several Yorkies running around her large Tudor apartment in New York City before her death in the 1960s.

While Mrs. Alfred A. Knopf veered from Yorkshire Terriers long enough to establish the Borzoi as a trademark for her husband's publishing firm, she eventually returned to Yorkshire Terriers as pets before her death in June 1966.

Ginna Carr Faye, wife of comedian Joey Faye, was another Yorkie devotee who worked in Obedience with her tiny Yorkie, Peanuts, right up until the time of her death in the 1970s.

Elizabeth Taylor had Yorkshires among other Toy breeds. There was a great deal of publicity regarding one of her trips to England with Richard Burton—and all the dogs—when she rented a large yacht to be moored off shore for the dogs in order to avoid the strict British quarantine laws.

Oscar de la Renta, the famous fashion couturier, and his wife have several Yorkies running around their equally fashionable house. Betty Bruce, of stage and movie fame, delighted in her Yorkie, as did musical movie star Mary Carlisle. Miss Carlisle's mother, Mrs. Leota Whytock, was a breeder of Yorkshires along with her daughter during the 1930s. Their kennel was based on imported Soham lines. They owned Champion Fritty, imported in 1938 by Mr. and Mrs. Arthur Mills.

Other Hollywood notables who owned Yorkies were Mr. and Mrs. Efrem Zinbalist, Jr., who had two of Aileen Martello's dogs. The second Mrs. Johnny Carson was awarded custody of Muffin in the divorce proceedings from the talk show host. Pasha was the name of Patricia Nixon's Yorkie. Hermione Gingold's Yorkie was the victim of a dognapping, but her Yorkie eventually was returned safely. Actress Eva Le Gallienne had a Yorkie, as did Lucy Arnaz, Erma Bombeck, and Shari Lewis. Former Senator and Mrs. Harrison Williams also owned Yorkshire Terriers.

Darling Yorkie figurines by artist Cindy A. Conter of Phoenix, Arizona, who works with stoneware clay.

A ceramic Yorkshire Terrier rendered by Carol Moorland Marshall of Pacific Palisades, California, A famous artist, Ms. Marshall's works have been sold all over the world, and at one time exclusively through Abercrombie and Fitch. This ceramic is from the author's collection.

Dot's Rockin Country Jamboree was a winner at his first show. Owned and handled by Dorothy Gaunt of West Covina, California.

CHAPTER SEVEN

The Dog Show World

Ch. Silk N Satin Talk of the Town started off her show career at the tender age of four months with this Best Junior Puppy win at a match show. Handled by her breeder, Clara Powanda.

Let us assume that after a few months of tender loving care, you realize your dog is developing beyond your wildest expectations and that the dog you selected is very definitely a show dog! Of course, every owner is prejudiced. But if you are sincerely interested in going to dog shows with your dog and making a champion of him, now is the time to start casting a critical eye on him from a judge's point of view.

There is no such thing as a perfect dog. Every dog has some faults, perhaps even a few serious ones. The best way to appraise your dog's degree of perfection is to compare him with the standard for the breed, or before a judge in a show ring.

MATCH SHOWS

For the beginner there are "mock" shows, called match shows, where you and your dog go through many of the procedures of a regular dog show, but do not gain points toward championship. These shows are usually held by kennel clubs, annually or semiannually, and much ring poise and experience may be gained there. The age limit is usually reduced to two months at match shows to give puppies four months of training before they compete at the regular shows when they reach six months of age. Classes range from two to four months, four to six months, six to nine months, and nine to twelve months. Puppies compete with others of their own age for comparative purposes. Many breeders evaluate their litters in this manner, choosing which is the most outgoing, which is the most poised, the best showman, and so on.

For those seriously interested in showing their dogs to full championship, these match shows provide important experience for both the dog and the owner. Class categories may vary slightly, according to number of entries, but basically include all the classes that are included at a regular point show. There is a nominal entry fee and, of course, ribbons and usually trophies are given for your efforts as well. Unlike the point shows, entries can be made on the day of the show right on the show grounds. They are unbenched and provide an informal, usually congenial atmosphere for the amateur, which helps to make the ordeal of one's first adventure in the show ring a little less nerve-wracking.

This young hopeful from the Dorchester Kennels of Commander and Mrs. John Leonard wins Best Puppy at an all-breed match show under judge Robert Jacobson.

POINT SHOWS

It is not possible to show a puppy at an American Kennel Club sanctioned point show before the age of six months. When your dog reaches this eligible age, your local kennel club can provide you with the names and addresses of the show-giving superintendents in your area who will be staging the club's dog show for them, and where you must write for an entry form.

The forms are mailed in a pamphlet called a premium list. This also includes the names of the judges for each breed, a list of the prizes and trophies, the name and address of the show-giving club and where the show will be held as well as rules and regulations set up by the American Kennel Club which must be abided by if you are to enter.

A booklet containing the complete set of show rules and regulations may be obtained by writing to the American Kennel Club, Inc., 51 Madison Avenue, New York, N.Y., 10010.

When you write to the dog show superintendent, request not only your premium list for this particular show, but ask that your name be added

Best Senior Puppy and Best in Match went to Denaire Joe Cool at a recent Gold Coast Yorkshire Terrier Club match show in Florida. Owner-handled by Joyce Watkins, Miami, Florida.

to their mailing list so that you will automatically receive all premium lists in the future. List your breed or breeds and they will see to it that you receive premium lists for specialty shows as well.

Unlike the match shows where your dog will be judged on ring behavior, at the point shows he will be judged on conformation to the breed standard. In addition to being at least six months of age (on the day of the show), he must be purebred for a point show. This means he and both of his parents are registered with the American Kennel Club. There must be no alterations or falsifications regarding his appearance. Females cannot have been spayed, and males must have both testicles in evidence. No dyes or powders may be used to enhance the appearance, and any lameness or deformity or major deviation from the standard for the breed constitutes a disqualification.

With all these things in mind, groom your dog to the best of your ability in the area specified for this purpose in the show hall, and *exercise your dog before taking him into the ring!* Too many Yorkshire Terrier owners are guilty of making their dogs remain in their crates so they do not get dirty, and the first thing the animals do when they start to show is stop to empty themselves. There is no excuse for this. All it takes is a walk *before* grooming. If your dog is clean, well groomed, *empty*, and leash trained, you should be able to enter the show ring with confidence and pride of ownership, ready for an appraisal of your dog by the judge.

The presiding judge on that day will allow each and every dog a certain amount of time and consideration before making his decisions. It is never permissible to consult the judge regarding either your dog or his decision while you are in the ring. An exhibitor never speaks unless spoken to, and then only to answer such questions as the judge may ask—the age of the dog, the dog's bite, or to ask you to move your dog around the ring once again.

However, before you reach the point where you are actually in the ring awaiting the final decisions of the judge, you will have had to decide in which of the five classes in each sex your dog should compete.

POINT SHOW CLASSES

The regular classes of the American Kennel Club are: PUPPY, NOVICE, BRED-BY-EXHIBITOR, AMERICAN-BRED, OPEN; if your dog is undefeated in any of the regular classes (divided by sex) in which it is entered, he or she is *required* to enter the Winner's Class. If your dog is placed second in the class to the dog which won Winner's Dog or Winner's Bitch, hold the dog or bitch in readiness as the judge must consider it for Reserve Winners.

PUPPY CLASSES shall be for dogs which are six months of age and over but under twelve months, which were whelped in the United States or Canada, and which are not champions.

Ch. Broomhill's Kissed A Toad is pictured winning at a fun match in 1979 at just three months of age. Sired by Ch. Trivar's Tycoon ex Clark's Kandy Girl, she was bred and is owned by Eugene Hauff, Broomhill Kennels, Anoka, Minnesota.

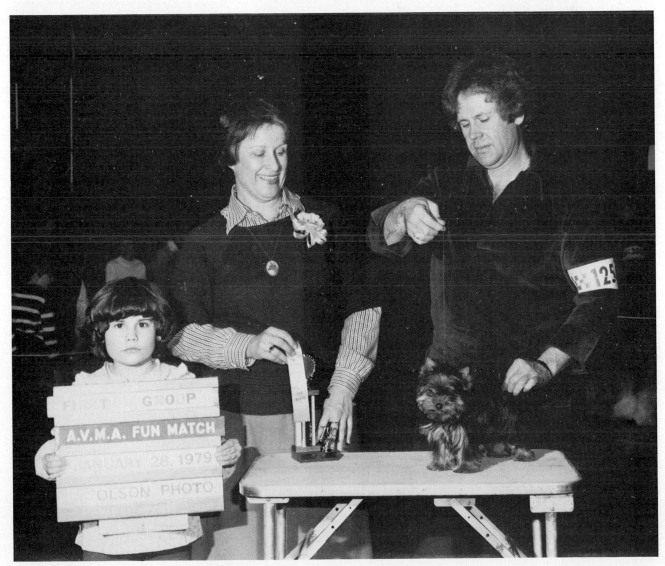

155

Classes are often divided six and (under) nine, and nine and (under) twelve months. The age of a dog shall be calculated up to and inclusive of the first day of a show. For example, a dog whelped on January first is eligible to compete in a puppy class on July first, and may continue to compete up to and including December thirty-first of the same year, but is not eligible to compete January first of the following year.

THE NOVICE CLASS shall be for dogs six months of age or over, whelped in the United States or Canada, which have not, prior to the closing entries, won three first prizes in the Novice Class, a first prize in Bred-by-Exhibitor, American-bred or Open Class, nor one or more points toward a championship title.

THE BRED-BY-EXHIBITOR CLASS shall be for dogs whelped in the United States which are six months of age and over, which are not champions, and which are owned wholly or in part by the person or by the spouse of the person who was the breeder or one of the breeders of record. Dogs entered in the BBE Class must be handled by an owner or by a member of the immediate family.

THE AMERICAN-BRED CLASS is for all dogs (except champions) six months of age or over, whelped in the United States by reason of a mating that took place in the United States.

THE OPEN CLASS is for any dog six months of age or over, except in a member specialty club show held for only American-bred dogs, in which case the class is for American-bred dogs only.

Dot's Rockin Country Jamboree winning in puppy class under judge Mona Berkowitz. The sire was Ch. Dot's Top Banana ex Dot's Blue Melody.

Ch. Carnaby Hot Rocks, finishing for his championship from the Bred-by-Exhibitor Class under judge Geraldine Hess. Handling is Joseph R. Champagne, co-owner of the Carnaby Yorkshire Terriers.

Noted Toy judge Frank Oberstar awards Ch. Windsor Gayelyn Prima Donna the win at this 1973 show. Prima Donna is co-owned by Glen Barr and Kathleen Kolbert. She is a daughter of Ch. Windsor Gayelyn Robin.

WINNERS DOG and WINNERS BITCH: After the above male classes have been judged, the first-place winners are then *required* to compete in the ring. The dog judged "Winners Dog" is awarded the points toward his championship title.

RESERVE WINNERS are selected immediately after the Winners Dog. In case of a disqualification of a win by the American Kennel Club, the Reserve Dog moves up to "Winners" and receives the points. After all male classes are judged, the bitch classes are called.

BEST OF BREED OR BEST OF VARIETY COMPETITION is limited to Champions of Record or dogs (with newly acquired points, for a ninety-day period prior to American Kennel Club confirmation) which have completed championship requirements, and Winners Dog and Winners Bitch (or the dog awarded Winners if only one Winners prize has been awarded), together with any undefeated dogs which have been shown only in non-regular classes; all compete for Best of Breed or Best of Variety (if the breed is divided by size, color, texture, or length of coat hair).

BEST OF WINNERS: If the Winners Dog or Winners Bitch earns Best of Breed or Best of Variety, it automatically becomes Best of Winners; otherwise they will be judged together for Best of Winners (following Best of Breed or Best of Variety judging).

BEST OF OPPOSITE SEX is selected from the remaining dogs of the opposite sex to Best of Breed or Best of Variety.

OTHER CLASSES may be approved by the American Kennel Club: STUD DOGS, BROOD BITCHES, BRACE CLASS, TEAM CLASS; classes consisting of local dogs and bitches may also be included in a show if approved by the American Kennel Club.

The MISCELLANEOUS CLASS shall be for purebred dogs of such breeds as may be designated by the American Kennel Club. No dog shall be eligible for entry in this class unless the owner has been granted an Indefinite Listing Privilege (ILP) and unless the ILP number is given on the entry form. Application for an ILP shall be made on a form provided by the American Kennel Club and when submitted must be accompanied by a fee set by the Board of Directors.

OBEDIENCE TRIALS

Some shows also offer Obedience Trials, which are considered as separate events. They give the dogs a chance to compete and score on performing a prescribed set of exercises intended to display their training in doing useful work.

Ch. Jusbecus Blue Creek Muffin, owned by Lori and Gary Williams of Shoshone, Idaho.

Best in Show Champion Wildweir Respected Legend, bred by Nancy Donovan and owned by Zinaida J. Daricek of Avondale, Pennsylvania. Co-owned by Laurel J. Howard of the Royal Row Yorkies.

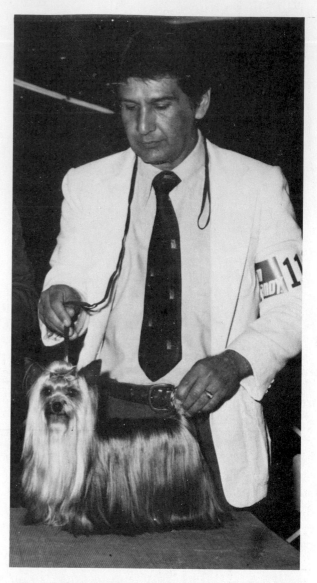

Ch. Estugo Wynsippi Shogun wins Best of Opposite Sex at a recent show. Hugo Ibanez handles and is co-owner and breeder wtih Stephen Maggard, Estugo Kennels, Charlotte, North Carolina.

All Miscellaneous breeds shall be shown together in a single class except that the class may be divided by sex if so specified in the premium list. There shall be *no* further competition for dogs entered in this class. Ribbons for First, Second, Third, and Fourth shall be Rose, Brown, Light Green and Gray, respectively.

There are three obedience titles for which they may compete: first, the Companion Dog or C.D. title; second, the Companion Dog Excellent or C.D.X.; and third, the Utility Dog or U.D. Detailed information on these degrees is contained in a booklet entitled *Official Obedience Regulations* and may be obtained by writing to the American Kennel Club.

JUNIOR SHOWMANSHIP

Junior Showmanship competition is for boys and girls in different age groups handling their own dogs or ones owned by their immediate family. There are four divisions: Novice A (10 to 12-year-olds) and Novice B (13 to 16-year-olds) for competitors with no previous Junior Showmanship wins, Open A (10 to 12-year-olds) and Open B (13 to 16-year-olds) for competitors with one or more JS awards.

DOG SHOW PHOTOGRAPHERS

Every show has at least one official photographer who will be more than happy to take a photograph of your dog with the judge, ribbons, and trophies, along with you or your handler. These make marvelous remembrances of your top show wins and are frequently framed along with the ribbons for display purposes. Photographers can be paged at the show over the public address system, if you wish to obtain this service. Prices vary, but you will probably find it costs little to capture these happy moments, and the photos can always be used in the various dog magazines to advertise your dog's wins.

TWO TYPES OF DOG SHOWS

There are two types of dog shows licensed by the American Kennel Club. One is the All-Breed show which includes classes for all the recognized breeds, and groups of breeds; i.e., all Terriers, all Toys, etc. Then there are the specialty shows for one particular breed which also offer championship points.

Ch. Nikko's Nicholas Nickleby, owned by Gloria Lipman and handled by Barbara Humphries, takes Group First under judge Anna Cowie.

TOWN & COUNTRY KNL CLUB
NORMAN OKLAHOMA
OCT 5 1980
TOY GROUP

JUDGE
MRS ANNA E COWIE

PHOTO BY
PETRULIS

TOWN & COUNTRY

TOY

BENCHED OR UNBENCHED DOG SHOWS

The show-giving clubs determine, usually on the basis of what facilities are offered by their chosen show site, whether their show will be benched or unbenched. A benched show is one where the dog show superintendent supplies benches (cages for toy dogs). Each bench is numbered and its corresponding number appears on your entry identification slip which is sent to you prior to the show date. The number also appears in the show catalogue. Upon entering the show you should take your dog to the bench, where he should remain until it is time to groom him before entering the ring to be judged. After judging, he must be returned to the bench until the official time of dismissal from the show. At an unbenched show, the club makes no provision whatsoever for your dog other than an enormous tent (if an outdoor show) or an area in a show hall where all crates and grooming equipment must be kept.

Benched or unbenched, the moment you enter the show grounds you are expected to look after your dog and have it under complete control at all times. This means short leads in crowded aisles or getting out of cars. In the case of a benched show, a "bench chain" is needed. It should allow the dog to move around, but not get down off the bench. It is also not considered "cute" to have small tots leading enormous dogs around a dog show.

IF YOUR DOG WINS A CLASS

Study the classes to make certain your dog is entered in a proper class for his or her qualifications. If your dog wins his class, the rule states: *You are required* to enter classes for Winners, Best of Breed and Best of Winners (no additional entry fees). The rule states, "No eligible dogs may be withheld from competition." It is not mandatory that you stay for group judging. *If your dog wins a group,* however, *you must stay for Best In Show competition.*

Marcris A Touch of Midas winning at a Gold Coast Yorkshire Terrier Club match show under noted Toy judge Joe Rowe. Owner-handled by Joyce Watkins, Marcris Kennels, Miami, Florida.

Topaz Robin Red, bred by Margery May and handled under judge Thomas Conway at this 1980 show for owners Elda and Nathan Tropper by Deborah E. Green. The sire was Ch. Topaz Chances Are ex Topaz Toi Fan. Missy Yuhl photo.

THE PRIZE RIBBONS AND WHAT THEY STAND FOR

No matter how many entries there are in each class at a dog show, if you place first through fourth position you will receive a ribbon. These ribbons commemorate your win and can be impressive when collected and displayed to prospective buyers when and if you have puppies for sale, or if you intend to use your dog at public stud.

All ribbons from the American Kennel Club licensed dog shows will bear the American Kennel Club seal, the name of the show, the date and the placement. In the classes, the colors are blue for first, red for second, yellow for third and white for fourth. Winners Dog or Winners Bitch ribbons are purple, while Reserve Dog and Reserve Bitch ribbons are purple-and-white. Best of Winners ribbons are blue-and-white; Best of Breed, purple-and-gold; and Best of Opposite Sex ribbons are red-and-white.

In the six groups, first prize is a blue rosette or ribbon, second placement is red, third yellow, and fourth white. The Best In Show rosette is either red, white, and blue or incorporates the colors used in the show-giving club's emblem.

Ch. Jusbecus Blue Creek Muffin winning a 4-point major on the way toward championship status. Owners are Lori and Gary Williams, Lor Dean's Kennels, Shoshone, Idaho.

QUALIFYING FOR CHAMPIONSHIP

Championship points are given for Winners Dog and Winners Bitch in accordance with a scale of points established by the American Kennel Club based on the popularity of the breed in entries, and the number of dogs competing in the classes. This scale of points varies in different sections of the country, but the scale is published in the front of each dog show catalogue. These points may differ between the dogs and the bitches at the same show. You may, however, win additional points by winning Best of Winners, if there are fewer dogs than bitches entered, or vice versa. Points never exceed five at any one show, and a total of fifteen points must be won to constitute a championship. These fifteen points must be won under at least three different judges, and you must acquire at least two major wins. Anything from a three to five point win is a major, while one and two point wins are minor wins. Two major wins must be won under two different judges.

Carlen's I. W. Harper wins at the 1973 Bryn Mawr Kennel Club show. Bred, owned, and shown by Helen Stern.

PROFESSIONAL HANDLERS

If you are new in the fancy and do not know how to handle your dog to his best advantage, or if you are too nervous or physically unable to show your dog, you can hire a reliable professional handler who will do it for you for a specified fee. The more successful or well-known handlers charge slightly higher rates, but generally speaking there is a pretty uniform charge for this service. As the dog progresses with his wins in the show ring, the fee increases proportionately. Included in this service is professional advice on when and where to show your dog, grooming, a statement of your wins at each show, and all trophies and ribbons that the dog accumulates. Any cash award is kept by the handler as a sort of "bonus."

When engaging a handler, it is advisable to select one that does not take more dogs to a show than he can properly and comfortably handle. You want your dog to receive his individual attention and not be rushed into the ring at the last moment because the handler has been busy with too many other dogs in other rings. Some handlers require that you deliver the dog to their establishment a few days ahead of the show, so they have ample time to groom and train him. Other handlers will accept well-behaved and trained dogs that have been groomed from their owners at ringside, if they are familiar with the dog and the owner. This should be determined well in advance of the show date.

There are several sources for locating a professional handler. Dog magazines carry their classified advertising. A note or telephone call to the American Kennel Club will also put you in touch with several in your area.

Sun Sprite Wendy, handled by Barbara Bedsted for breeder-owners Elda and Nathan Tropper of Los Angeles, California. Judge Stewart Makley awards the blue ribbon to Wendy at this 1982 show.

DO YOU REALLY NEED A HANDLER?

The answer to that question is sometimes yes, sometimes no! However, the answer that must be determined first of all is, "But can I *afford* a professional handler?" or, "I want to show my dog myself. Does that mean my dog will never do any big winning?"

Do you *really* need a handler to win? If you are mishandling a good dog that should be winning and isn't because it is made to look bad in the ring by its owner, the answer is yes. If you don't know how to handle a dog properly, why make your dog look bad when a handler could show it to its best advantage?

Some owners simply cannot handle a dog well, and still wonder why their dogs aren't winning in the ring, no matter how hard they try. Others are nervous and this nervousness travels down the leash to the dog, and the dog behaves accordingly. Some people are extroverts by nature, and these are the people who usually make excellent handlers. Of course, the biggest winning dogs at the shows usually have a lot of "show off" in their nature, too, and this helps a great deal.

Ch. Melodylane Smooth Sailing, bred and owned by Mary Purvis, was handled by Freeman Purvis to this win under judge Glen Sommers.

163

Bob's Beau Brummell, owned and handled by Mrs. Robert E. Quick of Kansas City, Missouri. Lewis Spence judged as Beau took the breed over an entry of 53.

Ch. Trivars Fiddlesticks wins the Breed at a 1981 show. Owned and handled by Alan Harper of Alexandria, Virginia.

THE COST OF CAMPAIGNING A DOG

At present many champions are shown an average of twenty-five times before completing a championship. In entry fees at today's prices, that adds up to over $250. This does not include motel bills, traveling expenses, or food. There have been dog champions finished in fewer shows, say five to ten shows, but this is the exception rather than the rule. When and where to show should be thought out carefully so that you can perhaps save money on entries. This is one of the services a professional handler provides that can mean a considerable saving. Hiring a handler can save money in the long run if you just wish to make a champion. If your dog has been winning reserves and not taking the points and a handler can finish him in five to ten shows, you would be ahead financially. If your dog is not really top quality, the length of time it takes even a handler to finish it (depending upon competition in the area) could add up to a large amount of money.

Campaigning a show specimen that not only captures the wins in his breed but wins Group and Best in Show awards gets up into the big money. To cover the nation's major shows and rack up a record as one of the top dogs in the nation usually costs an owner between ten and fifteen thousand dollars a year. This includes not only the professional handler's fee for taking the dog into the ring, but the cost of conditioning, grooming, board, advertising in the dog magazines, photographs, and so on.

There is great satisfaction in winning with your own dog, especially if you have trained and cared for it yourself. With today's enormous entries at the dog shows and so many worthy dogs competing for top wins, many owners who said "I'd rather do it myself!" and meant it, became discouraged and eventually hired a handler anyway.

However, if you really are in it just for the sport, you can and should handle your dog if you want to. You can learn the tricks by attending training classes, and you can learn a lot by carefully observing the more successful professional handlers as they perform in the ring. Model yourself after the ones that command respect as being the leaders in their profession. But, if you find you'd really rather be at ringside looking on, then do get a handler so that your worthy dog gets his deserved recognition in the ring. To own a good dog and win with it is a thrill, so good luck, no matter how you do it.

Ch. Park Royal Starlight Melodie, bred
and owned by Kathleen Park, is pictured
winning under judge Stewart Makley,
handled by Jo Ann Noffsinger.

Winning sweep for the Melodylane Ken-
nels under judge Henry Stoecker. Ch.
Melodylane Mini Trail wins Best of
Breed, and his littermate, Ch.
Melodylane Top of the Tower, takes Best
of Winners. They were handled to these
wins by breeder-owners Freeman and
Mary Purvis of Centerville, Iowa.

Ch. Carnaby Rondelay winning at the 1977 Delaware Valley Yorkshire Terrier Club Specialty. Terence Childs is handling.

CHAPTER EIGHT

Showing and Judging the Yorkshire Terrier

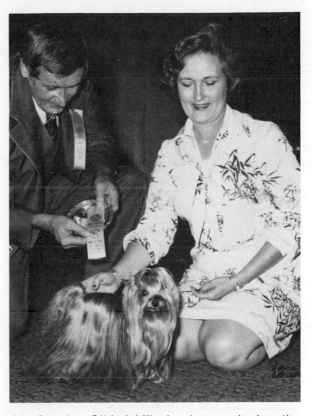

Ch. Gayelyn Gilded Lilly is shown winning the Veterans Class at the age of 13, handled by owner Kathleen B. Kolbert of Oxford, Connecticut.

Ever since I started judging dogs in 1961, I never enter a show ring to begin an assignment without thinking back to what the late, great judge Alva Rosenberg told me when we discussed my apprentice judging under his watchful eyes. His most significant observation I find still holds true for me today—that a judge's first and most lasting impression of a dog's temperament and bearing will be made the moment it walks into the ring.

It has always been a source of amazement to me the way so many exhibitors ruin that important first impression of their dog before the judge. So many are guilty of dragging their dogs along behind them, squeezing through the ringside crowds and snapping at people to get out of their way, just to arrive in the ring with a dog whose feet have been stepped on by people pushing to get closer to ringside, and whose coat has been ruined by food and cigarette ashes. After all this, the dog is expected to turn on its charm once inside the ring, fascinate the crowds, captivate the judge, and bring home the silverware and ribbons! All this on a day that invariably is either too hot or too cold—or too rainy—not to mention the hours of standing rigidly on a crate, being sprayed in the face and all over their bodies with a grooming substance that doesn't smell or taste too good, and then brushed and trimmed until dry to their handler's satisfaction.

Add this to the lengthy bath and grooming session the day before the show, and the bumpy ride to the show grounds, and, well Alva Rosenberg had a point! Any dog that can strut into the ring after what it regards as a forty-eight-hour torture treatment *does* have to have an excellent disposition and a regal bearing. How fortunate we are that so many of our flashy little Yorkies do have such marvelous temperaments in spite of our grooming rituals!

There is no reason an exhibitor cannot allow sufficient time to get to ringside with a few minutes to spare, in order to wait calmly somewhere near the entrance to the ring. They need only walk directly ahead of the dog, politely asking the people along the way to step aside with a simple statement to the effect that there is a "dog coming through." It works. I have seen spectators promptly step aside, not only to oblige this simple request when politely stated, but also to observe the beauty of the show dog passing by. Those who prefer to carry their dogs, and know how to do it without disturbing the coat, can make the same request for the same result.

The short waiting period at ringside also allows time for the dog to gain his footing and perspective, and gives the exhibitor time to get his armband on securely so it won't drop down the arm and onto the dog's head during the first sprint around the ring. These few spare moments will also allow a great deal of the "nervousness" that travels down the lead to your dog to disappear as the realization occurs to you that you have arrived at your class on time and you and your dog can both relax.

Ch. Wildweir Royal Credit, winner of two Bests of Breed and two Group Placings. Whelped in 1979, the sire was Gleno Credit Card ex Wildweir Stepping Stone. Bred, owned, and shown by Mrs. Leslie Gordon, Jr., and Miss Janet Bennett.

ENTERING THE RING

When the ring steward calls out the numbers for your class, there is no need for you to try to be first in the ring. There is no prize for being first. If you are new at the game, you would do well to get behind a more experienced exhibitor or professional handler where you can observe and perhaps learn something about ring behavior. The judges will be well aware of your presence in the ring when they make a small dot or a small check mark in their judge's book as you enter. The judges must also mark all absentees before starting to evaluate the class, so you can be sure no one will be overlooked as they "count noses."

Simply enter the ring as quickly and calmly as possible with your dog on a loose lead, and at the first opportunity make sure you show your armband to the judge. Then take a position in the line-up already forming in the ring (usually at the opposite side from the judge's table). Set your dog up in the show pose so that once the judge has checked in all the dogs in the class, he will have an immediate impression of the outline of your dog in show stance. This is also referred to as "stacking" your dog.

The judge will then go up and down the line of dogs in order to compare one outline with another, while getting an idea of the symmetry and balance of each profile. This is the time when you should see that your dog maintains the show stance. Don't be nervously brushing your dog, constantly adjusting his feet, tilting his head, and primping his tail. All of this should have been done while the judge was walking down the line with his eyes on the other dogs.

By the time the judge gets to your dog, it should be standing as still as a statue, with your hands off it if at all possible. Far too many exhibitors handle show dogs as if they were puppets with strings attached to all the moving parts. They are constantly pushing them in place, prodding them to a desired angle for the judge to see, placing the head and tail and feet according to their idea of perfection. More often than not, their fingers are covering the dog's muzzle or they are employing their thumbs to straighten out a topline, or using a finger to tilt a tail to the proper angle. Repeatedly moving a dog's feet tends to make the judge believe the dog can't stand correctly by itself. If a dog is standing incorrectly, the judge might assume that it just happened to be standing incorrectly at that moment, and that the exhibitor couldn't imagine such a thing and therefore never noticed it!

Fussing over a dog only calls attention to the fact that the exhibitor either has to do a lot to make the dog look good, or is a rank amateur and is nervously mis-handling the dog. A free, natural stance, even when a little "off base," is still more appealing to the judge than a dog presented with all four feet barely touching the ground. All Yorkshire Terriers are beautiful on their own, and unnecessary handling can only be regarded as a distraction, not as indulgence on the part of the exhibitor. Do not get the mistaken idea that if the judge thinks you are working hard with your dog you deserve to win.

MOVE THEM OUT

Once the judge has compared the outlines (or profiles) of each dog, he will ask the exhibitors to move the dogs around the ring so that he might observe the dogs in action. This usually means two complete circles of the ring, depending on the size of the ring and the number of dogs competing in it. This is the time when the judge must determine whether the dog is moving properly or if it is limping or lame. The judge will check out the dog for proper gait and observe if the dog is moving freely on its own—not strung up on the end of a lead with the handler holding the head high.

Be careful not to hamper your dog in any way in the limited time and space you have to show the judge how your dog moves. This means gaiting on a loose lead. Move next to your dog at a safe distance to the side so that you do not step on it going around corners or pull it off balance on turns. You must also keep in mind that you should not get too close to the dog ahead of you and that you must keep far enough ahead of the dog behind you so that your dog doesn't get spooked—or that you don't break the gait.

Once the judge has had the time to observe each dog in motion, the signal will be given to one person to stop at a specific spot in the ring, forming the line-up for closer inspection of each dog individually. At the judge's discretion, the individual evaluation may be done either in place or on a small table placed in the ring. Whether the judge chooses to evaluate each dog on the ground or on a table, the judge must go over the dog completely in order to evaluate it in accordance with the Standard for the breed.

Mamie Gregory is handling Dansel Senator Bob at a 1970 show at Fort Wayne, Indiana. E.H. Frank photo.

Gintique's Funny Magic, bred and owned by Virginia Miller of Mentor, Ohio, pictured here at the age of ten months.

Ch. Harriet Ovale Love of Carlen, owned by Helen Stern of Brooklyn, New York.

JUDGING THE HEAD

As the judge approaches your dog, he will get his first close look at the expression. The judge will want to see the dark eye, will check the stop, the muzzle, the occiput, ear leather and set, and the head in its entirety for excellence. During this examination, the exhibitor must make sure the dog remains perfectly still and in correct show stance. Since the dangers of the various virus infections and contagious diseases that can be passed from dog to dog at the shows has been made known to us, it is hoped the judge will ask that you show your dog's bite. It is permissible, however, for the judge to open the dog's mouth to check out the bite, especially if the judge has reason to believe there is a fault. The judge will also evaluate the head from straight on as well as in profile.

Next, the neck and shoulders will be checked. The judge will lift up the ears to see just how long the neck really is and how well placed the shoulders are. Shoulders play an important part

in the proper placement of the front legs and pasterns. Running his hands down the front leg, the judge will go all the way to the foot, picking it up and checking the foot pads and nails, and paying particular notice to whether the dog puts its foot down correctly in place when released.

The judge will check the brisket and the tuck-up as well as the topline. At this point, with his hands going over the dog, the judge can determine the proper texture of the coat, the profusion of feathering, and the general weight of the dog. Tail length and carriage are to be considered as well. Judging the hindquarters should prove the dog's legs are sturdy and well placed and strong enough to provide the strength for proper gait and movement. This is also the time when the judge will check to see that on male dogs both testicles are present and descended.

Once the judge has gone over the dog completely, he will usually take a step or two away from the dog to give it a final over-all view, keeping a complete picture of it in his mind to make the comparison with the dog he has judged just before and will judge after yours. This is the time you must still keep your dog "on his toes," so that when the judge glances ahead or behind, your dog is not sitting down, chasing butterflies, or lifting his leg on the number markers. Remember, training is done at home—*performance* is required in the show ring at all times.

This lovely formal portrait is of Kathleen Park's American and Mexican Ch. Park Royal Centennial Eagle. The Park Royal Kennels are in Hacienda Heights, California.

Elm City Blue Atom, handled by Jane Forsythe for owner Rosemary Vernon, winning in the mid-1960s under judge William Burrow.

INDIVIDUAL GAITING

Once the judge has gone over each dog individually, he will go to the end of the ring and ask each handler to gait his dog. It is important at this point to pay strict attention to the judge's instructions as to how this is to be done. Some judges require the "T" formation, others the half-triangle. Further observation of your dog may bring a request for you to repeat the pattern, especially if your dog did not show well during the first trip. It is important that you hear whether the judge wants you to repeat the entire exercise or merely to gait your dog "down and back" this time.

When each dog has been gaited, the judge will want a last look at all of them lined up together before making his final decisions. Usually the procedure will be to once again present the left side of your dog as the judge weaves in and out of the line to check once more the fronts or rears or other individual points of comparison. Some dogs may be asked to gait a third time, or to gait side by side with one of the other dogs should the judge want to "break a tie" as to which dog is the better mover. Because such deciding factors cannot be predicted or anticipated, it is necessary for the handler to always be ready to oblige once the request is given by the judge.

171

After the decisions are made, the judge will point to his four placements and those four will set their dogs up in front of the designated number markers on the side of the ring. Be ready at this point to show the numbers on your armband so that the judge can mark his judge's book. The judge then will present the winners with the appropriate color ribbons and any trophies won, and you may leave the ring.

Contrary to popular opinion, it is not necessary or even correct to thank the judge for the ribbon. It is to be assumed that the dog *deserved* the ribbon or the judge would not have awarded it. Handing you the ribbon is part of the procedure and does not warrant a thank-you. The club, not the judge, is responsible for the donation of the trophies. It is not called for that the exhibitor speak to the judge, but if the win is significant enough so that you feel compelled to say *something*, a simple and not overly exuberant "I'm so pleased that you like my dog," or something similar is still more than is necessary.

The "thank-you" for the ribbon has on occasion become what some exhibitors like to think of as a "weapon." At ringside you can sometimes hear words to the effect that, "I didn't even thank him for that rotten red ribbon!" As if the judge had even noticed! However, it *is* expected that you take with you from the ring a

Silk N Satin Fabulous Fanny is pictured winning under judge James P. Cavallaro at nine months of age. Owner-handled by Clara Powanda of Wheeling, West Virginia.

Genie's Lil Duke, owned by Sheri and Willowe Linde of Rapid City, South Dakota. This win was under judge Jean Fancy for two points toward championship.

ribbon of *any color*. To throw it on the ground or leave it behind in the ring so that the steward is obliged to call you back into the ring for the judge to hand it to you again is most unsportsman-like. You must play the game according to the rules. Your entry fee is to obtain the opinion of your dog by the judge. You must take the opinion and behave accordingly. If you do not like it, do not give them another entry, but you owe the judge the courtesy of respect for that title.

After this judging procedure is followed in the five classes for dogs, and Winners Dog and Reserve Winners Dog have been determined, the bitches are judged in this same manner. After Winners Bitch and Reserve Winners Bitch awards have been made, the Best of Breed judging follows. Class procedures here are discussed elsewhere in this chapter. Once the judge has completed his assignment and signed his judge's book, it is permissible to request any photographs that you may wish to have taken of your wins. At this time it is also permissible to ask the judge his motives in his judging of *your* dog. If you wish to, it should be done in a polite and calm manner. It must be remembered that the judge is not going to make comparisons rating one dog against another, but can, if he chooses, give a brief explanation as to how he evaluated your dog.

It is helpful to remember that "no one wins them all." You will win some and lose some no matter how good your dog is. Judges are human and, while no one is perfect, they have earned the title of "judge" for some mighty good reasons. Try to recall that this is a sport and it should be fun—tomorrow is another day.

THE GAMES PEOPLE PLAY

If you are new to the game of dog-show exhibiting, there are a few things you should know about, such as how to protect yourself and your

dog so that you do not get too discouraged and disillusioned right at the start.

There may be an occasion where your dog is winning a great deal and jealousy will arise from others competing in the ring with you. It has been known that some of these bad sports will try to get between you and the judge so the judge cannot see your dog at his best. Others may try stepping on your dog, breaking his gait so that he cannot be adequately judged, bringing bitches in season into the ring, throwing bait around to distract your dog, and so on. Needless to say, most judges are aware of these nasty tricks people play and will not tolerate them. Just be on your guard. Do not leave your dog alone or leave it in the care of others. Thefts have been known at dog shows, as well as poisoning and physical abuse.

The Specialty Best in Show and Group-winning Ch. Melodylane El Toro Del Busque pictured at the Yorkshire Terrier Club of Greater St. Louis Specialty under judge Bettie Krause. Bred by Mary Purvis, Toro is owned by her and Joy Wieland. The sire was Ch. Loveland's Good Buddy ex Melodylane Sunrise.

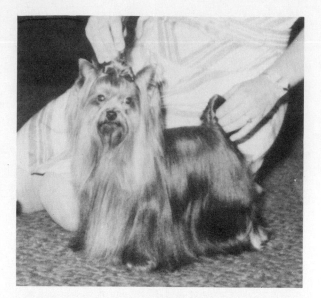

Ch. Hampshire Flying Nun finishing for her championship in 1975. Co-owned by Mary Ressler and Bonnie Jean James of Oak Ridge, New Jersey. Jayne Langdon photo.

CHILDREN IN THE SHOW RING

No one is more approving than I of children learning to love and to care for animals. It is beautiful to see a child and an animal sharing complete rapport and companionship or performing as a team in the show ring. Those of us who have been around dog shows for any length of time have all been witness to some remarkable performances by children and their dogs. Junior Showmanship is one example; dogs caring for or standing guard over babies and infants is another example.

However, there is nothing "cute" about a child being allowed to handle a dog where the welfare of both the child and the general public are in danger. Dogs have been known to pull children to the ground with resulting injury to either child or dog, or both. I have seen frightened children let go of leashes or become tangled up in them in the middle of dog fights that left all three participants injured.

If a child shows the natural desire to exhibit a dog after having attended handling classes where they are taught how to properly show a dog, they must also be taught ring procedure. It is not fair to expect other exhibitors to show patience while a judge or the steward informs the child where to stand, or waits for the child exhibitor to gait the dog several times before it is done in the formation requested. Lack of knowledge or repeated requests delay the judging, look bad to the ringside crowds, and certainly don't make the dog look good.

If necessary, parents might stay after the dog-show judging and actually train the child in an empty ring. Parents should also sit ringside with the children to explain the judging procedures to them so they will know what to expect when they enter the ring. Many match show appearances should precede any appearance in a point show ring also. Certainly no parent could possibly expect a judge to give them a win just because they are a cute pair—even though they are!

BAITING

No matter how one feels about baiting a dog in the ring, we must acknowledge that almost everyone at one time or another has been guilty of it. Certain breeds are particularly responsive to it, while others show little or no interest with so much going on all around them.

There is no denying that baiting can be an aid to basic training. But in the show ring some judges consider it an indication that the training of the dog for the show ring is not yet complete. It becomes obvious to the judge that the dog still needs an incentive to respond to what other dogs are doing in the name of performance and showmanship.

Frequently, squeaky toys will work as well. Using conversation and pet nicknames in trying to encourage the dog is equally inappropriate.

Futsong of Cygnet Reach was winner of the breed at the 1961 Long Island Kennel Club show. Evelyn Shafer photo.

Sun Sprite Frisbee, handled by Barbara Bedsted, bred and owned by Elda and Nathan Tropper of Los Angeles, California. This 1982 photo pictures Frisbee winning under judge Raphael Schulte.

DOUBLE-HANDLING

You can be sure the competent judge becomes aware of any double-handling to which some of the more desperate exhibitors may resort.

Double-handling is both distracting and frowned upon by the American Kennel Club. Nonetheless, some owners go to all sorts of ridiculous lengths to get their apathetic dogs to perform in the ring. They hide behind trees or posts at ringside or may lurk behind the ringside crowd until the exact moment when the judge is looking at or gaiting their dog, and then pop out in full view perhaps emitting some familiar whistle or noise, or wave of a hat, or whatever, in hopes that the dog will suddenly become alert and express a bit of animation.

Don't be guilty of double-handling. The day may come when you finally have a great show dog, but the reputation of an owner guilty of double-handling lives on forever! You'll be accused of the same shady practices and your new show dog is apt to suffer for it.

Ch. Indigo Macho Munchken pictured at two years of age, owner-handled by Grace Stanton of Indigo Yorkies, Wayne, New Jersey. This win under Frank Landgraf represented points toward his championship at this 1979 show.

JUDGING ON THE TABLE

Most Yorkshire Terrier judges will require that you place your dog on a table in the ring, so that they may go over your dog thoroughly without having to bend over or stoop down. You must watch for the judge to indicate this and be ready to place your dog on the table facing the judge as he or she approaches. As the judge goes over your dog—which you have set up in show stance—be prepared to move around the table so that the judge will get to see your dog from every angle.

At times the judge may require you to place your dog on the table with another dog, if the judge is trying to make a comparison between two choices being considered for placement. You also must be alert to this suggestion and place your dog in show stance at a safe distance from the other dog, thus allowing the judge to once again go over each dog individually, at close quarters.

At outdoor shows you will find the judges will always want to see your dog at least once on the table. Since they must gait in the grass at outdoor shows, the table examination becomes all the more important in making an appraisal.

APPLAUSE, APPLAUSE!

Another "put-on" by some of our less secure exhibitors is the practice of bringing their own cheering section to applaud vigorously every time the judge happens to cast an eye on their dog.

The judge is concentrating on what he is doing and will not pay attention to this or will not be influenced by the cliques set up by those trying to push their dogs to a win, supposedly by popular approval. The most justified occasions for applause are during a Parade of Champions, during the gaiting of an entire Specialty Best of Breed Class, or during the judging awards for Stud Dog, Brood Bitch, and Veterans Class. At these thrilling moments the tribute of spontaneous applause—and the many tears—are understandable and well received, but to try to prompt a win or stir up interest in a particular dog during the normal course of class judging is amateurish.

"Koko" gets his reward from Barbara Wolferman for winning at Westminster in 1981. Co-owners and co-breeders of Ch. Mayfair Barban Verikoko are Ms. Wolferman and Ann Seranne, Mafair Yorkie House, Newton, New Jersey.

If you have ever observed this practice, you will notice that the dogs being applauded are sometimes the poorest specimens whose owners seem to subconsciously realize they cannot win under normal conditions.

CARDINAL SINS WHEN SHOWING A YORKSHIRE TERRIER

* DON'T forget to exercise your dog before entering the ring! Do it before grooming if you are afraid the dog will get wet or dirty after the grooming is completed.

* DON'T be late for your class and enter the ring with both you and your dog in a nervous state.

* DON'T drag the dog around the ring on a tight lead and destroy the proud carriage.

* DON'T alter the appearance of your Yorkie by catching hairs up in rubber bands or bows. If your Yorkie isn't show-worthy in its natural state, *don't* show it.

* DON'T talk to the judge in the ring. Watch the judge closely and follow instructions. Don't talk to people at ringside or others that are competing with you in the ring.

* DON'T strike or in any way abuse your dog—especially not in the ring. The time for training and discipline is at home or in a class and not in front of the judge or the public. Even outside the ring we know that the reward system, not punishment, is the most successful method of training a dog.

* DON'T be a bad loser! Win or lose, be a good sport. You can't win them all, so if you win today, be gracious; if you lose, be happy for the exhibitor who won today. Your turn may come tomorrow.

* DON'T shove your dog in a crate or leave it on the bench and forget about him until it's time to go home. A drink of water or something to eat and a little companionship will go a long way toward making dog shows more enjoyable for him, so that he will show even better next time!

A show winner from the 1950s the Houston's Yorkie takes the breed win at a 1958 Ox Ridge Kennel Club show.

American and Canadian Ch. Carnaby Rock N Roll is pictured winning a Best in Show at the 1976 Riverhead Kennel Club with owner-breeder-handler Terence Childs. This is one of six Bests in Show won by Rocky during his career.

Yorkie figurines by artist and sculptor Bradley Odagiri of Hawaii. While Mr. Odagirl creates figurines for all breeds of dogs, he specializes in Yorkshire Terriers and shows them in the show ring.

American and Bermudian Ch. Chriswards Mayflower of Carlen is pictured winning under judge Iris Bueno on the way to her championship.

Two adorable Yorkies bred and owned by Virginia Bull of Blairstown, New Jersey, were photographed during a visit to Bermuda for the dog shows.

Ch. Phirno Emerald Earl demonstrates what it looks like to be up in curlers. Dick and Bronya Johnston of Tyler, Texas, submitted this "between shows" picture.

CHAPTER NINE

Grooming Your Yorkshire Terrier

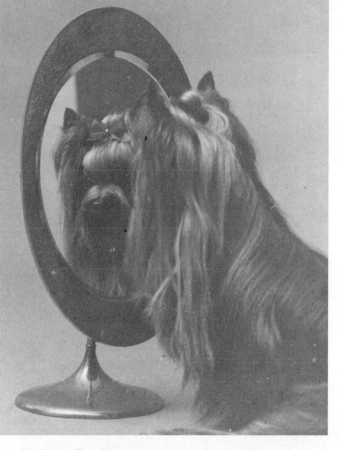

Ch. Dot's Top Banana, photographed by Missy Yuhl for owner Dot Gaunt of West Covina, California.

In 1886, the fifth edition of Stonehenge's *The Dogs of the British Islands* appeared, and in it Hugh Dalziel wrote—among other things complimentary to our breed—that the Yorkshire Terrier was "undoubtedly a manufactured article" and that "his distinctive character is in his coat—well carded, soft, and long. . .free from even a suspicion of shoddy."

He also included a comparison to the Irish and Scottish terrier breeds "with their ragged unkempt coats." He further referred to the other terriers as "bog trotters," "stack o'duds," and "sects of the doggy family."

Theo Marples, founder and editor of the sporting magazine *Our Dogs*, wrote glowingly of the Yorkshire Terrier's elegance. He stated, "The Yorkshire Terrier is still the prettiest and most elegant morsel of Toy Dog flesh on the British show bench."

Mr. Dobson's famous little dog, Harpurhey Hero, was reported to have had the longest coat in his time, measuring thirty-six inches.

Impressive to say the least, but no matter how much acclaim was given to our breed in the past,

no one in those days could have visualized by the furthest stretch of imagination the glorious beauty we see in the flowing coats on our dogs today. Modern grooming aids, the benefits of correct nutrition, and the indulgence of caring owners who are well aware that it takes all three, plus a certain inheritance factor, have produced our modern-day beautifully coated Yorkies.

All dogs, and especially the long-coated breeds such as our Yorkshire Terrier, require regular, careful grooming. Done on a regular basis, it can be a relatively simple task. It can remain a beautifully coated dog which proudly wears the silky, luxurious coat, clearly indicating the time and trouble you have taken to cultivate it—and that is a joy to behold, both in and out of the show ring. Once it is ruined or let go beyond repair, the coat will take endless time and energy to restore it to its original natural lustre and length. It is wise to take a little time each day to keep your dog in top condition, rather than to try to repair the damage that has been done by accumulated neglect. This is especially true if a dog is to be presented in the show ring.

Ch. Trivar's Fiddlesticks, owned by Alan L. Harper of Alexandria, Virginia.

To establish grooming as a common practice in the daily routine, you'll find matters simplified by choosing a particular spot for grooming the dog each time. You'll make it easier for yourself by placing a grooming table where the light is good and where the dog will have the least distractions. Make the table top a rather small area which will reduce the temptation for the dog to "wander off." Eliminate other temptations by keeping toys, bones, biscuits, and other family pets out of sight of the grooming area; the dog will become restless if he thinks he's missing something. Make the dog realize there is work to be done and that you mean to do it. Be firm—but gentle—about it.

How you choose to position your dog for the various aspects of grooming is a matter of choice for your own convenience. Teaching the dog to be comfortable in various positions will aid and speed the grooming. First considerations should be that the table is steady and is covered by a rubber mat so that the dog has firm footing and feels secure at that height.

You must establish your own amount of time for grooming. There is no set time for grooming a Yorkie. Naturally, the more heavily coated the dog is, the more time must be allotted for going over the entire dog each time it is put on the table. What you skip on one grooming will be twice as hard to remedy by the time the next grooming session rolls around. And you also run the risk of pulling out more hair when a certain spot has been allowed to get twice as tangled. This simply will not do for a show dog.

A natural-bristle hair brush should be used, and the coat should be brushed out in layers from the skin to the ends of the hair. If the brush is gathering too much hair on one side of the bristles, you are not holding it properly. The dead hair you brush out should be evenly distributed over the surface of the bristles. The coat should be brushed in the direction in which it is to fall. The one exception to this is in the case of puppies. Here, the method of grooming or brushing the coat can be said to be "every which way." At this tender age, it does the hair itself no actual harm and stimulates the skin and hair cells to encourage the growth of the coat. Hair on the legs and face can be fluffed up and adds to that typical, darling puppy expression.

Special attention should be given to the feet. The feet are usually the first part of the dog to get dirty and may stay that way. Wiping them off with wet paper towels will help, especially in winter if the dog has been walking on sidewalks that have been sprinkled with salt to help melt the ice. It is irritating to the feet and not good for the dog if it licks its feet.

Ch. Melodylane Holiday, owned by Kay Jainer. Bred by Mary Purvis of Melodylane Kennels, Centerville, Iowa, the sire was Ch. Melodylane Razzle Dazzle ex Lazy Acres Candy Apple.

182

Silverwinds Lion of the Sea, by Ch. Wildweir Bumper Sticker ex Silverwinds Song Maiden. Owned by Elissa Taddie of West Chester, Pennsylvania.

GROOMING AIDS

The stores are filled with various kinds of grooming aids and coat conditioners that can help you keep your dog well groomed and smelling like a rose. They are on sale at all pet shops and at the concession booths at all the dog shows. It is up to you to decide which is best suited to your particular dog and gives you the best results. Consult the breeder of your dog if you have any questions, and learn what the professionals use. For the most part, these coat conditioners are sprayed on with atomizers and then brushed into the coat. However, it is wise to read —and re-read—the instructions for best results.

If your Yorkie is outdoors a great deal or lives in a city where soot and excessive dirt plagues him, you will more than likely want to use one of the dry shampoos or lather-dry bath preparations between tub baths. Do not expect miracles from these man-made preparations. They are only "aids" that will help you maintain a clean, healthy coat which will be acceptable to live with.

Grooming Equipment List

Natural bristle brush
A wide and a narrow width comb
Spray bottles or atomizers for your coat preparations
Wrapping paper—rice paper, waxed paper, porous paper, net, or plastic wrap cut to size
Baby powder and/or corn starch
Tangle remover lotion
Shampoo—a brand best suited to your dog
Balsam creme rinse
Hair control spray
Knitting or crochet needle (for making the part)
Rubber bands for topknot (or wrappings)
Hair bows
Nail clipper

Ch. Beauvior Melodylane Pizazz, co-bred and co-owned by Mary Purvis and Lois Phelan of Centerville, Iowa.

GROOMING POSITIONS

The first job to be taken care of when grooming your Yorkie is to remove any tangles that might have gathered since the last grooming session. These will probably be found mostly on the underside of the dog and behind the elbows. One of the easiest ways to elimate these is to turn the dog over on its back (on your lap or perhaps later on the table). Spray with a tangle remover and brush loose hair gently away from the area around the mat. Take a little bit of the mat in your hand and try to shred it gently apart with your fingers. Next take a comb and carefully work it out from the ends of the hair, working up toward the body until you get to the skin. When the mat has all been separated, start brushing out the tangled hairs until all remaining hairs are free. Then brush them back into the rest of the coat.

While the puppy or dog is on its back, it is a good time to trim the nails. If your Yorkie is trained to this position at a very early age, it will save you much grief in later years when a heavier coat may tangle. Rubbing the puppy's stomach and talking to it will also help in getting it to tolerate this position. The puppy should also be taught to lie on its side as well as to stand still so that the body coat can be given full attention.

One of Mrs. F.P. Fox's Yorkshire Terriers, this one out of Assam ex Remarkable. Bred in the 1950s.

Standing for grooming is also good practice for the show ring. The noose on the grooming arm also can help accustom the dog to the feel of a show lead. Just be certain that the noose does not "hang" the dog or he will not like grooming or the show ring! Need I remind you, *never* leave the dog alone when he is attached like this. If it should slip off the table, it might break its neck or hang itself. When the telephone or door bell rings, put the dog on the floor or take it with you.

When the coat is all brushed out, use a knitting needle to make the part from the neck to the end of the tail and brush the coat downward on each side.

When grooming the head, special care should be taken to protect the dog's eyes. Steel combs and sharp bristles on a brush can damage eyes permanently, and the dogs themselves seem to sense this. Since your dog is likely to be extremely uncomfortable about this, a little reassuring conversation at this point will help tremendously.

THE TOPKNOT

One of the most charming features of the Yorkshire Terrier is the characteristic topknot, a gathering of the hair on the top of the head secured with a rubber band, barrette, or ribbon bow. Rubber bands will hold it adequately, but ribbons, being more decorative, are seen in the show ring as well as used on an everyday basis at home.

The small rubber bands can be purchased at most five-and-ten-cent stores and pet shops and also at concession booths at the dog shows. Also available are a specially designed rubber bands which do not risk pulling out as much hair as regular rubber bands. These are especially recommended for show dogs whose every hair must be preserved.

When learning to make the topknot, you will find you get the best results by observing and learning from the person from whom you buy your dog. A simple guide for putting up a topknot is to gather all the hair from the outside corners of the eyes and all over the top of the head between the ears, including a small "V" down the back of the neck. When this hair is neatly and evenly gathered and brushed up together, place the rubber band around it securely. It may be necessary to double over the band to be sure it is tight enough to hold the hair in place.

Once the rubber band is secured, be certain that it is not so tight that it pulls the eyes or ears out of their natural position. Move the band back and

Karen McIntire with Ch. Chelsea Nimar Finders Keepers. "Fuzzy" was bred by Nina McIntire of the Chelsea Nimar Kennels, Dallas, Texas.

forth and around in place to be sure there is no pulling, or the dog will scratch at it and break a lot of hairs in the process. If there is any pulling or tightness, loosen the hair between the band and the skin until the tension is relieved.

Once you are certain it is comfortable, spread the hair above the band ever so slightly and gently toward the back of the head until it resembles a little "palm tree." Then attach the bow, if desired, and tell the dog how beautiful it looks! When you put the animal down on the floor, watch for a moment to see that it is not going to scratch at the bow. If he does scratch or try to "rub it off" against the furniture, floor, or with its paws, remove the band gently and immediately, and re-do it until you get it right.

Practice makes perfect, and there is a knack to preparing a topknot correctly and comfortably. Once you learn, it quickly becomes second nature. You might want to practice on a wig, or even on a doll, before risking the hair on your dog. At any rate, you will soon become adept at making topknots or *pien ji* (pronounced been dye), as the Chinese call them.

Remove rubber bands with scissors. Trying to slip them off tends to break too many hairs and may be painful for the dog.

185

Jill, Jody, and Andy make up this handsome trio owned by Shirlee and Francis Sly of Overland Park, Kansas. Photographed in 1976, their official names are Ch. Jody's Handyman, Ch. Newsham's Glitter' n Gold, and Newsham's Lady Sapphire.

GROOMING THE WHISKERS

Even if you tie the side and bottom whiskers in papers or rubber bands while your Yorkie eats, food will undoubtedly stick to the fur and a washing will be necessary to prevent the hair from smelling. If just rubber bands are used, you can rinse the whiskers in a small bowl of water, squeeze dry with paper towels, sprinkle with corn starch, and brush them dry. You must be sure that all food is rinsed away. Make sure that, when applying the rubber bands, the chin hairs are not pulled or are so tight that they interfere with the dog's ability to eat. If the lips, for instance, are pulled back too tightly, he may not even *want* to eat, or may not be able to chew or swallow naturally. After applying the bands and/or wraps, check to see if the mouth is held in a normal position.

Ch. Trivar's Trifle of Bel Tel, owned by Mike Lytle of Los Angeles, California. Missy Yuhl photo.

EARS

Naturally, you want your dog's ears to be clean and clean-smelling. There is no set time for this; once again it will depend on each individual dog. While some dogs require daily maintenance, others need to be checked only once a week.

A periodic check with a cotton swab will soon give you an indication of what your dog requires, and you can act accordingly. The main thing to remember is that the ear is an extremely sensitive organ and must be handled with care. Do not "dig" down or try to penetrate the inner canal. A hint would be to draw an imaginary line from the ear to the nose along the side of the face and keep the cotton swab in that direction. Gently twirl it rather than rub out any matter you may find there. If it continues to build or becomes dark in color, a visit to the veterinarian is recommended, since this may indicate a more serious condition than normal ear wax.

Use eyebrow tweezers to pull out any matted hair from within the ear canal. This allows air to enter the ear canal which will help keep the ears clean. The hair on the outer ear will prevent dust and dirt from entering this canal.

Only the very outside edge of the ear is trimmed for the show ring.

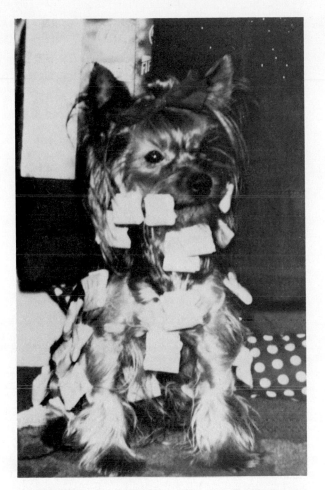

Mayfair's Loup-de-Mer in his papers "between shows." Owned and bred by Mayfair Yorkie House, Newton, New Jersey.

ways to cut and fold the "wraps," to apply the rubber bands to hold them in place, and to still allow for comfort for the dog. It must also be remembered that a dog cannot be wrapped and left that way indefinitely. The wraps must be removed at least every couple of days and the dog given a complete grooming to assure that the coat gets sufficient air and the skin proper stimulation. Wrapping should never be considered a subsitute for grooming.

We suggest that you consult the breeder or person from whom you bought your dog for advice and, better still, ask for a demonstration on how to wrap its coat. It is actually a breeder's obligation to teach you all necessary procedures required to maintain your dog as a worthy specimen. Your breeder will also be familiar with the proper wraps and grooming aids that best suit the breeder's line. A breeder who is proud of his line will willingly offer this advice and you would do well to listen carefully and observe his technique. It may not be easy for you at first, but it will be well worth your while over a long period of time to preserve the long, beautiful, flowing coat for which our breed is known and admired.

WRAPPING THE COAT

Many owners, especially owners of show dogs, put up their dogs' coats in "papers" between shows to prevent the ends of the hairs from breaking off and to insure the longest possible growth. Coats that trail on the floor have a tendency to break or wear off and never attain any greater length.

The art of putting dogs up in papers, netting, or any of the other things used for this purpose, is truly an "art" which requires observation, learning, and lots of practice in order not to do more harm than good to the coat. *How* to wrap the hair, *where* to wrap the coat, *how long* to keep it wrapped, and *what* is best to wrap the coat with are all very much a matter of individual preference and experience.

It is possible to have a show dog's coat in good condition without wrapping it. Rather than do it wrong, it is better not to do it at all if you don't learn from a good teacher. There are specific

A television addict of the first order, the Johnston's Ch. Phirno Emerald Earl doesn't want to miss anything.

If you haven't done so already, study the diagrams on the wrapping procedure in this book, and if there are any questions in your mind as to whether or not you are doing it correctly, a call to your breeder, a grooming salon, or another Yorkie owner who shows his dog is in order.

WRAPPING INSTRUCTIONS

You will be dealing with between twenty-six and twenty-eight wraps, depending on the length and thickness of your dog's coat. Once you've decided on what you are going to use, cut your papers ahead of time—while watching television is a good time to get ahead. Each cut paper should be approximately eight inches long by three inches wide. Waxed paper is the most commonly used, though many people are now using Handywipes because they are porous. A porous wrap is essential in a damp climate.

Ch. Trivar's Friar Tuck is a Group-winning Yorkshire Terrier owned by Johnny Robinson and Morris Howard of the Trivar Kennels in Potomac, Maryland. "Tuck" is pictured here as he looks between shows with his beautiful coat wrapped in papers.

Ch. Newshams Glitter N Gold, owned by Shirlie and Francis Sly of Overland Park, Kansas.

The papers should never be put on over a dirty coat, or one that is matted, and only the longer hair need be wrapped. Fold your wrap in three sections lengthwise and place a strand of hair half way down the middle section. Fold and crease one third of the paper into the right over the hair, then fold and crease the other side into the left. Fold up and under once and then fold up and under again. Twist a rubber band around the entire folded section.

Test to see if there is any hair pulling uncomfortably, and on tail and ears especially make sure you have not included any skin or ear leather! You can do this by making sure you can get a comb through the hair between the paper and the skin. Make sure eyes and lip and ears are not pulled out of shape to make the dog uncomfortable and scratch at them.

Yorkie Wraps

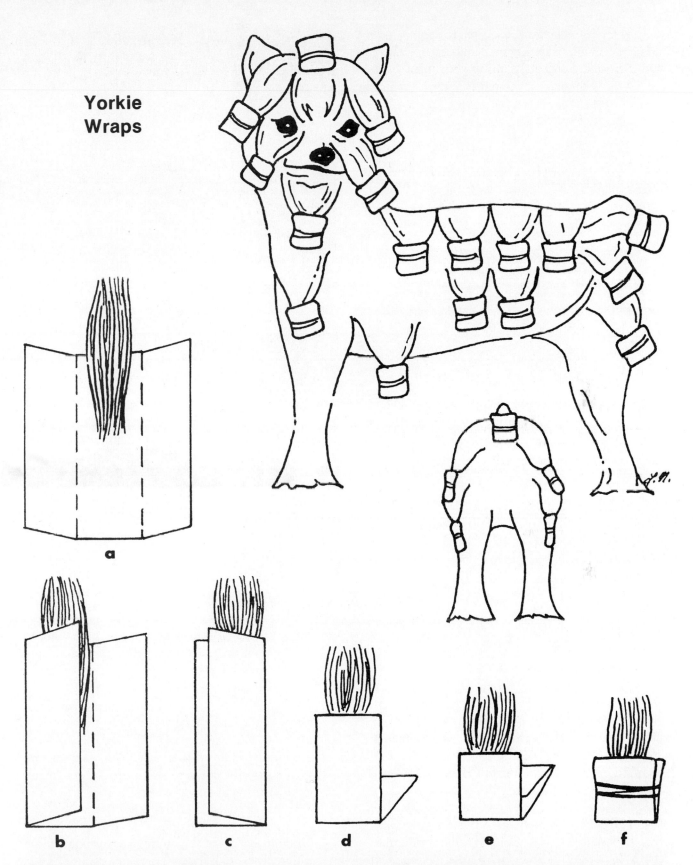

a

b

c

d

e

f

The diagrams above may be helpful in understanding the procedure for wrapping a Yorkshire Terrier. After folding a strip of paper into thirds and then re-opening it, (**a**) lay hairs about halfway down the center section, (**b**) fold one of the thirds over the center section, and (**c**) fold the other third also over the center section. Then (**d**) fold the paper under once, (**e**) fold it under a second time, and (**f**) put rubber bands around the final package to keep it securely together. Since this procedure will be repeated perhaps as many as thirty times each time you wrap your Yorkshire, be sure you have an adequate supply of papers and rubber bands available before you start.

This Myers Studio photo shows one Yorkshire Terrier with its coat in papers and the other Yorkie in "puppy coat."

SPECIAL YORKSHIRE HAIRCUTS

Many people who love the breed and own Yorkshire Terriers do not have either the time or the ability to keep their little dogs in show coat at all times. Even those of us who specialize in show dogs find that after a Yorkie is no longer being shown and we have new little hopefuls coming along who deserve their fame in the show ring, there is less and less time available to keep all the "stay at homes" in show coat.

Many of us have come to realize that there are alternatives which make care quite simple and that still keep Yorkies close to looking like the show dogs they used to be. These alternatives consist of several different kinds of "haircuts" which make grooming much easier without drastically changing the appearance or characteristic expression we have come to love in the Yorkshire. These special haircuts also allow pet

owners, and all others who don't have time to groom their dogs as often as they should, the opportunity to own the breed by making just a few adjustments to the normal coat pattern.

Although the true, staunch breed advocate gasps at the shaved dog with only fluffy ears, a topknot, and feathery tail left after a visit to the grooming parlor or after they've taken a scissors to the dog themselves, there are far too many Yorkies seen cut down to the skin in this fashion. The list of selections for other grooming patterns allows for variations that are far more acceptable and more becoming. For instance, there is no reason at all that a Yorkshire cannot be put back into a puppy-length coat. Then there is the pattern seen on many Cocker Spaniels. The major portion of the body hair is cut down and the leg hair thinned out and shortened. The ears are trimmed down to just below the ear leather,

190

whiskers shortened, topknot shortened, and tail as well. There also is the cut to which the Old English Sheepdog people often resort, cutting the hair one inch long over the entire body but leaving the entire head in tact. With this cut, the topknot remains along with the cute little bows, but the body coat seldom mats.

Of course, anyone who is handy with a pair of scissors can also create his or her own personal haircut that will make grooming easier. However, the grooming parlors are also getting to know the various shortcuts and might make suggestions for other haircuts. If you tell them what you want, they will very likely do a good job no matter which pattern you choose.

GROOMING BEHAVIOR

If your Yorkie wiggles and squirms or backs off and fights you every bit of the way when grooming time rolls around, chances are you are being a little too rough. True enough, there are dogs that just never do get to like being groomed.

These dogs require extra patience and, quite possibly, extra work, since they will employ every scheme known to canines to put you off and hamper your progress. But more than likely, if you meet resistance it's because the dog is genuinely uncomfortable.

The main tactic is to be gentle, especially in the sensitive areas around the groin, the feet, under the tail, around the eyes, the testicles, etc. The calmest of dogs will flinch when he sees the bristles of a brush or the shiny teeth of a steel comb flashing overhead. You can be pretty brisk on the body and chest, but such fervor in the tender regions can resemble a Chinese torture!

Since we are dealing with a long-coated breed, it will pay off later to get the dog accustomed to being groomed from the time he is a newborn puppy. Grooming will probably never seem easy, but it can be a gratifying experience for both dog and master if approached with common sense and patience. Let your dog see that you take a definite pride in taking care of him.

Photographer Burt Murphy snapped this picture of a darling little Yorkie all set to go to a show, complete with all his grooming equipment, waiting patiently for his handler.

He will appreciate this interest, gentleness, and attention, and it will result in a closer communication between you and your dog through this time spent together. And he'll certainly look more beautiful.

Try starting the grooming process when the puppies are just a few days old, using a toothbrush for the coat. Play with their feet, singling out their toes, standing them briefly in future show pose, propping up their tail, and holding up their heads—giving a little scratching under the neck at the same time. Repeat the words "stay," and "good dog," as a clue to future ring procedure. It all adds to a bright future and an outgoing personality.

BATHING THE PUPPY

Here again there are two schools of thought on the advisability of bathing the very young puppy. If you are an advocate of the bath, the same technique can be used for the puppy that is advised for the adult dog. Remember that drafts are very dangerous for puppies; *never* leave a puppy only partially dry, nor put it outdoors in the cold while still damp.

If you believe a bath exposes and endangers a puppy unnecessarily, it is wise to know about the dry shampoos when a cleaning job is deemed advisable. These dry shampoos, plus regular brushings, will keep the puppy reasonably clean as well as stimulate the hair follicles and encourage the natural hair oils necessary for a good coat.

Ch. Wildweir Fairly Obvious is owned by the Cupoluv Kennels of Zinaida Daricek of Avondale, Pennsylvania.

Ch. Cupoluv's Fair LeGrand. "Reggie" is owned and bred by Zinaida Daricek.

Bathing a dog can be hard work, and if you don't know a few of the tricks of the trade, it can be a disaster with a long-haired dog, with everyone and everything ending up equally wet. We would suggest a rubber apron or an old, lightweight raincoat with the sleeves cut off at the elbows as proper attire, because sooner or later your dog is going to shake himself.

BATHING THE ADULT YORKSHIRE

There are probably as many theories on how, and how often, to bathe a dog as there are dog owners. There is, however, no set rule on frequency or method, although it is certain that show dogs, or dogs that spend a great deal of time outdoors in all kinds of weather, yet still spend time indoors with the family, will require a bath on occasion.

Once you've made up your mind that the time for the bath has come, remove all mats from the coat, insert a wad of cotton in each ear and perhaps a drop of mineral oil in each eye to prevent soap burning, and you are almost ready to begin—provided, of course, that you have already placed a rubber mat in the bottom of the sink for sure footing, gathered the towels and shampoos, rinses, combs, brushes, and a dryer.

For a dog the size of a Yorkie, the kitchen sink is about the best place for a bath, and the water pressure and drainage are ideal for the several soapings and many rinsings you will want.

Soaping should provide a good thick lather, and this can best be accomplished by giving the dog a thorough rinsing with warm water first.

You must decide if your dog requires one or two shampoos—usually two is best—which are then followed by a good, long rinsing to make sure every last bit of soap is out of the coat. Soap left in the coat will dry it and cause it to break off or be "gummy."

Start the rinsings and soapings at the rear end of the dog. The noise and feel of the water will be more readily accepted if it is away from the face, and felt first on the more heavily coated areas of the body. Let a little water gather in the sink so that the feet are well soaked, which will help melt away any heavy dirt that might be stuck to the pads or toes. When you get to the head, be sure to hold the head back and protect the eyes from any direct stream of water or soap. Cup your hands with water to wet the head, then gradually work up to the spray. Separate the coat as you rinse. Use a cream rinse after the two shampoos, following the directions on the bottle very carefully. Once you are sure that you have given several thorough rinsings, do it once more for good measure.

THE DRYING PROCESS

Let the water from the rinsings run off and make sure the feet have not gathered any of the soap or residue washing down the sink. Let the dog "drip dry" for a few minutes while you gently squeeze out the heavily coated parts of the body, then throw a turkish towel over the dog and gently squeeze dry the coat into the towel. Once you have most of the drippings into the towel, pick up the dog in the wrapped towel and move it onto the grooming table. While the excess water is still soaking into the towel, turn on your dryer and let it warm up before you direct it at the dog for the blow-dry. This will also give the dog time to get used to the sound of the dryer. We must remember that their hearing is much more acute than ours, and this must be a most unpleasant sound for them.

When the dryer has warmed up, gently start brushing the entire body in the current of warm air. Allow approximately one foot of space between the dog and dryer, and once again brush in layers or in the direction in which the coat is to fall. Be sure to dry evenly all over the body, and not just in one spot with the rest of the dog still soaking wet. When brushing the feet and legs, it is helpful to place the dog's feet at the edge of the table so that you can brush from the skin to the ends of the hair without hitting the table.

A little windblown in this photograph taken several years ago is Ch. Redway Buster, owned by Mrs. Merle E. Smith of Mill Valley, California.

Your Yorkie should never be allowed to dry on the outside while remaining wet next to the skin, so don't bathe your dog unless you are prepared to finish the job properly once you've started it. When the dog is completely dry, you may continue with normal grooming procedures. Watch out for drafts or a room that is too cold.

Also sporting the windblown look is this Yorkie owned by Charlene Ginn of Kennett Square, Pennsylvania.

Ch. Chelsea Nimar For Keeps, son of Ch. Chelsea Nimar Finders Keepers. Both are leading show dogs from Nina McIntire's Chelsea Nimar Kennels in Dallas, Texas.

PREPARING THE SHOW DOG

If your Yorkshire Terrier is to be a show dog, there are several additional steps to be taken which will further enhance its coat and appearance in the ring. Sooner or later, every owner or handler comes up with what they consider the ideal way to prepare a Yorkie for the ring, having achieved what they believe to be the perfect combination of sprays, creme rinses, oil baths, and so on. This is not as simple as it may sound. All one has to do is pass a concessionaire's booth at a dog show and view the myriad of grooming aids and products on display to realize how long it takes to give all of them a fair trial before settling on the "perfect" way to present your dog.

With so many procedures and combinations available, the entire process might seem to be one of trial and error. Since all products, with rare exception, are of good quality, the selection may be said to be "to each his own." Rather than working by the trial-and-error method, let the professionals groom your dog until you have procedures down pat. This will avoid damage to the coat, which may take months to repair. Watch the pros groom at the dog shows. You will almost be able to pick out the winners by the outstanding way the dogs look and behave while still up on the grooming tables. Do not expect the handlers to take time out to teach you while they are preparing to go into the ring. But the breeder of your dog should be able to tell you how to go about learning for yourself or where to attend a grooming school.

Some Yorkies love the water, but not a bath, so be sure to talk to the dog reassuringly so the next bath will be even easier. And every once in a while pick it up and hug it and get a whiff of that marvelous sweet freshness! It can make all the effort worthwhile.

How often to bathe is another personal decision. The general consensus of opinion among exhibitors of show dogs seems to be around every seven to ten days. Others stand by once a month. For the pet dog, bathe as often as seems necessary.

Everblue's Seven No Trump, sired by Nitetrain Desparado ex Ch. Nitetrain Painted Lady. She had major points toward championship at the time this photo was taken. Owner is Arlene Mack of Westlake, Ohio.

Bridget's Silver Dream, sired by Toy Tuffen ex Wee Bridget II. The owner is Mrs. Hilde Rozera of Portland, Oregon, who also makes the adorable bows for her dogs and for others on special order.

USING THE CLIPPERS

Many exhibitors will use the corner of an Oster clipper to trim away excess hair around the anus and to clean off the hair on the stomach. This is another procedure which requires practice and skill so as not to cut or burn these delicate areas of the body. A good teacher should be sought before attempting this procedure.

All scissors used to shape the feet and ears should have blunt edges, and be kept away from the dog's eyes while trimming the hair off the outside of the ear.

CONDITIONING

While we have already discussed that diet, inheritance, and wrapping play a large part in a good coat, there are additional aids if a dog is inclined to have a poor, dry coat. Hot oil treatments, or "putting a dog down in oil" between shows, is yet another contributing factor to a good coat.

Warm olive oil applied to the roots after a bath and gently worked into the coat clear out to the ends will help if heat is also applied by means of hot towels or a warm dryer for several minutes. Mineral oil, baby oil, or corn oil are also used, but caution must be taken to see that the dog does not soil furniture before bathing it out of the coat. Once again, it is advisable to check with your breeder on the best conditioners, or if they are necessary at all.

Never brush the dog if the coat is dirty or dry. Even a spraying with water as you brush will help. After a bath, a spray of half water and half creme rinse will put on a lovely finishing touch.

BRAIDING

More and more Yorkshire Terriers are being seen with their hair braided, or plaited as it is sometimes called. In the past, the hair was put up in either one topknot with a bow and hair falling in a cascade down the neck or in two little topknots, one over each eye. Here again, it is strictly a matter of choice.

The tiny little braids serve several purposes. They keep the hair out of the eyes and also train the "part" for the show ring. They also alleviate the need for barrettes, bows, or rubber bands in most cases, thus preventing scratching by the dog.

The braids are easy to make, once the technique is properly learned. They should lie close to the body and not stick out from it. The silky quality of the hair has a natural tendency to fall this way, so if they stick out, re-do them. Just as you would take down their wrappers every couple of days, the braids also should be redone. Matting also will be greatly reduced. The hair must be quite long in order to make a decent braid, so don't give up too soon.

Mrs. Hilde Rozera's Tinkerbelle gives us that "questioning" look.

195

Retrieving the dumbbell during one of the obedience title trials is Ch. Trivar's Zarin Tinsel, C.D.X., owned and trained to this coveted title by Marie V. Huffman, of New Carrollton, Maryland.

CHAPTER TEN

Yorkshire Terriers in Obedience

The C.D.X. titlist Ch. Trivar's Zarin Tinsel, groomed and ready for the show ring. Owner is Marie Huffman.

Dog shows and conformation classes had a tremendous head start on obedience in the United States. It was in 1933 that the first obedience tests were held in Mount Kisco, New York. Mrs. Helene Whitehouse Walker inaugurated these initial all-breed obedience tests which she had brought from England. Along with Blanche Saunders, her kennel maid at that time, she was responsible for the staging of the first four obedience tests held in the United States.

Obedience training and tests for dogs were an immediate success from the moment those first 150 spectators saw the dogs go through their paces.

Mrs. Walker was instrumental in getting the American Kennel Club to recognize and even sponsor the obedience trials at their dog shows, and her discussions with Charles T. Inglee (then the vice president of the AKC) ultimately led to their recognition. In 1935 she wrote the first published booklet on the subject, called simply *Obedience Tests*. These tests were eventually incorporated into the rules of the AKC obedience requirements in March 1936. It developed into a twenty-two-page booklet that served as a manual for judges, handlers, and the show-giving clubs. The larger version was called *Regulations and Standards for Obedience Test Field Trials*.

Mrs. Walker, Josef Weber (another well-known dog trainer), and Miss Saunders added certain refinements, basic procedures, and exercises, and these were published in the April 1936 issue of the *American Kennel Gazette*.

On June 13 of that same year, the North Westchester Kennel Club held the first AKC-licensed obedience test in conjunction with their all-breed dog show. There were twelve entries for judge Mrs. Wheeler H. Page. The exercises for Novice and Open classes remain virtually unchanged today—half a century later. Only Tracking Dog and Tracking Dog Excellent have been added in the intervening years.

By June of 1939, the American Kennel Club realized that obedience was here to stay and saw the need for an advisory committee. One was established and chaired by Donald Fordyce, with enthusiastic members from all parts of the country willing to serve on it. George Foley of Pennsylvania was on the board. He was one of the most important of all men in the fancy, being superintendent of most of the dog shows on the eastern seaboard. Mrs. Radcliff Farley, also of Pennsylvania, was on the committee, along with Miss Aurelia Tremaine of Massachusetts, Samuel Blick of Maryland, and Frank Grant of Ohio, as well as Josef Weber and Mrs. Walker.

197

A little of the emphasis on dog obedience was diverted with the outbreak of World War II, when talk switched to the topic of dogs serving in defense of their country. As soon as peace was declared, however, interest in obedience reached new heights. In 1946, the American Kennel Club called for another obedience advisory committee, this time headed by John C. Neff. This committee included Blanche Saunders, Clarence Pfaffenberger, Theodore Kapnek, L. Wilson Davis, Howard P. Calussen, Elliott Blackiston, Oscar Franzen, and Clyde Henderson.

Under their leadership, the obedience booklet grew to forty-three pages. Rules and regulations were even more standardized than before, and there was the addition of the requirements for the Tracking Dog title.

In 1971, an obedience department was established at the American Kennel Club offices to keep pace with the growth of the sport and to review and give guidance to show-giving clubs. Judge Richard H. D'Ambrisi was the director until his untimely death in 1973, at which time his duties were assumed by James E. Dearinger, along with his two special consultants, L. Wilson Davis for Tracking and Reverend Thomas O'Connor for Handicapped Handlers.

Anderleigh Rockin Robbie, C.D., owned and trained by Clara Powanda of Wheeling, West Virginia.

A darling little Yorkie being trained in tracking, captured on film by Bill Huffman.

The members of this 1973 committee were Thomas Knott of Maryland, Edward Anderson of Pennsylvania, Jack Ward of Virginia, Lucy Neeb of Louisiana, William Phillips of California, James Falkner of Texas, Mary Lee Whiting of Minnesota, and Robert Self (co-publisher of the important *Front and Finish* obedience newspaper) of Illinois.

While the committee functions continuously, meetings of the board are tentatively held every other year unless a specific function or obedience question arises, in which case a special meeting is called.

During the 1975 session, the committee held discussions on several old and new aspects of the obedience world. In addition to their own ever-increasing responsibilities to the fancy, they discussed seminars and educational symposiums, the licensing of tracking clubs, a booklet with suggested guidelines for obedience judges, Schutzhund training, and the aspects of a Utility Excellent Class degree.

Through the efforts of succeeding advisory committee members, the future of the sport has been insured, as well as the continuing emphasis on the working abilities for which dogs were originally bred. Obedience work also provides novices an opportunity to train and handle their dogs in an atmosphere that provides maximum pleasure and accomplishment at minimum expense—which is precisely what Mrs. Walker and Blanche Saunders intended.

When the advisory committee met in December 1980, many of the familiar names were among those listed as attending and continuing to serve the obedience exhibitors. James E. Dearinger, James C. Falkner, Rev. Thomas V. O'Connor, Robert T. Self, John S. Ward, Howard E. Cross, Helen F. Phillips, Samuel W. Kodis, George S. Pugh, Thomas Knott, and Mrs. Esme Treen were present and accounted for.

As we look back on a half century of obedience trials, we can only surmise that the pioneers—Mrs. Helene Whitehouse Walker and Blanche Saunders—would be proud of the progress made in the obedience rings, founded on their original ideas and enthusiasm.

THE OBEDIENCE RATING SYSTEMS

Just as the Phillips System mushroomed out of the world of show dogs, it was almost inevitable that a "system" or "systems" to measure the successes of obedience dogs would become a reality.

By 1974, Nancy Shuman and Lynn Frosch had established the "Shuman System" of recording the Top Ten All-breed Obedience Dogs in the country. They also listed the Top Four in every breed, if each dog had accumulated a total of fifty or more points according to their requirements. Points were accrued on a scale based on qualifying scores from 170 and up. No Yorkshire Terrier qualified among the Top Ten Obedience Dogs in the all-breed category that year, but two qualified in the Top Ten Toys. In fact, they were Number Four and Number Five. J. Gidden's Yorkie, Mr. Ragtag of Appoline, went all the way to the U.D. title, and L. E. Sullivan's Yorkie, Sully's Li'L Bit Orum, was C.D.X.

1975 OBEDIENCE WINNERS

Front and Finish, the dog trainers' newspaper, also publishes the Delaney System for the Top Ten Obedience Dogs, compiled by Kent Delaney, which rates the dogs in a different manner from the Shuman System.

In the Delaney System, points are awarded for High in Trial or for class placements only, and are based on the published results in the *American Kennel Gazette*. High in Trial winners get a single point for each dog in competition. First place in the class earns a point for each dog competing in that class; second place in the class earns a point for each dog competing in the class minus one; third place in the class earns a point minus two; and the fourth place winner in the class earns a point for each dog competing minus three.

In 1975, no Yorkshire Terrier made the list of Top Ten Obedience Dogs in the all-breed category, but two Yorkies made the list of Top Ten in Toys. Number Nine was M. Ashby's Marys Mighty Mai Tai, C.D.X., and Number Ten was D. and W. Wieland's Teena's Tinker Belle, C.D.X. Following those two in the listing of Top Ten Yorkshire Terriers were third, Mr. Rag Tag of Appoline, U.D., owned by J. Giddens; fourth, My Muffin, C.D., owned by Mr. and Mrs. B. Worknar; fifth, Appolines Wee Spark of Magic, also owned by J. Giddens; sixth, Braunstars Little Tuffy, C.D., owned by M. Johns and M. Braun; seventh, Womacks Ebony Emp, C.D., owned by C. Hayden; eighth, Two Ms Tuppence An Inch, C.D., owned by M. and M. Longec; ninth, Brandy B, U.D., owned by B. and J. Baratono; and tenth, Mar Dels Cricket of Dolru, C.D., owned by D. Densten.

1976 WINNERS

There were no Yorkies listed in the Top Ten All-breeds or the Top Ten Toys in 1976. There were, however, the following winners in the breed, listed here in order from first to eighth: Kendra Kim, owned by P. Astorga; Mr. Rag Tag of Appoline, U.D., owned by J. Giddens; Radnors Winsome Willie, C.D., owned by L. and A. Blum; Annas Little Sugar Plum, owned

The eagerness to work is evident in this Bill Huffman photo of a little Yorkie taking the dumbbell over a jump.

Robyn Huff's Pagan Place Simply Charmin, U.D., takes one of the jumps during an obedience trial. Charmin was the first Utility Dog titlist in the state of Georgia.

by A. Espersen and S. Wortman; Cinder Blu V Schrolucke, C.D., owned by D. Wood; Miss Muffitt of Appoline, C.D.X., owned by J. Giddens; Mar Dels Cricket of Dolru, C.D.X., owned by D. Densten; Champion Ravenrush Raffle Ticket, owned by J. Copple. There was a tie for ninth between Beerex Nobility C.D.X., owned by D. Densten and B. Kramer, and Mayfairs Little Tyke, owned by J. and W. Volhad.

The 1976 Shuman System produced different results for this year. There were no Yorkies in the Top Ten All-breed or Toy category, and just five winners were listed in the breeds: Number One was Mr. Rag Tag of Appoline, U.D.; Number Two, Mar Dels Cricket of Dolru; Number Three, Two Ms Tuppence An Inch; and a tie for Number Four between Braunstar Fanci Poo and Donnybens Little Noel.

1977 WINNERS

In 1977, Mar Dels Cricket of Dolru, U.D. was a Number One obedience dog, followed by Mayfairs Little Tyke, Radnors Winsome Willie, and Wildweir Meet Mr. Chips.

And so it went in the obedience rings during the second half of the 1970s, with dogs amassing thousands of points to reach the top of the various systems. Unfortunately, no Yorkshire Terrier made it again to either the All-breed or the Top Ten Toy lists in either the Delaney or the Shuman Systems, but a refreshing number of newcomers to the lists of title holders gave evidence of the continuing interest in obedience within the ranks of the breed.

THE FIRST U.D. YORKSHIRE TERRIER

Miss California of 48 was truly a winner! She won her championship in conformation classes and went on to win three obedience titles as well. Champion Miss California was the first Yorkshire Utility Dog titlist in America, and second of all Toy breeds. Ruby Erickson was the breeder, and Champion Petite Wee Billy Boy was the sire. Mrs. Erickson also owned several champions, and much of her stock went back to Goldie Stone's breeding. Perhaps her greatest claim to fame is the tremendous accomplishment Miss California achieved in the obedience ring, which served as an inspiration for all the others to come.

Pagan Place Simply Charmin, U.D., became Number One Obedience Yorkie in the 1977-1978 season. Owned and trained by Robyn Huff of Lawrenceville, Georgia.

Lord Casey of Eastwood, C.D.X., top obedience dog for 1981 according to the *Yorkie Tales* magazine statistics, made his U.D. title in 1982. His sire was The Duke of Abruzzi ex Shir-el's Little Lulu. Bred by Donna Tenopir, owned and trained by Marjorie Davis of Glencoe, Illinois.

OTHER U.D. YORKIES

As this book goes to press, there are about twenty Yorkies which have earned their U.D. titles. In the 1960s, Helen and Merrill Cohen's Mardels Terrence earned his title, as did Yam Snevets, owned by Tepe Stevens; Mrs. Lewis's Durgin's Tinkerbell; Edythe Parvis's Girleen of Fortfield; and Donneykin's Cafe Snevets, also owned by Ms. Stevens. Others to finish in the footsteps of Miss California were George Reed's Durgin's York of Woodlawn, Lois Noyes Patoot's Mr. Boo of Sher-lo, and Mrs. Mahne's Patrick Emmet. From the 1970s through the time of this writing were Destiny, owned by Elizabeth Strully; Carnival Queen, owned by Kathleen James; Brandy B., owned by B. and J. Baratono; Wee Laddie Pippin; Dolores and William Wieland's Teena's Tinker Belle; Mardel's Cricket, owned and trained by Dolores Densten; Robyn Huff's Pagan Place Simply Charmin (in 1981); and Marjorie Davis's Lord Casey of Eastwood (in 1982).

Congratulations are due all of them for this remarkable accomplishment!

OBEDIENCE IN CANADA

Caraway's Token of Highland has many titles —the latest one being the coveted Tracking Dog award. Token, owned and trained by Jay Jay Rasing of Canada, is working on his show ring career as well.

"Sunshine," as Token is better known, completed his C.D. title with scores of 198½, 196, and 198, and was also High in Trial twice. Sunshine and Jay Jay trained for four months, and they earned the C.D., C.D.X., and T.D. degrees within a period of seven months.

Sunshine was trained strictly on the food reward method, and barks when he finds the article to be retrieved that has been dropped by the tracklayer. Jay Jay started the training by teaching Sunshine to speak for a cookie, then for a cookie on a glove, and then for the glove with a treat for the barking. He has a natural affinity for tracking work and has been justly rewarded by earning this advanced title. He was also the first North American Tracking Yorkshire Terrier.

OTHER CANADIAN U.D. YORKIES

By no means a complete list, Canadian U.D. dogs include Barbway's Marquis Mackduff, owned by Mrs. L. Mahood; Lady Blue Daisey of Sarabette, owned by Mrs. E. Kadarik, and Almost A Tiger of Lucky-Dais, also owned by E. Kadarik. These three deserve much credit for their achievements.

Bob Mahood of Richmond, British Columbia, puts one of the Kelim Yorkies through his paces. His "Tuffy" is the most titled obedience dog in the breed.

THE DOG OBEDIENCE CLASSICS

Within the dog fancy there are, of course, opportunities for obedience achievement other than through the Delaney and Shuman Systems featured in *Front and Finish*.

In March 1976, the Gaines Dog Research Center, located in White Plains, New York, began its sponsorship of the United States Dog Obedience Classic. Founded by the Illini Obedience Association in 1975, the first classic was held in Chicago.

Gaines' motive in the support of the regional events and the Classic was to emphasize to dog owners, both present and future, their belief that an obedience-trained dog is a better citizen and an asset to any community. Their support was to offer rosettes, trophies, and plaques, as well as prize money, for a series of regional competitions and for the Classic at the year's end. Prize money for the regional awards was almost $3000, while the Classic prize money was in excess of $5000. Each year the Classic is held in another area, where a local obedience club plays host to participants from all over the country.

By 1978, when the two-day Classic was held in Los Angeles at the Sports Arena, people from twenty-three states exhibited with an entry well over the 180-dog limit and with dogs going through their paces in eight rings. The top winner in this competition earns the title of Super Dog, and along with other prizes and money, takes home the sterling silver dumbbell trophy.

The Gaines Dog Obedience Classic competition is open to all breeds and owners who qualify and who enjoy the challenge of teamwork with their dogs—no matter how big or small they may be!

American and Canadian Ch. Jentres Tia Tia, C.D., owned by Ruth Jenkins of Lakeside, California.

THE YORKIE SQUARE DANCERS

At the first Yorkshire Terrier Club of America Specialty Show held in conjunction with the Beverly-Riviera Kennel Club Show (September 18, 1954, in Santa Monica, California), the obedience devotees staged a highly successful square dance for their Yorkies. The little Yorkies all wore golden ribbons and had blue leads, while their handlers wore full circular skirts and black blouses with a turquoise, blue, and black color scheme.

The performance of the square dance incorporated every exercise required in the C.D. title, mostly off lead, and was performed along with music, a professional caller, and specially written words to the tune.

There were approximately twenty-five Yorkshires participating at this first parent club Specialty, and the highest scoring dog, Muriel Kreig's Ginger Lei, won a large ceramic Yorkshire Terrier made and donated by the club's president, Kay Finch. Ginger Lei was one of four participants in the Square Dance exhibition, along with Frances Davis and "Mike," Sally Meyers and "Little Peanut," and Pearl Kincarte and "Pearl."

While many of the Yorkie clubs have obedience-trained dogs among their membership and support obedience competition, the first National Obedience Trial held with the Yorkshire Terrier Club of America Specialty was in February 1981. Merrill Cohen was the judge for the thirty-six entries. Fay Gold was the obedience chairperson; Helen Stern served as trophy chairperson for this initial, very successful, event. Highest score in Trials at this first National was Ricki Abrams' Red Stag's Nik Nak, with a score of 196½.

ANOTHER YORKIE "FIRST"

At the 1973 Crufts Dog Show in London, England, a little Yorkshire Terrier named Shandy accomplished an amazing feat. It was the first time a Toy dog—of any breed—had competed in the obedience rings at Crufts. While this was amazing in itself, Shandy is to be further congratulated on his placing fifth with a score of 295 points out of a possible 300. This win was made while competing against no less than twenty-nine of England's top Working breeds, and his win caused a great deal of comment and praise.

Mrs. Joyce Burton, who owns, trains, and handles her little dog, had to overcome tremendous odds, since the British obedience rules make *no allowance for size.* Judge N. Braithwaite wrote in his critique on Shandy's performance, "My how those little legs did travel round the great big ring!. . .Kept pace with big dogs all the time, a grand performance by handler and dog." Perhaps Shandy might have done even better had he not been ill recently, but Mrs. Burton attributed the success to the fact that Shandy's chief aim in life was to please her. She has made everything a game for him, and in spite of his not being up to snuff on that particular day, the combination of trainer and dog worked, and together they made Yorkshire history!

OTHER OBEDIENCE ACTIVITIES

For those interested in the obedience sport, there are many other activities connected with dog training.

There are scent dog seminars, hurdle races, World Series of Dog Obedience in Canada, and the Association of Obedience Clubs and Judges, to name just a few. The best possible way to keep informed of activities on both a national and local scale is by membership in kennel and obedience clubs—and by reading dog magazines and newspapers published by obedience experts and enthusiasts.

Front and Finish, the dog trainers' newspaper, is perhaps the leading publication. It features the Delaney System obedience results, along with many columns of wide interest on all phases of obedience. Current subscription rates may be obtained by writing to H. and S. Publications, Inc., 113 S. Arthur Avenue, Galesburg, Illinois 61401. A. J. Harler and Robert T. Self are co-editors of this most worthy and informative publication.

UNDERSTANDING AN OBEDIENCE TRIAL

For those interested in attending a trial, it is suggested they read a booklet entitled "How To Understand and Enjoy an Obedience Trial," available free of charge from the Ralston Purina Company, Checkerboard Square, St. Louis, Missouri 63188.

The American Kennel Club publishes the Obedience Regulations booklet and offers it free of charge when single copies are requested. A check or money order for fifteen cents per copy is required when ordering in quantities for clubs or organizations. Anyone thinking about becoming active in obedience training should read this booklet before joining an obedience club.

Future Ch. Tivar's Zarin Tinsel, C.D.X., is enjoying the snow as a young puppy. Owned by Marie Huffman of New Carrollton, Maryland.

TO TRAIN OR NOT TO TRAIN

There are those obedience buffs who will tell you that the Yorkshire Terrier—or any other Toy breed—is not too well suited for obedience training. In some instances this may be true. There is nothing more frustrating than trying to train a dog that just doesn't "get the call." Training becomes uphill work all the way, and there is always the doubt lingering in the back of your mind whether the dog will or won't perform in the ring, which is far from the satisfaction one gets from *knowing* that your dog is a willing worker and just as anxious as you are to put on a good show.

However, more and more Yorkshire Terriers are receiving their degrees, and more and more training methods and devoted owners are succeeding where others have failed, proving that Yorkies are intelligent and can be trained—especially if they want to be! Some Yorkies do seem to take a special delight in convincing their owners that they aren't suited for obedience, when actually it is just that they don't want to and have convinced their trainers that it is a hopeless cause. Others just need to be coaxed.

While it is not advisable to force a dog into working toward a degree, basic training is good for every dog just for the sake of good manners. If approached correctly, training will not make a dog dislike taking orders. Those who wish to go farther should make sure that their dog displays a natural desire to "please" its owner and that the dog will take pleasure from the experience of obedience training.

Davis' Smokey, U.D., owned and trained by Marjorie Davis of Glencoe, Illinois, is a perfect example of the willing worker in the obedience ring. He earned his title in 1978.

TRAINING YOUR DOG

While the American Kennel Club will gladly send along booklets with rules and regulations for competition at the shows, you must be prepared to start "basic training" with your dog long before you start thinking about entering obedience trials. There are few things in the world a dog would rather do than please his master; therefore, obedience training—even the learning of his name—will be a pleasure for your dog. If taught correctly, it will certainly make him a much nicer animal to live with the rest of his life.

EARLY TRAINING AT HOME

Some breeders believe in starting the training as early as two weeks of age. Repeating the puppy's name and encouraging the puppy to come when called is a good start, as long as you don't expect too much too soon. Some recommend placing a narrow ribbon around the puppy's neck to get him used to the feel of what will later be a collar and leash. The puppy can play with it and learn the pressure of the pull on his neck before he is actually expected to respond to it.

If you intend to show your puppy, there are other formalities which you may observe as early as four weeks of age that will help later on. One of the most important points is setting him up on a table in show stance while repeating "stand" and "stay." If this is repeated gently several times a day, it can be handled like a game. And don't forget the lavish praise when the dog obeys.

WHEN TO START FORMAL TRAINING

Official training should not start until the puppy is about six months of age unless it shows a natural tendency toward learning very early. Most obedience trainers will not take dogs in their classes much before this age. As the puppy grows, however, you can certainly get him used to his name, to coming when he is called, and to the meaning of words like "no," and "come," and other basic commands. Repetition and patience are the keys to success since most dogs are not ready for a wide range of words in their rather limited attention span. If your dog is to be a show dog, it would be wise to concentrate on the "stand" and "stay" commands.

THE REWARD METHOD

The only acceptable kind of training is the kindness-and-reward method which will build a strong bond between dog and master. Try to establish respect and attention, not fear of punishment. Give each command, preceded by the dog's name, and make it stick. Do not move on to another command or lesson until the first one is mastered. At first, train where there are no distractions, and never when the dog is tired or right after eating. When interest wanes, quit until another session later in the day. Two or three sessions a day with a bright dog, increasing the time from, say, five minutes to fifteen minutes, might be right. Each dog is different, and you must establish and set your own schedule according to your own dog's learning ability.

WHAT YOU NEED TO START TRAINING

The soft nylon show leads available at all pet stores are best for early training. Later, a choke chain may be used. Let the puppy play with the lead or even carry it around when you first put it on. Too much pressure pulling at the end of a lead is likely to get him off to a bad start.

Ch. Trivars Zarin Tinsel, C.D.X., owned and trained by Marie V. Huffman, goes over the jumps during a training exercise.

FORMAL SCHOOL TRAINING

The time will come when your dog is ready to join obedience classes to work along with other dogs amid outside distractions.

The yellow pages of your telephone book can lead you to dog training schools or classes for this official training. Usually the lessons are moderately priced, and you should start making inquiries when the puppy is about four months of age so you will be ready for the start of the next class. Adult education classes usually feature dog training sessions also.

If you intend to show your dog, training *yourself* along with the dog will benefit both of you.

OBEDIENCE DEGREES

Several obedience titles are recognized by the American Kennel Club. Dogs may earn these through a process of completed exercises. The Companion Dog, or C.D. degree, is divided into three classes: Novice, Open, and Utility, with a total score of 200 points. After a dog has qualified with a score of at least 170 points, it has earned the right to have included the letters *C.D.* after its name, and is eligible to compete in Open Class competition and earn a Companion Dog Excellent degree, or *C.D.X.* After qualifying in three shows for this title, it may compete for the Utility Dog title, or *U.D.* Tracking Dog and Tracking Dog Excellent titles also may be earned, the requirements for which may be obtained from the American Kennel Club.

Powanda's Mr. Red, C.D., is owned by Mark Powanda of Wheeling, West Virginia.

OBEDIENCE TRIAL CHAMPIONSHIPS

The Board of Directors of the American Kennel Club approved Obedience Trial Championship titles in July 1977. Points for these championship titles are recorded only for those dogs that have earned the U.D. title. Any dog that has been awarded the title of Obedience Trial Champion may continue to compete. Dogs that complete requirements receive an Obedience Trial Championship Certificate from the American Kennel Club and are permitted the use of the letters *O.T. Ch.* preceding their name.

March Winds Little Joker, C.D.X., whelped in 1979, and owned and trained by the breeder Donna Tenopir of St. David, Arizona. The sire was The Duke of Abruzzi ex Shir-Els Little Lulu.

There is great satisfaction for both owner and dog in earning those titles, and when considering such training for your dog, you would do well to recall St. Mathilde's Prayer:

O, God,

Give unto me by grace

that obedience which thou hast

given to my little dog

by nature.

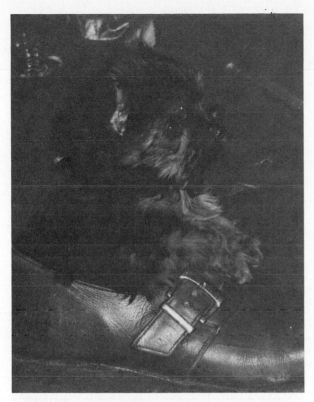

This ten-week-old puppy "who jumped in a shoe" grew up to be both a champion and a C.D.X. title holder. Owned by Marie Huffman.

CHECK POINTS FOR OBEDIENCE COMPETITORS

- Do your training and have your lessons down pat before entering the show ring.
- Make sure you and your dog are ready before entering a show.
- Don't expect more than your dog is ready to give. Obedience work is progressive, not all learned in the first few lessons.
- It's okay to be nervous, but try not to let your dog know it by your over-handling or fidgeting.
- Do not punish your dog in or out of the ring; if the dog isn't working well, it is probably your fault and not his.
- Pay attention to the judge, and follow instructions exactly.
- Pay attention to your own dog, and don't talk or advise or criticize others.
- Don't forget to exercise your dog before entering the ring.
- Be a good loser; if you don't win today, you can try again another day.
- Have confidence in your dog's intelligence; his greatest desire is to please you if you have earned his respect.
- If it isn't fun for you and your dog, stay out of the ring and try another sport!

Anderleigh Rockin Robbie, C.D., is owned by Clara Powanda.

A little Yorkie goes through its paces during an obedience trial, photographed by H. Weihermann.

Already a champion and obedience titlist, Ch. Trivar's Zarin Tinsel, C.D.X., takes time out for a litter. Owner, breeder, and trainer is Marie V. Huffman of New Carrollton, Maryland. This is a perfect example of why our Yorkies can be considered as "all-around" dogs.

CHAPTER ELEVEN

Breeding Your Yorkshire Terrier

American and Canadian Ch. Windsor Gayclyn Strut N Stuff, owned by Suzanne M. Jones of New York Mills, New York, and a chief stud force at her kennels.

Let us assume the time has come for your dog to be bred, and you have decided you are in a position to enjoy producing a litter of puppies that you hope will make a contribution to the breed. The bitch you purchased is sound, her temperament is excellent and she is a most worthy representative of the breed.

You have a calendar and have counted off the ten days since the first day of red staining, and have determined the tenth to fourteenth day, which will more than likely be the best days for the actual mating. You have additionally counted off sixty to sixty-five days before the puppies are likely to be born to make sure everything necessary for their arrival will be in good order by that time.

From the moment the idea of having a litter occurred to you, your thoughts should have been given to the correct selection of a proper stud. Here again, the novice would do well to seek advice on analyzing pedigrees and tracing bloodlines for the best breedings. As soon as the bitch is in season and you see color (or staining) and a swelling of the vulva, it is time to notify the owner of the stud you selected and make appointments for the breedings. There are several pertinent questions you will want to ask the stud owners after having decided upon the pedigree.

The owners, naturally, will also have a few questions they wish to ask you. These questions will concern your bitch's bloodlines, health, age, and how many previous litters she's had, if any.

THE POWER IN PEDIGREES

Someone in the dog fancy once remarked that the definition of a show prospect puppy is one third the pedigree, one third what you see, and one third what you *hope* it will be! Well, no matter how you break down your qualifying fractions, we all quite agree that good breeding is essential if you have any plans at all for a show career for your dog. Many breeders will buy on pedigree alone, counting largely on what they themselves can do with the puppy by way of feeding, conditioning, and training. Needless to say, that very important piece of paper commonly referred to as the "pedigree" is mighty reassuring to a breeder or buyer new at the game, or to one who has a breeding program in mind and is trying to establish his own bloodline.

One of the most fascinating aspects of tracing pedigrees is the way the names of the really great dogs of the past keep appearing in the pedigrees of the great dogs of today—positive proof of the strong influence of heredity and witness to a great deal of truth in the statement that great

Precious Blue Tuttles, brood bitch at Sue Lively's Yorkie kennels in North East, Maryland. Whelped in 1976, her sire was Ch. Phirno Emerald Earl, an English import, ex Candytops Blue Grace.

dogs frequently reproduce themselves, though not necessarily in appearance only. A pedigree represents something of value when one is dedicated to breeding better dogs.

To the novice buyer or one who is perhaps merely switching to another breed and sees only a frolicking, leggy, squirming bundle of energy in a fur coat, a pedigree can mean everything! To those of us who believe in heredity, a pedigree is more like an insurance policy—so always read it carefully and take heed.

For the even more serious breeder of today who wishes to make a further study of bloodlines in relation to his breeding program, the American Kennel Club library stud books can and should be consulted.

Ch. Wildweir Fairly Obvious, pictured in full coat. "Michael" was the foundation stud at Mrs. James Daricek's Cupoluv Kennels in Avondale, Pennsylvania. Bred by Nancy Donovan, he is now the sire of several champions.

THE HEALTH OF THE BREEDING STOCK

Some of your first questions should concern whether the stud has already proved himself by siring a normal healthy litter. Also inquire as to whether the owners have had a sperm count made to determine just exactly how fertile or potent the stud is. Determine for yourself whether the dog has two normal testicles.

When considering your bitch for this mating, you must take into consideration a few important points that lead to a successful breeding. You and the owner of the stud will want to recall whether she has had normal heat cycles, whether there were too many runts in the litter, and whether a Caesarean section was ever necessary. Has she ever had a vaginal infection? Could she take care of her puppies by herself, or was there a milk shortage? How many surviving puppies were there from the litter, and what did they grow up to be in comparison to the requirements of the breed standard?

Two puppies bred by Sue Lively. The sire was Ch. Wildweir Fairly Obvious ex Precious Blue Tuttles. This litter was whelped in 1978.

Don't buy a bitch that has problems in heat and has never had a live litter. Don't be afraid, however, to buy a healthy maiden bitch, since chances are, if she is healthy and from good stock, she will be a healthy producer. Don't buy a monorchid male, and certainly not a cryptorchid. If there is any doubt in your mind about his potency, get a sperm count from the veterinarian. Older dogs that have been good producers and are for sale are usually not too hard to find at good established kennels. If they are not too old and have sired quality show puppies, they can give you some excellent show stock from which to establish your own breeding lines.

WHEN TO BREED A GROWN BITCH

The best advice used to be not until her second heat. Today with our new scientific knowledge, we have become acutely aware of such things as hip dysplasia, juvenile cataracts, and other congenital diseases. The best advice now seems to be aimed at not breeding your dogs before two years of age, when both the bitch and the sire have been examined by qualified veterinarians and declared—in writing—to be free and clear of these conditions.

THE DAY OF THE MATING

Now that you have decided upon the proper male and female combination to produce what you hope will be—according to the pedigrees—a fine litter of puppies, it is time to set the date. You have selected the two days (with a one day lapse in between) that you feel are best for the breeding, and you call the owner of the stud. The bitch always goes to the stud, unless, of course, there are extenuating circumstances. You set the date and the time and arrive with the bitch *and* the money.

Standard procedure is payment of a stud fee at the time of the first breeding, if there is a tie. For the stud fee, you are entitled to two breedings with ties. Contracts may be written up with specific conditions on breeding terms, of course, but this is general procedure. Often a breeder will take the pick of a litter to protect and maintain his bloodlines; this can be especially desirable if he needs an outcross for his breeding program or if he wishes to continue his own bloodlines if he sold you the bitch to start with, and this mating will continue his line-breeding program. This should all be worked out ahead of time and written and signed before the two dogs are bred. Remember that the payment of the stud fee is for the services of the stud—not for a guarantee of a litter of puppies. This is why it is so important to make sure you are using a proven stud. Bear in mind also that the American Kennel Club will not register a litter of puppies sired by a male that is under eight months of age. In the case of an older dog, they will not register a litter sired by a dog over twelve years of age, unless there is a witness to the breeding in the form of a veterinarian or other responsible person.

Many studs over twelve years of age are still fertile and capable of producing puppies, but if you do not witness the breeding there is always the danger of a "substitute" stud being used to produce a litter. This brings up the subject of sending your bitch away to be bred if you cannot accompany her.

The disadvantages of sending a bitch away to be bred are numerous. First of all, she will not be herself in a strange place, so she'll be difficult to handle. Transportation, if she goes by air (while reasonably safe), is still a traumatic experience. There is always the danger of her being put off at the wrong airport, not being fed or watered properly, etc. Some bitches get so upset that they go out of season and the trip—which may prove expensive, especially on top of a substantial stud fee—will have been for nothing.

If at all possible, accompany your bitch so that the experience is as comfortable for her as it can be. In other words, make sure, before setting this kind of schedule for a breeding, that there is no stud in the area that might be as good for her as the one that is far away. Don't sacrifice the proper breeding for convenience, since bloodlines are so important, but put the safety of the bitch above all else. There is always a risk in traveling, since dogs are considered cargo on a plane.

Juana Phillips is showing her American and Canadian Ch. Trail West High and Miley. He was the sire of five champions at the time this book was being written.

K-9 TRANSPORTATION

Shipping puppies by air, or sending bitches away for stud service is frequently a disturbing decision. The horrible tales of unfortunate mishaps linger in our ears as we tuck our little Yorkies into their crates and turn them over to the men who load them aboard those enormous aircraft.

However, when we compare the large number of dogs that are safely shipped these days to the relatively few bad experiences, perhaps we can take heart and hope that with a few ordinary precautions, a safe journey can be almost assured.

Planning ahead of time is the key to a smooth trip. Making the reservations ahead of time for non-stop flights—even if it means considerable traveling on each end—is good for starters. And not shipping puppies in summer heat is another important consideration. Night flying is always an advantage, and so is shipping your dog midweek when vacationers are not also traveling, in order to avoid crowded conditions. Try, if possible, to ship your dog in your own crate as it will smell of home. Also include a toy or blanket that is comforting and familiar. Just make sure the crate is substantial and large enough to meet plane requirements, and won't get lost "in the shuffle." Crates may be purchased at the airport, and you can work it out with the party on the other end as to who will pay for it.

A visit to the veterinarian is another prerequisite. Each state has different rules and regulations concerning vaccinations, so there is no purpose in stating them here. But it is wise to call the airline to find out the current rules and vaccinations necessary at that time. Most airlines also require the animal to be present at least two hours before the flight departure time. Needless to say, feed a light diet on the day of the flight, and walk the dog before crating it. This practice not only enables the dog to relieve itself, but gives it exercise, and hopefully it will be able to sleep en route. Make sure water is included in the crate. Not so much as to spill over, but enough to give it a drink en route.

The ideal way to ship is to take the dog on board with you in a small carrier to be put under your seat. Most airlines will allow this if reservations are made far enough in advance, and if not too many pets are booked on the same flight.

If the dog must travel in the baggage section, make sure the crate is marked "LIVE ANIMAL" with full instructions as to where it has come from and where it will be going, complete with telephone numbers. If the trip takes a reasonable time, leave instructions not to remove the dog from the crate. If it is a matter of several days, be sure to leave complete instructions and a leash attached to the crate. Dog biscuits will usually suffice as food. On long trips, put a heavy layer of sawdust or newspaper on the bottom of the crate. Secure the door to prevent an accidental bump from opening the crate and having your dog escape. However, do not lock the crate in case of an emergency.

Once the dog is airborne, head for a telephone and let the people on the other end of the line know all the details: when it ate last, what it eats, arrival time, and so on. Then go home and wait by the phone to learn of its safe arrival!

Puppies bred at the Wildweir Kennels in Glenview, Illinois.

212

A family portrait at Elissa Taddie's Silverwinds Kennels in West Chester, Pennsylvania. American, Canadian Ch. Wildweir Candytuft, Silverwinds Rose Fairy, Goria Queen, and Silverwinds Spirit of Apollo (Candytuft's son).

HOW MUCH DOES THE STUD FEE COST?

The stud fee will vary considerably—the better the bloodlines, the more winning the dog does at shows, the higher the fee. Stud service from a top winning dog could run $500.00 and up. Here again, there may be exceptions. Some breeders will take part cash and then, say, third pick of the litter. The fee can be arranged by a private contract rather than the traditional procedure we have described.

Here again, it is wise to get the details of the payment of the stud fee in writing to avoid trouble.

THE ACTUAL MATING

It is always advisable to muzzle the bitch. A terrified bitch may fear-bite the stud, or even one of the people involved, and the wild or maiden bitch may snap or attack the stud to the point where he may become discouraged and lose interest in the breeding. Muzzling can be done with a lady's stocking tied around the muzzle with a half knot, crossed under the chin and knotted at the back of the neck. There is enough "give" in the stocking for her to breathe or salivate freely, and yet not open her jaws far enough to bite. Place her in front of her owner, who holds onto her collar and talks to her and calms her as much as possible.

If the male will not mount on his own initiative, it may be necessary for the owner to assist in lifting him onto the bitch, perhaps even in guiding him to the proper place. Usually, the tie is accomplished once the male gets the idea. The owner should remain close at hand, however, to make sure the tie is not broken before an adequate breeding has been completed. After a while the stud may get bored, and try to break away. This could prove injurious. It may be necessary to hold him in place until the tie is broken.

We must stress at this point that while some bitches carry on physically, and vocally, during the tie, there is no way the bitch can be hurt. However, a stud can be seriously or even permanently damaged by a bad breeding. Therefore, the owner of the bitch must be reminded that she must not be alarmed by any commotion. All concentration should be devoted to the stud and a successful and properly executed service.

Many people believe that breeding dogs is simply a matter of placing two dogs, a male and a female, in close proximity, and letting nature take its course. While often this is true, you cannot count on it. Sometimes it is hard work, and in the case of valuable stock, it is essential to supervise to be sure of the safety factor, especially if one or both of the dogs are inexperienced. If the owners are also inexperienced, it may not take place at all.

Three of a kind are these ten-month-old littermates from the Silk N Satin kennels of Clara Powanda, Wheeling, West Virginia. Anastasia Delight, Wind of Miranda, and Sherlock Min Venn all carry the Silk N Satin prefix.

ARTIFICIAL INSEMINATION

Breeding by means of artificial insemination is usually unsuccessful, unless under a veterinarian's supervision, and can lead to an infection for the bitch and discomfort for the dog. The American Kennel Club requires a veterinarian's certificate to register puppies from such a breeding. Although the practice has been used for over two decades, it now offers new promise, since research has been conducted to make it a more feasible procedure for the future.

There now exists a frozen semen concept that has been tested and found successful. The study, headed by Dr. Stephen W.J. Seager, M.V.B., an instructor at the University of Oregon Medical School, has the financial support of the American Kennel Club, indicating that organization's interest in the work. The study is being monitored by the Morris Animal Foundation of Denver, Colorado.

Dr. Seager announced in 1970 that he had been able to preserve dog semen and to produce litters with the stored semen. The possibilities of selective world-wide breedings by this method are exciting. Imagine simply mailing a vial of semen to the bitch! The perfection of line-breeding by storing semen without the threat of death interrupting the breeding program is exciting also.

As it stands today, the technique for artificial insemination requires the depositing of semen (taken directly from the dog) into the bitch's vagina, past the cervix and into the uterus by syringe. The correct temperature of the semen is vital, and there is no guarantee of success. The storage method, if successfully adopted, will present a new era in the field of purebred dogs.

THE GESTATION PERIOD

Once the breeding has taken place successfully, the seemingly endless waiting period of about sixty-three days begins. For the first ten days after the breeding, you do absolutely nothing for the bitch—just spin dreams about the delights you will share with the family when the puppies arrive.

Around the tenth day, it is time to begin supplementing the diet of the bitch with vitamins and calcium. We strongly recommend that you take her to your veterinarian for a list of the proper or perhaps necessary supplements and the correct amounts of each for your particular bitch. Guesses, which may lead to excesses or insufficiencies, can ruin a litter. For the price of a visit to your veterinarian, you will be confident that you are feeding properly.

The bitch should be free of worms, of course, and if there is any doubt in your mind, she should be wormed now, before the third week of pregnancy. Your veterinarian will advise you on the necessity of this and proper dosage as well.

PROBING FOR PUPPIES

Far too many breeders are overanxious about whether the breeding "took" and are inclined to feel for puppies or persuade a veterinarian to radiograph or x-ray their bitches to confirm it. Unless there is reason to doubt the normalcy of a pregnancy, this is risky. Certainly sixty-three days is not too long to wait, and why risk endangering the litter by probing with your inexperienced hands? Few bitches give no evidence of being in whelp, and there is no need to prove it for yourself by trying to count puppies.

ALERTING YOUR VETERINARIAN

At least a week before the puppies are due, you should telephone your veterinarian and notify him that you expect the litter and give him the date. This way he can make sure that there will be someone available to help, should there be any problems during the whelping. Most veterinarians today have answering services and alternative vets on call when they themselves are not

A charming trio of Yorkshire Terriers from the Pequa Kennels. Eleanor Rost was the photographer.

available. Some veterinarians suggest that you call them when the bitch starts labor so that they may further plan their time, should they be needed. Discuss this matter with your veterinarian when you first take the bitch to him for her diet instructions, and establish the method that will best fit in with his schedule.

DO YOU NEED A VETERINARIAN IN ATTENDANCE?

Even if this is your first litter, I would advise that you go through the experience of whelping without panicking and calling desperately for the veterinarian. Most animal births are accomplished without complications, and you should call for assistance only if you run into trouble.

When having her puppies, your bitch will appreciate as little interference and as few strangers around as possible. A quiet place, with her nest, a single familiar face, and her own instincts are all that is necessary for nature to take its course. An audience of curious children squealing and questioning, other family pets nosing around, or strange adults, should be avoided. Many a bitch that has been distracted in this way has been known to devour her young. This can be the horrible result of intrusion into the bitch's privacy. There are other ways of teaching children the miracle of birth, and there will be plenty of time later for the whole family to enjoy the puppies. Let them be born under proper and considerate circumstances.

Ch. Fardust's Femme Fatale, owned by Barbara Beissel of Minneapolis, Minnesota. "Whitney" is one of the important brood bitches at Barbara's Lamplighter Kennels.

Yorkfold Satin Lady, one of the breed bitches at Clara Powanda's Silk N Satin Kennels.

LABOR

Some litters—many first litters—do not run the full term of sixty-three days. So, at least a week before the puppies are actually due, and at the time you alert your veterinarian as to their expected arrival, start observing the bitch for signs of the commencement of labor. This will manifest itself in the form of ripples running down the sides of her body that will come as a revelation to her as well. It is most noticeable when she is lying on her side—and she will be sleeping a great deal as the arrival date comes closer. If she is sitting or walking about, she will perhaps sit down quickly or squat peculiarly. As the ripples become more frequent, birth time is drawing near, and you will be wise not to leave her. Usually within twenty-four hours before whelping she will stop eating, and as much as a week before she will begin digging a nest. The bitch should be given something resembling a whelping box with layers of newspaper (black and white only) to make her nest. She will dig more and more as birth approaches, and this is the time to begin making your promise to stop interfering unless your help is specifically required. Some bitches whimper and others are silent, but whimpering does not necessarily indicate trouble.

THE ARRIVAL OF THE PUPPIES

The sudden gush of green fluid from the bitch indicates that the water or fluid surrounding the puppies has "broken" and they are about to start down the canal and come into the world. When the water breaks, birth of the first puppy is imminent. The first puppies are usually born within minutes to a half hour of each other, but a couple of hours between the later ones is not uncommon. If you notice the bitch straining constantly without producing a puppy, or if a puppy remains partially in and partially out for too long, it is cause for concern. Breech births (puppies born feet first instead of head first) can often cause delay or hold things up, and this is often a problem that requires veterinarian assistance.

Mother and babies are doing just fine, thank you. Precious Blue Tuttles with her litter of five whelped in January, 1982. Bred by Mrs. Bobby Lively of North East, Maryland.

FEEDING THE BITCH BETWEEN BIRTHS

Usually the bitch will not be interested in food for about twenty-four hours before the arrival of the puppies, and perhaps as long as two or three days after their arrival. The placenta that she cleans up after each puppy is high in food value and will be more than ample to sustain her. This is nature's way of allowing the mother to feed herself and her babies without having to leave the nest and hunt for food during the first crucial days. In the wild, the mother always cleans up all traces of birth so as not to attract other animals to her newborn babies.

Orion's Fayleen, foundation bitch at Fay Gold's Fago Kennels in New York City.

However, there are those of us who believe in making food available should the mother feel the need to restore her strength during or after delivery—especially if she whelps a large litter. Raw chopped meat, beef bouillon, and milk are all acceptable and may be placed near the whelping box during the first two or three days. After that, the mother will begin to put the babies on a sort of schedule. She will leave the whelping box at frequent intervals, take longer exercise periods and begin to take interest in other things. This is where the fun begins for you. Now the babies are no longer soggy little pinkish blobs. They begin to crawl around and squeal and hum and grow before your very eyes!

Eight-week-old puppies at the Silk N Satin Kennels in Wheeling, West Virginia.

217

A charming candid shot of American and Canadian Ch. Wildweir Candytuft and her son, Silverwinds Spirit of Apollo. Owner is Elissa Taddie of West Chester, Pennsylvania.

BREECH BIRTHS

Puppies normally are delivered head first; however, some are presented feet first or in other abnormal positions, and this is referred to as a "breech birth."

Aid can be given by grasping the puppy with a piece of turkish toweling and pulling gently during the dam's contractions. Be careful not to squeeze the puppy too hard; merely try to ease it out by moving it gently back and forth. Because even this much delay in delivery may mean the puppy is drowning, do not wait for the bitch to remove the sac. Do it yourself by tearing the sac open to expose the face and head. Then cut the cord anywhere from one-half to three-quarters of an inch away from the navel. If the cord bleeds excessively, pinch the end of it with your fingers and count five. Repeat if necessary. Then pry open the mouth with your finger and hold the puppy upside down for a moment to drain any fluids from the lungs. Next, rub the puppy briskly with turkish or paper toweling. You should get it wriggling and whimpering by this time.

DRY BIRTHS

Occasionally the sac will break before the delivery of a puppy and will be expelled while the puppy remains inside, thereby depriving the dam of the necessary lubrication to expel the puppy normally. Inserting vaseline or mineral oil via your finger will help the puppy pass down the birth canal. This is why it is essential that you be present during the whelping—so that you can count puppies and afterbirths and determine when and if assistance is needed.

THE TWENTY-FOUR HOUR CHECKUP

It is smart to have a veterinarian check the mother and her puppies within twenty-four hours after the last puppy is born. The veterinarian can check the puppies for cleft palates or umbilical hernia and may wish to give the dam—particularly if she is a show dog—an injection of Pituitin to make sure of the expulsion of all afterbirths and to tighten up the uterus. This can prevent a sagging belly after the puppies are weaned and the bitch is being readied for the show ring.

FALSE PREGNANCY

The disappointment of a false pregnancy is almost as bad for the owner as it is for the bitch. She goes through the gestation period with all the symptoms—swollen stomach, increased appetite, swollen nipples—even makes a nest when the time comes. You may even take an oath that you noticed the ripples on her body from the labor pains. Then, just as suddenly as you made up your mind that she was definitely going to have puppies, you will know that she definitely is not! She may walk around carrying a toy as if it were a puppy for a few days, but she will soon be back to normal and acting just as if nothing happened—and nothing did!

CAESAREAN SECTION

Should the whelping reach the point where there is complication, such as the bitch's not being capable of whelping the puppies herself, the "moment of truth" is upon you and a Caesarean section may be necessary. The bitch may be too small or too immature to expel the puppies herself, her cervix may fail to dilate enough to allow the young to come down the birth canal, there may be torsion of the uterus, a dead or monster puppy, a sideways puppy blocking the canal, or perhaps toxemia. A Caesarean section will be the only solution. No matter what the cause, get the bitch to the veterinarian immediately to insure your chances of saving the mother and/or the puppies.

Ch. Chelsea Nimar Wild Flower and her son, future Champion Chelsea Nimar Snuff Box, bred and owned by Nina McIntire, Dallas, Texas.

The Caesarean section operation (the name derived from the idea that Julius Caesar was delivered by this method) involves the removal of the unborn young from the uterus of the dam by surgical incision into the walls through the abdomen. The operation is performed when it has been determined that for some reason the puppies cannot be delivered normally. While modern surgical methods have made the operation itself reasonably safe, with the dam being perfectly capable of nursing the puppies shortly after the completion of the surgery, the chief danger lies in the ability to spark life into the puppies immediately upon their removal from the womb. If the mother dies, the time element is even more important in saving the young, since the oxygen supply ceases upon the death of the dam, and the difference between life and death is measured in seconds.

After surgery, when the bitch is home in her whelping box with the babies, she will probably nurse the young without distress. You must be sure that the sutures are kept clean and that no redness or swelling or ooze appears in the wound. Healing will take place naturally, and no salves or ointments should be applied unless prescribed by the veterinarian, for fear the puppies will get it into their systems. If there is any doubt, check the bitch for fever, restlessness (other than the natural concern for her young), or a lack of appetite, but do not anticipate trouble.

EPISIOTOMY

Even though most dogs are generally easy whelpers, any number of reasons might occur to cause the bitch to have a difficult birth. Before automatically resorting to Caesarean section, many veterinarians are now trying the technique known as episiotomy.

Used rather frequently in human deliveries, episiotomy (pronounced *e-pease-e-ott-o-me*) is the cutting of the membrane between the rear opening of the vagina back almost to the opening of the anus. After delivery it is stitched together, and barring complications, heals easily, presenting no problem in future births.

Ch. Jentres Sheen of Queba, top-producing bitch for 1980, owned by Ruth Jenkins of Lakeside, California.

This Christmas package owned by Muriel Holman of Livonia, Michigan, is called "Lacey," pictured here at four weeks of age.

Brok Arro Business Manager, an eight-week-old puppy owned by Clara Powanda of Wheeling, West Virginia.

SOCIALIZING YOUR PUPPY

The need for puppies to get out among other animals and people cannot be stressed enough. Kennel-reared dogs are subject to all sorts of idiosyncrasies and seldom make good house dogs or normal members of the world around them when they grow up.

The crucial age that determines the personality and general behavior patterns that will predominate during the rest of the dog's life are formed between the ages of three and ten weeks. This is particularly true from the twenty-first through the twenty-eighth day. It is essential that the puppy be socialized during this time by bringing him into family life as much as possible. Walking on floor surfaces, indoor and outdoor, should be experienced; handling by all members of the family and visitors is important; preliminary grooming gets him used to a lifelong necessity; light training, such as setting him up on tables, cleaning teeth and ears, and cutting nails, has to be started early if he is to become a show dog. The puppy should be exposed to car riding, shopping tours, a leash around its neck, children —your own and others—and in all possible ways, relationships with humans.

It is up to the breeder, of course, to protect the puppy from harm or injury during this initiation into the outside world. The benefits reaped from proper attention will pay off in the long run with a well-behaved, well-adjusted grown dog capable of becoming an integral part of a happy family.

REARING THE FAMILY

Needless to say, even with a small litter there will be certain considerations that must be adhered to in order to insure successful rearing of the puppies. For instance, the diet for the mother should be appropriately increased as the puppies grow and take more and more nourishment from her. During the first few days of rest while the bitch just looks over her puppies and regains her strength, she should be left pretty much alone. It is during these first days that she begins to put the puppies on a feeding schedule, and feels safe enough about them to leave the

Marianette's Panhandle Pearl is pictured here at six months of age. Bred and owned by Marian and Michael Allen.

A darling twelve-week-old puppy bred at the Marianette Kennels of Marian and Michael Allen in Amarillo, Texas.

whelping box long enough to take a little extended exercise.

It is cruel, however, to try to keep the mother away from the puppies any longer than she wants to be because you feel she is being too attentive, or to give the neighbors a chance to peek in at the puppies. The mother should not have to worry about harm coming to her puppies for the first few weeks. The veterinary checkup will be enough of an experience for her to have to endure until she is more like herself once again.

The crucial period in a puppy's life occurs when the puppy is from twenty-one to twenty-eight days old, so all the time you can devote to it at this time will reap rewards later on in life. This is the age when several other important steps must be taken in a puppy's life. Weaning should start if it hasn't already, and it is the time to check for worms. Do not worm unnecessarily. A veterinarian should advise on worming and appropriate dosage.

EVALUATING THE LITTER

A show puppy prospect should be outgoing (probably the first one to fall out of the whelping box!), and all efforts should be made to socialize the puppy that appears to be the most shy. Once the puppies are about three weeks old, they can and should be handled a great deal by friends and members of the family.

During the third week they begin to try to walk instead of crawl, but they are unsteady on their feet. Tails are used for balancing, and the puppies begin to make sounds.

Exercise and grooming should be started at this time, with special care and consideration given to the diet. You will find that the dam will help you wean the puppies, leaving them alone more and more as she notices that they are eating well on their own. Begin by leaving them with her during the night for comfort and warmth; eventually when she shows less interest, keep them separated entirely.

222

By the time the fifth week arrives, you will already be in love with every member of the litter and desperately searching for reasons to keep them all. They recognize you—which really gets to you!—and they box and chew on each other, and try to eat your finger, and a million other captivating antics that are special with puppies. Their stomachs seem to be bottomless pits, and their weight will rise. At eight to ten weeks, the puppies will be weaned and ready to go.

SPAYING AND CASTRATING

A wise old philosopher once said, "Timing in life is everything!" No statement could apply more readily to the age-old question that every dog owner is faced with sooner or later . . . to spay or not to spay.

For the one-bitch pet owner, spaying is the most logical answer, for it solves many problems. The pet is usually not of top breeding quality, and therefore there is no great loss to the bloodline; it takes the pressure off the family if the dog runs free with children, and it certainly eliminates the problem of repeated litters of unwanted puppies or a backyard full of eager males twice a year.

But for the owner or breeder, the extra time and protection that must be afforded a purebred quality bitch can be most worthwhile—even if it is only until a single litter is produced after the first heat. It is then not too late to spay; the progeny can perpetuate the bloodline, the bitch will have been fulfilled—though it is merely an old wives' tale that bitches should have at least one litter to be "normal"—and she may then be retired to her deserved role as family pet once again.

With spaying, the problem of staining and unusual behavior around the house is eliminated, as is the necessity of having to keep her in "pants" or administering pills, sprays, or shots, which most veterinarians do not approve of anyway.

Two future champions from Nina McIntire's Chelsea Nimar Kennels in Dallas, out of Ch. Chelsea Nimar Lavendar Blue, and sired by Ch. Bim Bam I'm Your Man.

In the case of males, castration is seldom contemplated, which to me is highly regrettable. The owner of the male dog merely overlooks the dog's ability to populate an entire neighborhood, since he does not have the responsibility of rearing and disposing of the puppies. When you take into consideration all the many females the male dog can impregnate, it is almost more essential that the males rather than the females be taken out of circulation. The male dog will still be inclined to roam, but will be less frantic about leaving the grounds, and you will find that a lot of the *wanderlust* has left him.

STERILIZING FOR HEALTH

When considering the problem of spaying or castrating, the first consideration after the population explosion should actually be the health of the dog or bitch. Males are frequently subject to urinary diseases, and sometimes castration is a help. Your veterinarian can best advise you on this problem. Another aspect to consider is the kennel dog that is no longer being used at stud. It is unfair to keep him in a kennel with females in heat when there is no chance for him to be used. There are other more personal considerations for both kennel and one-dog owners, but

Wildweir Periwinkle and Wildweir Shining Star are pictured as young puppies.

Ch. Mayfair's Tiddlewinks, a three-pound Yorkie owned and bred at the Mayfair Yorkie House. Tiddlewinks was never used at stud because of his diminutive size.

when making the decision, remember that it is final. You can always spay or castrate, but once the deed is done, there is no return.

A BREEDING WARNING

Raising a litter of puppies can be a wonderful experience for those who love dogs, especially if there are children in the family who also love animals. However, there is one very important consideration before thinking about having a litter. That is, is your bitch big enough? We are hearing more and more about "tea cup" Yorkshires, or pocket-size Yorkshires, which should not be bred at all—ever! While they are highly desirable among pet owners, they still require special care and frequently have a considerably shorter life span than the normal-size dogs.

If your little bitch is small she should not be bred. How small is small, you ask? Consult your veterinarian if you are not an experienced breeder, and let him decide if it would be too risky. Just remember, if she is too small and you breed her, you are apt to lose the puppies and the bitch. If the puppy bitch you bought grows up to be small, too small for breeding, keep her as your mascot, and buy another bitch. If you have a "tiny" in any of your litters, and you decide to sell it, make sure you explain to the buyer she is not to be bred.

CULLING

Next to the importance of proper coat color in Yorkshire Terriers, perhaps the easiest way to start a heated debate is to discuss the merits of culling. Far too many breeders allow themselves to "play God" by evaluating and disposing of puppies, even though their experience in breeding dogs (or any animals) is practically nil.

Needless to say, many mistakes are made, and it is highly likely that over the years many valuable specimens have been lost because overzealous breeders, determined to breed the ideal dog, depended solely on their own judgment.

In explaining their attempts to save only the best puppies, some of the most ridiculous excuses are given for culling litters. If it is a large breed, they will cite monetary reasons, such as savings on food, or vet bills. Others will tell you they cull because the litter is too large. How many puppies represent a large litter? To some breeders, six is a large litter, especially if it is a large breed. Others will say eight puppies, or four puppies constitute a large litter.

Others go on to explain that culling also means less cleaning up after puppies, or that they will have fewer puppies to sell in a slow market. Actually the major consideration for culling should be a sort of "insurance" that the bitch is not over-taxed by feeding too many puppies, especially if she is to be bred again. Both bitch and breeder should be able to observe and enjoy the puppies individually and collectively.

Other legitimate reasons for culling may be consideration of breed disqualifications. Unacceptable breed colors or markings or structural faults are additional reasons given for culling.

Three typical puppies owned and bred by the Mayfair Yorkie House, photographed in 1977 by Mel McIntire.

These litter sisters bred by the Silk N Satin Kennels are Silk N Satin Executive Memo and Silk N Satin Executive Bonus.

These faults should be checked out carefully before a decision to cull is reached.

Once the decision is made to cull, the next question should be, What is the "best" time? At birth? Within hours after birth? Two weeks? Two months? And what is the "proper" method of disposing of the unwanted puppies? Is there such a thing as a painless death?

VETERINARY CONSIDERATIONS

Most breeders find they cannot depend on or expect the support of their veterinarians, if you ask them to put the "excess" puppies down. They will be quick to tell you that they are in business and dedicated to the preserving of life, not its termination. Some veterinarians will oblige rather than have the breeder do it, so they are sure it will be painless for the puppies. However, their attitude will more than likely be a suggestion to allow the puppies to live with spaying or neutering in the future as an alternative.

FOREIGN "CULLING"

In some foreign countries, culling is a government matter, and comes under the jurisdiction of the department of agriculture. However, the thought of a government or kennel club official coming to a breeder's home and culling a predetermined number of puppies from a litter without regard for quality or sex is abhorrent. Many of us would stop breeding before allowing ourselves and our bitches to be placed in such a position.

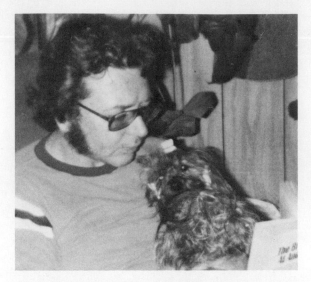

Gary Williams reads a bedtime story to one of the Yorkie puppies at the Lor-Dean Kennels, Shoshone, Idaho.

We have all heard of the Yorkshire puppy that was purchased in a pet shop and won a Best in Show. This is the living proof that "culling" is a talent few possess. Had the breeders of this puppy any inkling that it was show dog potential, they never would have parted with it. Breeders don't always know which to cull, or for what reasons, at any given age. This puppy, given a chance at life with the right owner far exceeded the breeder's expectations!

Culling is not to be entered into lightly. Those breeders who dare to "play God" must remember that we are NOT God. . . only humans, and humans make mistakes. Mother Nature is actually the most stringent of all "cullers," and it is usually wise to leave culling up to her. It is also unwise to try to keep a struggling puppy alive. The risks of continued ill-health, retardation, or growth problems are frequently the result. The final decision should be determined by the survival of the fittest.

LOSING A PUPPY

There is great joy in planning, whelping, and raising a litter of puppies. We give so much of ourselves and hold such hopes and dreams for our little charges. And there is nothing like a litter of puppies to give us even more respect and closeness for our bitches in recognition of their efforts and care in bearing a litter.

Those of us who are fortunate enough to raise healthy puppies know all too well that sometimes, in spite of our devotion, something can go wrong. Sometimes we lose a puppy.

In researching this book, I was so deeply touched by a little poem I came across in an old issue of the *Yorkshire Terrier Quarterly*, that I felt I wanted to include it in this book for all of us to share again.

I
Can never accept
The fading of a
New born
Puppy

I
Waited
For this one a
Long time

Gladly gave it
All my time
And all my
Love

Just to
Keep it
Alive
And then
It slipped away.

Unfortunately, nature gives no guarantees, and we all may lose a puppy at some future time. It is never easy, but perhaps realizing that someone else feels as deeply about it as we do may help.

Gintique's Funny Bambi, picutured at the weight of 2¼ pounds, was shown only once before an untimely death. Bred and owned by Warren and Virginia Miller of Mentor, Ohio.

Six-month-old Sweet Pleasure typifies the Yorkie expression. Owner is Hilde Rozera of Portland, Oregon.

Dot's Chopper One, posing on his favorite toy, is owned by Dorothy Gaunt of West Covina, California. This charming photograph was taken by Missy Yuhl when Chopper was seven months old and weighed less than two pounds.

What a Yorkie should do on a cold night is shown by Mt. View Sweet Babatte, owned by Mrs. Lloyd Rozera.

Petit Point All Jazzed Up is ready to travel. Bred and owned by Susan M. Sandlin, the Original Petit Point, Arlington, Virginia.

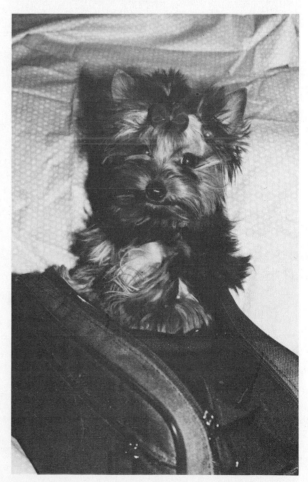

Chelsea Nimar Cat Ballou, photographed at ten weeks of age. "C.B." is owned by Nina McIntire, Chelsea Yorkshire Terriers, Dallas, Texas.

CHAPTER TWELVE

Buying Your Yorkshire Terrier Puppy

A puppy from the Robinwood Kennels of Bob and Doris Spiece of Greenfield, Wisconsin.

In searching for that special puppy, there are several paths that will lead you to a litter from which you may find the puppy of your choice. If you are uncertain as to where to find a reputable breeder, write to the parent club and ask for the names and addresses of members who have puppies for sale. The addresses of Yorkshire Terrier breed clubs may be obtained by writing directly to the American Kennel Club, 51 Madison Avenue, New York, N.Y. 10010. They keep an up-to-date, accurate list of breeders from whom you may seek information on obtaining a good, healthy puppy. The classified ad listings in dog publications and the major newspapers may also lead you to that certain pup. The various dog magazines generally carry a monthly breed column which features information and news on the breed that may aid in your selection.

It is advisable that you become thoroughly acquainted with the breed prior to purchasing your puppy. Plan to attend a dog show or two in your area at which you may view purebred dogs of just about every breed at their best in the show ring. Even if you are not interested in purchasing a show-quality dog, you should be familiar with what the better specimens look like so that you will at least purchase a decent representative of the breed for the money. You can learn a lot from observing the show dogs in action in the ring, or in a public place where their personalities are clearly shown. The dog show catalogue is also a useful tool to put you in contact with the local kennels and breeders. Each dog that is entered in the show is listed along with the owner's name and address. If you spot a dog that you think is a particularly fine and pleasing specimen, contact the owners and arrange to visit their kennel to see the type and color they are breeding and winning with at the shows. Exhibitors at the dog shows are usually more than delighted to talk to people interested in their dogs and the specific characteristics of their breed.

Once you've decided that the Yorkshire Terrier is the breed for you because you appreciate its exceptional beauty, personality, and intelligence, it is wise to thoroughly acquaint yourself by reading some background material on owning the breed. When you feel certain that this puppy will fit in with your family's way of life, it is time to start writing letters and making phone calls and appointments to see some puppies.

Some words of caution: don't choose a kennel simply because it is near your home, and don't buy the first "cute" puppy that romps around your legs or licks the end of your nose. All puppies are cute, and naturally some will appeal to you more than others. But don't let preferences sway your thinking. If you are buying your Yorkshire Terrier to be strictly a family pet, then preferences are permissible. If you are looking for a top-quality puppy for the show ring, you must evaluate clearly, choose wisely, and make the best possible choice. Whichever one you choose, you will quickly learn to love your Yorkie puppy. A careful selection, rather than a "love at first sight" choice will save a disappointment later on.

To get the broadest idea of what puppies are for sale and the going market prices, visit as many kennels as possible in your area and write to others farther away. With today's safe and rapid air flights on the major airlines, it is possible to purchase dogs from far-off places at nominal costs. While it is safest and wisest to first see the dog you are buying, there are enough reputable breeders and kennels to be found for you to take this step with a minimum of risk. In the long run, it can be well worth your while to obtain the exact dog or bloodline you desire.

Estugo Puppies, bred and owned by Hugo Ibanez and Stephen Maggard.

Photographed at Susan Sandlin's kennel in Arlington, Virginia, are Ginger Peachy and Peaches N Cream, both bearing the Petit Point prefix.

It is customary for the purchaser to pay the shipping charges, and the airlines are most willing to supply flight information and prices upon request. Rental on the shipping crate, if the owner does not provide one for the dog, is nominal. While unfortunate incidents have occurred on the airlines in the transporting of animals by air, the major airlines are making improvements in safety measures and have reached the point of reasonable safety and cost. Barring unforeseen circumstances, the safe arrival of a dog you might buy can pretty much be assured if both seller and purchaser adhere to and follow up on even the most minute details from both ends.

WHAT TO LOOK FOR IN A YORKSHIRE TERRIER PUPPY

Anyone who has owned a Yorkshire Terrier as a puppy will agree that the most fascinating aspect of raising the pup is to witness the complete and extraordinary metamorphosis that occurs during its first year of maturing. Your puppy will undergo a marked change in appearance, and during this period you must also be aware of the puppy's personality, for there are certain qualities visible at this time that will generally make for a good adult dog. Of course, no one can guarantee nature, and the best puppy does not always grow up to be a great dog. However, even the novice breeder can learn to look for certain specifics that will help him to choose a promising puppy.

Packed and ready to go! This twelve-week-old puppy doesn't want to be left behind. Sired by Wright's Tiny Fellow ex Wright's Simply Fantastic, the breeder-owner is Florence Wright, Poway, California.

Should you decide to purchase a six- to eight-week old puppy, you are in store for all the cute antics that little pup may dream up for you! At this age, the puppy should be well on its way to being weaned, wormed, and ready to go out into the world with its responsible new owner. It is better not to buy a puppy that is less than six weeks old; it simply is not ready to leave its mother or the security of the other puppies. By eight to twelve weeks of age you will be able to notice much about the behavior and appearance of the dog. Yorkie puppies, as they are recalled in our fondest childhood memories, are amazingly active and bouncy—as well they should be! The normal puppy should be alert, curious, and interested, especially about a stranger. However, if the puppy acts a little reserved or distant, don't necessarily construe these acts to be signs of fear or shyness. It might merely indicate that he hasn't quite made up his mind whether he likes you as yet! By the same token, though, he should not be openly fearful or terrified by a stranger—and especially should not show any fear of his owner!

In direct contrast, the puppy should not be ridiculously over-active either. The puppy that frantically bounds around the room and is never still is not especially desirable. And beware of the "spinners"! Spinners are the puppies or dogs that have become neurotic from being kept in cramped quarters or in crates, and that behave in an emotionally unstable manner when let loose in adequate space. When let out they run in circles and seemingly "go wild." Puppies with this kind of traumatic background seldom ever regain full composure or adjust to the big outside world. The puppy which has had the proper exercise and appropriate living quarters will have a normal, though spirited, outlook on life, and will do its utmost to win you over without having to go into a tailspin.

If the general behavior and appearance of the dog thus far appeal to you, it is time for you to observe him more closely for additional physical requirements. First of all, you cannot expect to find in the Yorkie puppy all the coat he will bear upon maturity. That will come with time and good food, and will be additionally enhanced by the many wonderful grooming aids which can be found in pet shops today. Needless to say, the healthy puppy's coat should have a nice shine to it, and the more dense at this age, the better the coat will be when the dog reaches adulthood.

Look for clear, dark, sparkling eyes that are free of discharge. From the time the puppy's eyes open until the puppy is about three months old, the eyes might have a slight blue cast to them. The darker the blue, the better are the chances for a good dark eye in the adult dog.

Jo-Lyles Sugar Cookie, pictured here at six months of age, is owned by Sara Jo Woodward, Jo-Lyle Yorkies of Orlando, Florida.

Silverwinds Spirit of Apollo, at just six months, owned by Elissa Taddie, West Chester, Pennsylvania.

Removing stubborn teeth is usually a job for your veterinarian, as it requires the administration of some type of pain-killer. Yorkies do not always take anesthesia well. A bad experience with an owner who wishes to pop them out with a thumb can make a dog hand shy as well as causing it pain.

It has become "fashionable" for owners to keep the teeth clean to start with, thus avoiding an accumulation of tartar on the teeth, and preventing a trip to the veterinarian. There are many ways to clean a dog's teeth. A baby toothbrush may be used with a mild solution of baking soda or a little salt. If the toothbrush is too rough, try using your finger, a wad of cotton, or a gauze bandage to rub over the surface of the teeth.

The best way to insure good teeth is still diet and exercising of the gums. Giving puppies something to chew on, such as a Nylabone, helps to clean their teeth and allow loose ones to fall out naturally.

Puppies usually have twenty-eight baby teeth. When these fall out and the jaw grows, they get forty-two permanent teeth. If all goes well, the dog will end up with either a level bite (all teeth matching each other), or a scissors bite (top teeth slightly extended over the lower teeth), both of which are acceptable in the breed. Bad bites occur when the top teeth extend too far out over the bottom teeth, and is referred to as a bad overbite; or when the teeth in the lower jaw extend too far out under the upper teeth, which is called an undershot bite.

Three-month-old Ondine's Continental Gent, young hopeful at the Ondine Kennels of Claire and Lisa Pollitzer of Irvington, New Jersey.

It is important to check the bite. Even though the puppy will cut another complete set of teeth somewhere between four and seven months of age, there will already be some indication of how the final teeth will be positioned. Too much of an overshot bite (top teeth are positioned too far *over* the bottom teeth) or too much of an undershot jaw (bottom teeth are positioned too far out *under* the top teeth) is undesirable as they are considered faults by the breed Standard.

Correcting the bite on a Yorkshire can involve many generations of breeding. The tiny toy breeds are notorious for problems with their teeth. Baby teeth must be removed if they do not fall out on their own, or they could destroy the correct placement of the permanent teeth.

Puppies take anything and almost everything into their mouths to chew on, and a lot of diseases and infections start or are introduced in the mouth. Brown-stained teeth, for instance, may indicate the puppy has had a past case of distemper, and the teeth will remain that way. This fact must be reckoned with if you have a show puppy in mind. The puppy's breath should be neither sour nor unpleasant. Bad breath can be a result of a poor mixture of food in the diet, or of eating meat of low quality, especially if fed raw. Some people say that the healthy puppy's breath should have a faint odor vaguely reminiscent of garlic. At any rate, a puppy should never be fed just table scraps, but should be raised on a well-balanced diet containing a good dry puppy chow and a good grade of fresh meat. Poor meat and too much cereal or fillers tend to make the puppy grow too fat.

Yorkie puppies are born with their ears down. During their puppyhood there will be a time when they will stand up of their own accord. In some cases, they may be slow in doing so. If this is the case, consultation should be held with either your veterinarian, or a breeder who has had experience in administering assistance in trying to solve the problem.

There are things that may be attempted, such as taping them up with pieces of nylon net, or lightweight cardboard and adhesive. Putting these devices on the ears can be dangerous to the puppy, and can result in establishing an improper ear set.

Sitting pretty are two Wildweir Kennels puppies photographed by the Glenview Studios for owners Mrs. Leslie Gordon and Miss Janet Bennett.

The typical, desired Yorkshire Terrier expression is shown by this puppy bred by Virginia Bull.

Most problems with ears going up and down will usually occur during the teething period. If the ears had been up before the teething began, don't panic. Chances are they will go up again. But if they persist in dropping, you might do well to seek advice and benefit from some other owner's experience.

Needless to say, the puppy should be clean. The breeder that shows a dirty puppy is one to steer away from. Look closely at the skin. Make sure it is not covered with insect bites or red, blotchy sores and dry scales. The vent area around the tail should not show evidences of diarrhea or inflammation. By the same token, the puppy's fur should not be matted with excretion or smell strongly of urine.

233

True enough, you can wipe dirty eyes, clean dirty ears, and give the puppy a bath when you get it home, but these things are all indications of how the puppy has been cared for during the important formative first months of its life, and can vitally influence its future health and development. There are many reputable breeders raising healthy puppies that have been reared in proper places and under the proper conditions in clean housing, so why take a chance on a series of veterinary bills and a questionable constitution?

The choice of sex in your puppy is also something that must be given serious thought before you buy. For the pet owner, the sex that would best suit the family life you enjoy would be the paramount choice to consider. For the breeder or exhibitor there are other vital considerations. If you are looking for a stud to establish a kennel, it is essential that you select a dog with both testicles evident, even at a tender age, and verified by a veterinarian before the sale is finalized if there is any doubt.

Future Ch. Wildweir Fair Victor, pictured here at four months of age, bred by the Wildweir Kennels, Glenview, Illinois. Photo by Ritter.

Cadbury's English Cookie, pictured at four months of age. Bred by V. Miller, the sire was Andora's Don Giovanni Ragamuchkin Touch of Class. Arlene Schwartz of Beachwood, Ohio, is the proud owner.

The visibility of only one testicle, known as monorchidism, automatically disqualifies the dog from the show ring or from a breeding program, though monorchids are capable of siring. Additionally, it must be noted that monorchids frequently sire dogs with the same deficiency, and to introduce this into a bloodline knowingly is an unwritten sin in the fancy. Also, a monorchid can sire dogs that are completely sterile. Dog with undescended testes are called cryptorchids, and are sterile.

An additional consideration for the private owner in the male versus female decision is that with males there might be the problem of leglifting, and with females there is the inconvenience while they are in season. However, this need not be the problem it used to be—pet shops sell "pants" for both sexes, which help to control the situation.

THE PLANNED PARENTHOOD BEHIND YOUR PUPPY

Never be afraid to ask pertinent questions about the puppy, as well as questions about the sire and dam. Feel free to ask the breeder if you

234

Eight-month-old future Ch. Kibet's Dancing Bear of J-Lo photographed in June, 1980. Owned by Shelby Stevens of Fort Lauderdale, Florida.

The normal time period for puppies (around three months of age) to eliminate is about every two or three hours. As the time draws near, either take the puppy out or indicate the newspaper for the same purpose. Housebreaking is never easy, but anticipation is about ninety per cent of solving the problem. The schools that offer to housebreak your dog are virtually useless. Here again, the puppy will learn the "place" at the schoolhouse, but coming home he will need special training for the new location.

A reputable breeder will welcome any and all questions you might ask and will voluntarily offer additional information, if only to brag about the tedious and loving care he has given the litter. He will also sell a puppy on a twenty-four hour veterinary approval basis. This means you have a full day to get the puppy to a veterinarian of your choice to get his opinion on the general health of the puppy before you make a final decision. There should also be veterinary certificates and full particulars on the dates and types of inoculations the puppy has been given up to that time.

Dot's Just Roudy Enough is pictured at six months of age. Roudy has won five Groups at puppy matches. His sire was Ch. Dot's Top Banana out of Dot's Blue Angel. Bred and owned by Dorothy Gaunt.

might see the dam; the purpose of your visit is to determine her general health and her appearance as a representative of the breed. Ask also to see the sire if the breeder is the owner. Ask what the puppy has been fed and should be fed after weaning. Ask to see the pedigree, and inquire if the litter or the individual puppies have been registered with the American Kennel Club, how many of the temporary and/or permanent inoculations the puppy has had, when and if the puppy has been wormed, and whether it has had any illness, disease, or infection.

You need not ask if the puppy is housebroken ... it won't mean much. He may have gotten the idea as to where "the place" is where he lives now, but he will need new training to learn where "the place" is in his new home! And you can't really expect too much from puppies at this age anyway. Housebreaking is entirely up to the new owner. We know puppies always eliminate when they first awaken, and sometimes dribble when they get excited. If friends and relatives are coming over to see the new puppy, make sure he is walked just before he greets them at the front door. This will help.

Dot's Just Roudy Enough, again pictured at six months of age. The owner-breeder is Dorothy Gaunt of West Covina, California. Photo by Missy Yuhl.

PUPPIES AND WORMS

Let us give further attention to the unhappy and very unpleasant subject of worms. Generally speaking, most puppies—even those raised in clean quarters—come into contact with worms early in life. The worms can be passed down from the mother before birth, or picked up during the puppies' first encounters with the earth or with their kennel facilities. To say that you must not buy a puppy because of an infestation of worms is nonsensical. You might be passing up a fine animal that can be freed of worms in one short treatment, although a heavy infestation of worms of any kind in a young dog is dangerous and debilitating.

The extent of the infection can be readily determined by a veterinarian, and you might take his word as to whether the future health and conformation of the dog has been damaged. He can prescribe the dosage and supply the medication at this time, and you will already have one of your problems solved.

VETERINARY INSPECTION

While your veterinarian is going over the puppy you have selected to purchase, you might just as well ask him for his opinion of it as a breed, as well as the facts about its general health. While few veterinarians can claim to be breed-conformation experts, they usually have a good eye for a worthy specimen, and can advise you where to go for further information. Perhaps your veterinarian could also recommend other breeders if you should want another opinion.

I would like to emphasize here that it is only through this type of close cooperation between owners and veterinarians that we may expect to reap the harvest of modern research in the veterinary field.

Most reliable veterinarians are more than eager to learn about various breeds of purebred dogs, and we in turn must acknowledge and apply what they have proved through experience and research in their field. We may buy and breed the best dog in the world, but when disease strikes, we are only as safe as our veterinarian is capable—so let's keep him informed breed by

Pictured when seven months old is American and Canadian Ch. Windsor Gayelyn Strut N Stuff, owned by Suzanne M. Jones of New York Mills, New York.

breed, and dog by dog. The veterinarian may mean the difference between life and death!

THE CONDITIONS OF SALE

While it is customary to pay for the puppy before you take it away with you, you should be able to give the breeder a deposit if there is any doubt about the puppy's health. You might also (depending on local laws) postdate a check to cover the twenty-four hour veterinary approval. If you decide to take the puppy, the breeder is required to supply you with a pedigree along with the puppy's registration papers. He is also obliged to supply you with complete information about the inoculations and American Kennel Club instructions on how to transfer ownership of the puppy to your name.

Some breeders will offer buyers time payment plans for convenience if the price on a show dog is very high, or if deferred payments are the only way you can purchase the dog. However, any such terms must be worked out between buyer and breeder, and should be put in writing to avoid later complications.

Ch. Chelsea Nimar Snuff Box, photographed at ten months of age. Bred and owned by Nina McIntire, Dallas, Texas.

Sun Sprite Wendy is pictured as a puppy in this 1981 photograph. Bred and owned by Elda and Nathan Tropper of Los Angeles, California.

You will find most breeders cooperative if they believe you are sincere in your love for the puppy and that you will give it the proper home and the show ring career it deserves (if it is sold as a show quality specimen of the breed). Remember, when buying a show dog, it is impossible to guarantee nature. A breeder can only tell you what he *believes* will develop into a show dog . . . so be sure your breeder is an honest one.

Also, if you purchase a show prospect and promise to show the dog, you definitely should show it! It is a waste to have a beautiful dog that deserves recognition in the show ring sitting at home as a family pet, and it is unfair to the breeder. This is especially true if the breeder offered you a reduced price because of the advertising his kennel and bloodlines would receive by your showing the dog in the ring. If you want a pet, buy a pet. Be honest about it, and let the breeder decide on this basis which is the best dog for you. Your conscience will be clear and you'll both be doing a real service to the breed.

BUYING A SHOW PUPPY

If you are positive about breeding and showing your Yorkie, make this point clear so that the breeder will sell you the best possible puppy. If you are dealing with an established kennel, you will have to rely partially, if not entirely, on their choice, since they know their bloodlines and what they can expect from the breeding. They know how their stock develops, and it would be foolish of them to sell you a puppy that could not stand up as a show specimen representing their stock in the ring.

However, you must also realize that the breeder may be keeping the best puppy in the litter to show and breed himself. If this is the case, you might be wise to select the best puppy of the opposite sex so that the dogs will not be competing against one another in the show rings.

THE PURCHASE PRICE

Prices vary on all puppies, of course, but a good show prospect at six weeks to six months of age will usually sell for several hundred dollars. If the puppy is really outstanding, and the pedigree and parentage are also outstanding, the price will be even higher. Honest breeders, however, will all quote around the same figure, so price should not be a strong deciding factor in your choice. If you have any questions as to the current price range, a few telephone calls to different kennels will give you a good average. Reputable breeders will usually stand behind the health of their puppies should something drastically wrong develop, such as hip dysplasia. Their obligation to make an adjustment or replacement is usually honored. However, this must be agreed to in writing at the time of the purchase.

A charming trio of Estugo puppies, bred and owned by Hugo Ibanez and Stephen Maggard, Charlotte, North Carolina.

THE COST OF BUYING ADULT STOCK

Prices for adult dogs fluctuate greatly. Some grown dogs are offered free of charge to good homes; others are put with owners on breeders' terms. But don't count on getting a "bargain" if it doesn't cost you anything! Good dogs are always in demand, and worthy studs or brood bitches are expensive. Prices for them can easily go up into the four-figure range. Take an expert with you if you intend to make this sort of investment. Just make sure the "expert" is free of professional jealousy and will offer an unprejudiced opinion. If you are reasonably familiar with the standard, and get the expert's opinion, you can usually come to a proper decision.

Right: Two Wildweir puppies join a mutual admiration society. **Below:** Almost a year old are Suzie and Joanie, bred by Clara Powanda of the Silk N Satin Kennels in Wheeling, West Virginia.

Ch. Chelsea Nimar Nanouchka. "Angel" was bred and owned by Nina McIntire of Dallas, Texas.

Chelsea Nimar Miss Money Penny, owned and bred by Nina McIntire of Dallas, Texas. This charming little Yorkie was pointed and on her way to championship at the time of this writing.

Gloria Lipman and Barbara Humphries, handler for the Nikko Yorkshire Terriers, enjoy a romp with the dogs in the fields outside Gloria and Stanley Lipman's kennels in Escondido, California.

A beautiful setting for a beautiful typey Yorkshire Terrier puppy owned and bred by the Nikko Kennels in Escondido, California. Owners are Gloria and Stanley Lipman.

Ch. Nikko's Rollys Royce Corniche, a Group-winning Yorkie owned by Gloria Lipman of Escondido, California. Barbara Humphries is handling to this 1982 win under judge Roland Adameck. Callea Photo.

BEST OF BREED
SANTA CLARA VALLEY
KENNEL CLUB
FEBRUARY 1982
CALLEA

These puppies, bred and owed by Estugo Kennels and featured on their Christmas card, are Estugo's Jenny Wren and Cock Robin.

Typical Estugo Yorkie puppies, bred and owned by Hugo Ibanez and Stephen Maggard.

Best in Show winner American and Puerto Rican Ch. Amwalk's Tigre de Oro, pictured at nine months of age in this charming study. Tigre is bred and owned by Audrey Walkmaster of San Juan, Puerto Rico, and has a Group First to his credit as well as several Group placings.

International (FCI), American, Venezuelan, Puerto Rican, and Dominican Republic Ch. Estugo Stargazer is pictured winning under breeder-judge Kathleen Kolbert at a 1981 show. Handled by Hugo Ibanez, who with Stephen Maggard co-owns Estugo Kennels, Charlotte, North Carolina.

Silverwinds Spirit of Apollo with Ch. Wildweir Candytuft, owned by Elissa Taddie of West Chester, Pennsylvania.

Ms Dinah-Mite of Lamplighter and daughter, Gucci Girl of Lamplighter. This charming photograph is used as the basis for the logo on stationery and kennel cards of owner Barbara Beissel of Minneapolis, Minnesota.

Sharo's Blue Magic Girl, whelped April 1977, and sired by Ka-Dolls Stormison ex Verzeys Nicole. "Kelli" is the pride and joy of Charlene B. Roland, Sharo's Yorkshire Terriers, Charleston, West Virginia.

Ch. Jacolyn Kibets Honey Bear, owned and bred by Joyce Watkins, Marcris Kennels, Miami, Florida.

Capri's Bedroom Bandit and sister Ch. Capri's Special Treat posed for famed dog photographer William P. Gilbert to commemorate their first birthday for breeder-owner Melba Clifton of Bethesda, Maryland. The sire was Ch. Jentres Charger of Mistangay ex Ch. Capri's Foolish Fancy. At the time of this writing, Bandit also had three majors toward his championship and required just two additional points.

Ten-month-old Sunsprite Mandy is owned by Alicia Lampert and Ruth Jenkins of Lakeside, California.

Beegee Dawn of Starfire, at her first show, goes Best of Winners and Best of Opposite Sex over Specials under judge Rutledge Gilliland. Dawn is always handled by her owner, Mrs. Anne Herzberg Goldman of Santa Monica, California.

This little "Japanese" Yorkie, owned by Mr. Kogai of Japan, was a winner of the April 1982 photo contest in *Yorkie Tales* magazine. Photo courtesy of Muriel Hunt, the editor.

Best Senior Puppy at the October 1981 Yorkshire Terrier Club of America Specialty held in Tulsa, Oklahoma, was Ga-Shire's Commander in Chief. Breeder and owner, Gail Drouin,

Pixie's Anna Versary Gift took a Group Second at just eight months of age. This win, under judge Hayden Martin, was with owner-handler Dixie Bletch of Clackamas, Oregon.

Opposite:
Canadian Ch. Marcliff's Blue Denim Patch is pictured winning a five-point major at nine months of age on the way to his championship title. Handling his dog to this important win under judge Mrs. Barbara Knoll was Dr. W.C. Hacking of Uxbridge, Ontario, Canada.

London Canine Club

Best of Winners Best Puppy in Breed

1981

Stonham Photography

Windfall's Carousel, a future champion hopeful owned by Gloria Knight-Bloch of Palm Bay, Florida.

Everblue's Mint Julep, pictured at four months of age in this photograph by Jim Easterday, is owned by Arlene Mack of Westlake, Ohio. "Mindy's" sire was Ch. Chelsea Nimar's For Pete's Sake ex Everblue's State Street Sadie.

Twelve-week-old future Ch. Jacolyn Kibets Honey Bear is owned by Shelby Stevens and Carolyn Servis.

CHAPTER THIRTEEN

Feeding and Nutrition

Six-month-old "Short-stop" is ready to eat. Owned by Clara Powanda.

There are many diets today for young puppies, including all sorts of products on the market for feeding the newborn, for supplementing the feeding of the young, and for adding "this or that" to diets, depending on what is lacking in the way of a complete diet.

When weaning puppies, it is necessary to put them on four meals a day, even while you are tapering off with the mother's milk. Feeding at six in the morning, noontime, six in the evening, and midnight is about the best schedule since it fits in with most human eating plans. Meals for the puppies can be prepared immediately before or after your own meals, without too much of a change in your own schedule.

6 A.M.

Two meat and two milk meals daily are best and should be served alternately, of course. Assuming the 6 A.M. feeding is a milk meal, the contents should be as follows: goat's milk is the very best milk to feed puppies, but is expensive and usually available only at drug stores, unless you live in farm country where it could be readily available fresh and less expensive. If goat's milk is not available, use evaporated milk (which can be changed to powdered milk later on) diluted as follows: two parts evaporated milk to one part water, mixed with raw egg yolk, honey, or Karo syrup, and sprinkled with high-protein baby cereal and some wheat germ. As the puppies mature, cottage cheese may be added or, at one of the two milk meals, it can be substituted for the cereal.

NOONTIME

A puppy chow that has been soaked in warm water or beef broth according to the time specified on the wrapper should be mixed with raw or simmered chopped meat in equal proportions with vitamin powder added.

6 P.M.

Repeat the milk meal—perhaps varying the type of cereal from wheat to oats, corn, or rice.

MIDNIGHT

Repeat the meat meal. If raw meat was fed at noon, the evening meal might be simmered.

Please note that specific proportions on this suggested diet are not given; however, it's safe to say that the most important ingredients are the milk and cereal, and the meat and puppy chow that forms the basis of the diet. Your veterinarian can advise on the portion sizes if there is any doubt in your mind as to how much to use.

Drax Gay Blade poses for his picture at three months of age at his Florida home in 1956.

If you notice that the puppies are cleaning their plates, you are perhaps not feeding enough to keep up with their rate of growth. Increase the amount at the next feeding. Observe them closely; puppies should each "have their fill," because growth is very rapid at this age. If they have not satisfied themselves, increase the amount so that they do not have to fight for the last morsel. They will not overeat if they know there is enough food available. Instinct will usually let them eat to suit their normal capacity.

If there is any doubt in your mind as to any ingredient you are feeding, ask yourself, "Would I give it to my own baby?" If the answer is no, then don't give it to your puppies. At this age, the comparison between puppies and human babies can be a good guide.

If there is any doubt in your mind, I repeat: ask your veterinarian to be sure.

Many puppies will regurgitate their food, perhaps a couple of times, before they manage to retain it. If they do bring up their food, allow them to eat it again, rather than clean it away. Sometimes additional saliva is necessary for them to digest it, and you do not want them to skip a meal just because it is an unpleasant sight for you to observe.

This same regurgitation process holds true sometimes with the bitch, who will bring up her own food for her puppies every now and then.

This is a natural instinct on her part that stems from the days when dogs were giving birth in the wild. The only food the mother could provide at weaning time was too rough and indigestible for her puppies; therefore, she took it upon herself to predigest the food until it could be taken and retained by her young. Bitches today will sometimes resort to this, especially bitches that love having litters and have a strong maternal instinct. Some dams will help you wean their litters and even give up feeding entirely once they see you are taking over.

WEANING THE PUPPIES

When weaning the puppies, the mother is kept away from the little ones for longer and longer periods of time. This is done over a period of several days. At first she is separated from the puppies for several hours, then all day, leaving her with them only at night for comfort and warmth. This gradual separation aids in helping the mother's milk to dry up gradually, and she suffers less distress after feeding a litter.

If the mother continues to carry a great deal of milk with no signs of its tapering off, consult your veterinarian before she gets too uncomfortable. She may cut the puppies off from her supply of milk too abruptly if she is uncomfortable, before they should be completely on their own.

There are many opinions on the proper age to start weaning puppies. If you plan to start selling them between six and eight weeks, weaning should begin between two and three weeks of age. (Here again, each bitch will pose a different situation.) The size and weight of the litter

Eight-week-old Marianette's Tiny Trojan is keeping an eye on things. Bred and owned by Marian and Michael Allen of Amarillo, Texas.

258

Two four-month-old Yorkie puppies, Dilly and Paddi-Wak, bred and owned by Virginia Bull.

should help determine the time, and your veterinarian will have an opinion as he determines the burden the bitch is carrying by the size of the litter and her general condition. If she is being pulled down by feeding a large litter, he may suggest that you start at two weeks. If she is glorying in her motherhood without any apparent taxing of her strength, he may suggest three to four weeks. You and he will be the best judges. But remember, there is no substitute that is as perfect as mother's milk—and the longer the puppies benefit from it, the better. Other food yes, but mother's milk first and foremost for the healthiest puppies.

ORPHANED PUPPIES

The ideal solution to feeding orphaned puppies is to be able to put them with another nursing dam who will take them on as her own. If this is not possible within your own kennel, or a kennel that you know of, it is up to you to care for and feed the puppies. Survival is possible but requires a great deal of time and effort on your part.

Your substitute formula must be precisely prepared, always served heated to body temperature, and refrigerated when not being fed. Esbilac, a vacuum-packed powder, with complete feeding instructions on the can, is excellent and about as close to mother's milk as you can get. If you can't get Esbilac, or until you do get Esbilac, there are two alternative formulas that you might use.

Mix one part boiled water with five parts of evaporated milk, and add one teaspoonful of dicalcium phosphate per quart of formula. Dicalcium phosphate can be secured at any drug store. If they have it in tablet form only, you can powder the tablets with the back part of a tablespoon. The other formula for newborn puppies is a combination of eight ounces of homogenized milk mixed well with two egg yolks.

You will need baby bottles with three-hole nipples. Sometimes doll bottles may be used for the newborn puppies, which should be fed at six-hour intervals. If they are consuming sufficient amounts, their stomachs should look full, or slightly enlarged, though never distended. The amount of formula to be fed is proportionate to the size, age, growth, and weight of the puppy, and is indicated on the can of Esbilac; or follow the advice of your veterinarian. Many breeders like to keep a baby scale nearby to check the weight of the puppies to be sure they are thriving on the formula.

At two to three weeks, you can start adding Pablum or some other high protein baby cereal to the formula. Also, baby beef can be licked from your finger at this age, or added to the formula. At four weeks, the surviving puppies should be taken off the diet of Esbilac and put on a more substantial diet, such as wet puppy meal or chopped beef; however, Esbilac powder can still be mixed in with the food for additional nutrition.

Kesar's That Girl and Kesar's Forget Me Not were bred by Barbara Bedsted. Owned by Elda and Nathan Tropper of Los Angeles, California, "Marlo" and "Flossie" were six months old when this photo was taken.

HOW TO FEED THE NEWBORN PUPPIES

When the puppy is a newborn, remember that it is vitally important to keep the feeding procedure as close to the natural mother's routine as possible. The newborn puppy should be held in your lap in your hand in an almost upright position with the bottle at an angle to allow the entire nipple area to be full of the formula. Do not hold the bottle upright so the puppy's head has to reach straight up toward the ceiling. Do not let the puppy nurse too quickly or take in too much air and possibly get colic. Once in awhile take the bottle away and let him rest a moment and swallow several times. Before feeding, test the nipple to see that the fluid does not come out too quickly, or by the same token, too slowly, so that the puppy gets tired of feeding before he has had enough to eat.

When the puppy is a little older, you can place him on his stomach on a towel to eat, and even allow him to hold on to the bottle or to "come and get it" on his own. Since most puppies enjoy eating, this will be a good indication of how strong an appetite he has, and of his ability to consume the contents of the bottle.

It will be necessary to "burp" the puppy. Place a towel on your shoulder and put the puppy over the towel as if it were a human baby, patting and rubbing it gently. This will also encourage the puppy to defecate. At this time, you should observe for diarrhea or other intestinal disorders. The puppy should eliminate after

Krizlamars Atom Bomb, photographed at six months of age, is owned by Mary Bratschi of Grand Ledge, Michigan.

DeeDee is pictured at six months of age. Her owner is Marjorie Mahan. The sire was Wildweir Respected Legend ex Ch. Nitetrain Painted Lady. Bred by Arlene Mack.

each feeding with occasional eliminations between times as well. If the puppies do not eliminate on their own after each meal, massage their stomachs and under their tails gently until they do.

You must keep the puppies clean. Under no circumstances should fecal matter be allowed to collect on their skin or fur.

All this—plus your determination and perseverance—might save an entire litter of puppies that would otherwise have died without their real mother.

FEEDING THE ADULT DOG

The puppies' schedule of four meals a day should drop to three by six months and then to two by nine months; by the time the dog reaches one year of age, it is eating one meal a day.

The time when you feed the dog each day can be a matter of the dog's preference or your convenience, so long as once in every twenty-four hours the dog receives a meal that provides it with a complete, balanced diet. In addition, of course, fresh clean water should be available at all times.

There are many brands of dry food, kibbles, and biscuits on the market that are all of good quality. There are also many varieties of canned dog food that are of good quality and provide a balanced diet for your dog. But, for those breeders and exhibitors who show their dogs, additional care should be given to providing a few "extras" that enhance the good health and good appearance of show dogs.

A good meal or kibble mixed with water or beef broth and raw meat is perhaps the best ration to provide. In cold weather, many breeders add suet or corn oil (or even olive or cooking oil) to the mixture, and others make use of the bacon fat after breakfast by pouring it over the dog's food.

Silverwinds Noblesse Oblige is pictured at six months of age after winning Best in Match over 51 adults at the Nation's Capital Yorkshire Terrier Club show. The sire was Ch. Wildweir Bumper Sticker ex Silverwinds Song Maiden. Owner-breeder is Elissa Taddie, West Chester, Pennsylvania.

Six-month-old Everblue's Grand Illusion is owned by Arlene Mack of Westlake, Ohio. The sire was Ch. Mayfair Barban Marzipan ex Ch. Niletrain Painted Lady.

Salting a dog's food in the summer helps replace the salt he "pants away" in the heat. Many breeders sprinkle the food with garlic powder to sweeten the dog's breath and prevent gas, especially in breeds that gulp or wolf their food and swallow a lot of air. I prefer garlic powder; the salt is too weak and the garlic clove is too strong.

There are those, of course, who cook very elaborately for their dogs, which is not necessary if a good meal and meat mixture is provided. Many prefer to add vegetables, rice, tomatoes, and so on, in with everything else they feed. As long as the extras do not throw the nutritional balance off, there is little harm, but no one thing should be fed to excess. Occasionally liver is given as a treat at home. Fish, which most veterinarians no longer recommend even for cats, is fed to puppies, but should not be given in excess of once a week. Always remember that no one food should be given as a total diet. Balance is most important; a 100 per cent meat diet can kill a dog.

Dot's Goldcoast Hooker is pictured winning at a 1982 show at nine months of age. Owned by Dorothy Gaunt of West Covina, California.

agency for establishing the nutritional requirements of dog foods. Most foods sold for dogs and cats meet these requirements, and manufacturers are proud to say so on their labels, so look for this when you buy. Pet food labels must be approved by the Association of American Feed Control Officials (AAFCO) Pet Foods Committee. Both the Food and Drug Administration and the Federal Trade Commission of the AAFCO define the word "balanced" when referring to dog food as follows:

"Balanced is a term which may be applied to pet food having all known required nutrients in a proper amount and proportion based upon the recommendations of a recognized authority (The National Research Council is one) in the field of animal nutrition, for a given set of physiological animal requirements."

With this much care given to your dog's diet, there can be little reason for not having happy well-fed dogs in proper weight and proportions for the show ring.

THE ALL-MEAT DIET CONTROVERSY

In March of 1971, the National Research Council investigated a great stir in the dog fancy about the all-meat dog-feeding controversy. It was established that meat and meat by-products constitute a complete balanced diet for dogs only when it is further fortified.

Therefore, a good dog chow or meal mixed with meat provides the perfect combination for a dog's diet. While the dry food is a complete diet in itself, the fresh meat additionally satisfies the dog's anatomically and physiologically meat-oriented appetite. While dogs are actually carnivores, it must be remembered that when they were feeding themselves in the wild, they ate almost the entire animal they captured, including its stomach contents. This provided some of the vitamins and minerals we must now add to the diet.

In the United States, the standard for diets that claims to be "complete and balanced" is set by the Subcommittee on Canine Nutrition of the National Research Council (NRC) of the National Academy of Sciences. This is the official

Dot's Costly Cargo, an eleven-month-old hopeful, bred and owned by Dorothy Gaunt is a son of her Ch. Dot's Top Banana. Photo by Missy.

OBESITY

As we mentioned before, there are many "perfect" diets for your dogs on the market today. When fed in proper proportions, they should keep your dogs in "full bloom." However, there are those owners who, more often than not, indulge their own appetites and are inclined to overfeed their dogs as well. A study in Great Britain in the early 1970's found that a major percentage of obese people also had obese dogs. The entire family was overfed and all suffered from the same condition.

Obesity in dogs is a direct result of the animal's being fed more food that he can properly "burn up" over a period of time, so it is stored as fat or fatty tissue in the body. Pet dogs are more inclined to become obese than show dogs or working dogs, but obesity also is a factor to be considered with the older dog since his exercise is curtailed.

A lack of "tuck up" on a dog, or not being able to feel the ribs, or great folds of fat that hang from the underside of the dog can all be considered as obesity. Genetic factors may enter into the picture, but usually the owner is at fault.

The life span of the obese dog is decreased on several counts. Excess weight puts undue stress on the heart as well as on the joints. The dog becomes a poor anesthetic risk and has less resistance to viral or bacterial infections. Treatment is seldom easy or completely effective, so emphasis should be placed on not letting your dog get fat in the first place!

GASTRIC TORSION

Gastric torsion, or bloat, sometimes referred to as "twisted stomach," has become more and more prevalent. Many dogs that in the past had been thought to die of blockage of the stomach or intestines because they had swallowed toys or other foreign objects, are now suspected of having been the victims of gastric torsion and the bloat that followed.

Though life can be saved by immediate surgery to untwist the organ, the rate of fatality is high. Symptoms of gastric torsion are unusual restlessness, excessive salivation, attempts to vomit, rapid respiration, pain, and the eventual bloating of the abdominal region.

The cause of gastric torsion can be attributed to overeating, excess gas formation in the stomach, poor function of the stomach or intestine, or general lack of exercise. As the food ferments in the stomach, gases form which may twist the stomach in a clockwise direction so that the gas is unable to escape. Surgery, where the stomach is untwisted counter-clockwise, is the safest and most successful way to correct the situation.

To avoid the threat of gastric torsion, it is wise to keep your dog well exercised to be sure the body is functioning normally. Make sure that food and water are available for the dog at all times, thereby reducing the tendency to overeat. With self-service dry feeding, where the dog is able to eat intermittently during the day, there is not the urge to "stuff" at one time.

If you notice any of the symptoms of gastric torsion, call your veterinarian immediately. Death can result within a matter of hours!

Blue Note Maggie of Silk N Satin Kennels, photographed at ten months of age. Owned by Clara Powanda, Wheeling, West Virginia.

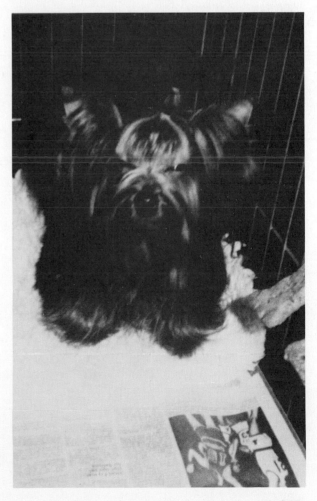

Ch. Bonny's Arielle, bred by Sonya and Mary Lees, owned by Elda and Nathan Tropper. This charming photo of Arielle was taken in 1978.

CHAPTER FOURTEEN

The Blight of Parasites

Bonny's Ginger Snap, owned by Elda Tropper of Los Angeles, California. Ginger was photographed here as a puppy in 1972.

Anyone who has ever spent hours peering intently at their dog's warm, pink stomach waiting for a flea to appear will readily understand why I call this chapter the "blight of parasites." It is that dreaded onslaught of the pesky flea that heralds the subsequent arrival of worms.

If you have seen even one flea scoot across that vulnerable expanse of skin, you can be sure there are more lurking on other areas of your dog. They seldom travel alone. So, it is now an established fact that *la puce*, as the French refer to the flea, has set up housekeeping on your dog! It is going to demand a great deal of your time before you manage to evict them—probably just temporarily at that—no matter which species your dog is harboring.

Fleas are not always choosy about their host, but chances are your dog has what is commonly known as *Ctenocephalides canis*, the dog flea. If you are a lover of cats also, your dog might even be playing host to a few *Ctenocephalides felis*, the cat flea, or vice versa. The only thing you can be really sure of is that your dog is supporting an entire community of them, all hungry and sexually oriented, and you are going to have to be persistent in your campaign to get rid of them.

One of the chief reasons fleas are so difficult to catch is that what they lack in beauty and eyesight (they are blind at birth, throughout infan-

cy, and see very poorly if at all during adulthood), they make up for in their fantastic ability to jump and scurry about.

While this remarkable ability to jump—some claim 150 times the length of their bodies—stands them in good stead with circus entrepreneurs, and has given them claim to fame as chariot pullers and acrobats in side show attractions, the dog owner can be reduced to tears at the very thought of the onset of fleas.

Modern research has provided a panacea in the form of flea sprays, dips, collars, and tags which can be successful to varying degrees. However, there are those who still swear by the good old-fashioned methods of removing them by hand, which can be a challenge to your sanity as well as your dexterity.

Since the fleas' conformation (they are built like envelopes, long and flat), with their spiny skeletal system on the outside of their bodies, is specifically provided for slithering through forests of hair, they are given a distinct advantage to start with. Two antennae on the head select the best spot for digging, and then two mandibles penetrate the skin and hit a blood vessel. It is also at this moment that the flea brings into play his spiny contours to prop himself against surrounding hairs to avoid being scratched off as he puts the bite on your dog. A small projecting tube is then lowered into the hole to draw out blood and another tube pumps saliva into the wound; this prevents the blood from clotting and allows the flea to drink freely. Simultaneously, your dog jumps into the air and gets one of those back legs into action, scratching endlessly and in vain, and ruining some coat at the same time!

If you should be so lucky as to catch an itinerant flea as it mistakenly shortcuts across your dog's stomach, the best hunting grounds in the world are actually in the deep fur all along the dog's back from neck to tail. However, the flea, like every other creature on earth, must have water, so several times during its residency it will make its way to the moister areas of your dog's anatomy, such as the corners of the mouth, the eyes, or the genital parts. This is when the

Ch. Oakshire's Mollie Brown, bred and owned by Shirlee and Francis Sly of Overland Park, Kansas.

flea collars and tags are useful. Their fumes prevent fleas from passing the neck to get to the head of your dog.

Your dog can usually support several generations of fleas, if it doesn't scratch itself to death or go out of its mind with the itching in the interim. The propagation of the flea is insured by the strong mating instinct and well-judged decision of the female flea as to the best time to deposit her eggs. She has the rare capacity to store semen until the time is right to lay the eggs after some previous brief encounter with a passing member of the opposite sex.

When that time comes for her to lay, she does so without so much as a backward glance and moves on. The dog shakes the eggs off during a normal day's wandering, and they remain on the ground until hatched and the baby fleas are ready to jump back onto a passing dog. If any of the eggs have remained on the original dog, chances are that in scratching an adult flea, he will help the baby fleas emerge from their shells.

Larval fleas are small and resemble slender maggots; they begin their lives eating their own egg shells until the dog comes along and offers them a return to the world of adult fleas, whose excrement provides the predigested blood pellets they must have to thrive. They cannot survive on fresh blood, nor are they capable at this tender age of digging for it themselves.

After a couple of weeks of this freeloading, the baby flea makes his own cocoon and becomes a pupa. This stage lasts long enough for the larval flea to grow legs, mandibles, and sharp spines, and to flatten out and in general become identifiable as the commonly known and obnoxious *Ctenocephalides canis*. The process can take several weeks or several months, depending on weather conditions, heat, and moisture, but generally three weeks is all that is required to enable the flea to start gnawing your dog in its own right.

And so the life-cycle of the flea is renewed and begun again. If you don't have plans to stem the tide, you will certainly see a population explosion that will make the human one resemble an endangered species. Getting rid of fleas can be accomplished by the aforementioned spraying of the dog, or the flea collars and tags, but air, sunshine and a good shaking out of beds, bedding, carpets, and cushions, certainly must be undertaken to get rid of the eggs or larvae lying around the premises.

Lor Dean's Spirit in the Sky, pictured at play at the kennels of Lori and Gary Williams, Shoshone, Idaho.

Should you be lucky enough to get hold of a flea, you must squeeze it to death (which isn't easy), or break it in two with a sharp, strong fingernail (which also isn't easy), or you must release it *underwater* in the toilet bowl and flush immediately. This prospect is only slightly easier.

There are those dog owners, however, who are much more philosophical about the flea, since, like the cockroach, it has been around since the beginning of the world. For instance, that old-time philosopher, David Harum, has been much quoted with his remark, "A reasonable amount of fleas is good for a dog. They keep him from broodin' on bein' a dog." We would rather agree with John Donne who, in his *Devotions*, reveals that, "The flea, though he kill none, he does all the harm he can." This is especially true if your dog is a show dog! If the scratching doesn't ruin the coat, the inevitable infestation of parasites left by the fleas will!

We readily see that dogs can be afflicted by both internal and external parasites. The external parasites are known as the aforementioned fleas, plus ticks and lice; while all of these are bothersome, they can be treated. However, the internal parasites, or worms of various kinds, are usually well-entrenched before discovery, and more substantial means of ridding the dog of them completely are required.

INTERNAL PARASITES

The most common worms are the round worms. These, like many other worms, are carried and spread by the flea and go through a cycle within the dog host. They are excreted in egg or larval form and passed on to other dogs in this manner.

Worm medicine should be prescribed by a veterinarian, and dogs should be checked for worms at least twice a year—or every three months if there is a known epidemic in your area— and during the summer months when fleas are plentiful.

Major types of worms are hookworms, whipworms, tapeworms (the only non-round worms on this list), ascarids (the "typical" round worms), heartworms, kidney, and lung worms. Each can be peculiar to a part of the country, or may be carried by a dog from one area to another. Kidney and lung worms are fortunately quite rare; the others are not. Some symptoms for worms are vomiting intermittently, eating grass, lack of pep, bloated stomach, rubbing the tail along the ground, loss of weight, dull coat, anemia and pale gums, eye discharge, or unexplained nervousness and irritability. A dog with worms will usually eat twice as much as he normally would.

Never worm a sick dog or a pregnant bitch after the first two weeks she has been bred, and never worm a constipated dog—it will retain the strong medicine within the body for too long a time.

Lively's Rhett, whelped in 1982 and sired by Ch. Jentre's Charger of Mistangay ex Precious Blue Tuttles. Owned and bred by Mrs. Bobby Lively of North East, Maryland.

Nestled amid some favorite stuffed animals is little "Lance," owned by Charlene Ginn of Kennett Square, Pennsylvania.

HOW TO TEST FOR WORMS

Worms can kill your dog if the infestation is severe enough. Even light infestations of worms can debilitate a dog to the point where he is more susceptible to other serious diseases that can kill.

Today's medication for worming is relatively safe and mild, and worming is no longer the traumatic experience for either the dog or owner that it used to be. Great care must be given, however, to the proper administration of the drugs. Correct dosage is a "must," and clean quarters are essential to rid your kennel of these parasites. It is almost impossible to find an animal that is completely free of parasites, so we must consider worming as a necessary evil.

However mild today's medicines may be, it is inadvisable to worm a dog unnecessarily. There are simple tests to determine the presence of worms, and this chapter is designed to help you learn how to administer these tests yourself. Veterinarians charge a nominal fee for this service, if it is not part of their regular office visit examination. It is a simple matter to prepare fecal slides that you yourself can read on a periodic basis.

All that is needed by way of equipment is a microscope with 100X power. These can be purchased in the toy department of a department or regular toy store for a few dollars. The basic, least expensive sets come with the necessary glass slides and attachments.

After the dog has defecated, take an applicator stick, a toothpick with a flat end, or even an old-fashioned wooden matchstick and gouge off a piece of the stool about the size of a small pea. Have one of the glass slides ready with a large drop of water on it. Mix the two together until you have a cloudy film over a large area of the slide. This smear should be covered with another slide or a cover slip—though it is possible to obtain readings with just the one open slide. Place your slide under the microscope and prepare to focus in on it. To read the slide you will find that your eye should follow a certain pattern. Start at the top and read from left to right, then right back to the left and then left over to the right side once again until you have looked at every portion of the slide from the top left to the bottom right side.

Make sure that your smear is not too thick or watery or the reading will be too dark and confused to make proper identification. If you decide you would rather not make your own fecal examinations, but would prefer to have the veterinarian do it, the proper way to present a segment of the stool is as follows:

After the dog has defecated, a portion of the stool, say a square inch from different sections of it, should be placed in a glass jar or plastic container and labeled with the dog's name and address of the owner. If the sample cannot be examined within three or four hours after passage, it should be refrigerated. Your opinion as to what variety of worms you suspect is sometimes helpful to the veterinarian, and may be noted on the label of the jar you submit to him for the examination.

Checking for worms on a regular basis is advisable not only for the welfare of the dog but for the protection of your family, since most worms are transmissible, under certain circumstances, to humans.

A Petit Point Yorkie belonging to Susan M. Sandlin, the Original Petit Point, Arlington, Virginia.

Silk N Satin Executive Memo, co-owned by Doris Rush of Rockford, Illinois, and breeder Clara Powanda of Wheeling, West Virginia.

Sitting on top of the world is Silverwinds Grand Prize with two of his friends, all owned by Elissa Taddie of West Chester, Pennsylvania.

Helen Stern contributed this adorable photograph of her grandson, a true Yorkie lover as it is plain to see.

Elissa Taddie's Garla Queen. While not a show dog (her ears never went up), her conformation was excellent and her personality was true Yorkie.

CHAPTER FIFTEEN

Your Dog, Your Veterinarian, and You

Gemineauxs Ready Cash, bred by Anita Wray of Houston, Texas. "Cash" was well on his way to a championship when a tragic encounter with a brown Recluse Spider put an end to his show ring career.

The purpose of this chapter is to explain why you should never attempt to be your own veterinarian. Quite the contrary, we urge emphatically that you establish a good liaison with a reputable veterinarian who will help you maintain happy, healthy dogs. Our purpose is to bring you up-to-date on the discoveries made in modern canine medicine, and to help you work with your veterinarian by applying these new developments to your own animals.

We have provided here "thumbnail" histories of many of the most common types of diseases your dog is apt to come in contact with during his lifetime. We feel that if you know a little something about the diseases and how to recognize their symptoms, your chances of catching them in the preliminary stages will help you and your veterinarian effect a cure before a serious condition develops.

Today's dog owner is a realistic, intelligent person who learns more and more about his dog —inside and out—so that he can care for and enjoy the animal to the fullest. He uses technical terms for parts of the anatomy, has a fleeting knowledge of the miracles of surgery, and is fully prepared to administer clinical care for his animals at home. This chapter is designed for study and/or reference, and we hope you will use it to full advantage.

We repeat, we do *not* advocate your playing "doctor." This includes administering medication without veterinary supervision, or even doing your own inoculations. General knowledge of diseases, their symptoms, and side effects will assist you in diagnosing diseases for your veterinarian. He does not expect you to be an expert, but will appreciate your efforts in getting a sick dog to him before it is too late and he cannot save its life.

ASPIRIN: A DANGER

There is a common joke about doctors telling their patients, when they telephone with a complaint, to take an aspirin, go to bed and let him know how things are in the morning. Unfortunately, that is exactly the way it turns out with a lot of dog owners who think aspirins are cure-alls, and who give them to their dogs indiscriminately.

Aspirin is not a panacea for everything—certainly not for every dog. In an experiment, fatalities in cats treated with aspirin in one laboratory alone numbered ten out of thirteen within a two-week period. Dogs' tolerance was somewhat better, as to actual fatalities, but there was considerable evidence of ulceration on the stomach linings in varying degrees when necropsy was performed.

271

Aspirin has been held in the past to be almost as effective for dogs as for people when given for many of the everyday aches and pains. The fact remains, however, that medication of any kind should be administered only after veterinary consultation and a specific dosage suitable to the condition is recommended.

While aspirin is chiefly effective in reducing fever, relieving minor pains, and cutting down on inflammation, the acid has been proven harmful to the stomach when given in strong doses. Only your veterinarian is qualified to determine what the dosage is or whether it should be administered to your particular dog at all.

Silk N Satin Wicked Wanda is pictured at home at the Silk N Satin Kennels.

Helen Stern's Carlen's Pompier and Ch. Carlen's I.W. Harper win Best Brace in Show at the 1977 Yorkshire Terrier Club of America Specialty show.

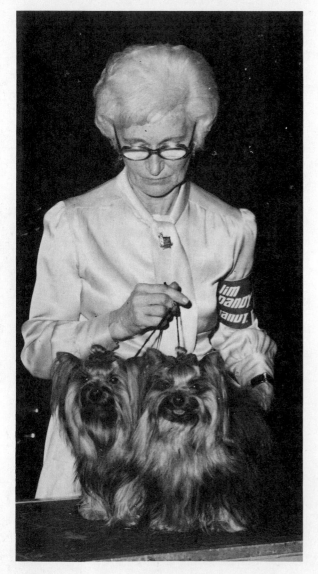

WHAT THE THERMOMETER CAN TELL YOU

You will notice in reading this chapter dealing with the diseases of dogs that practically everything a dog might contract in the way of sickness has basically the same set of symptoms: loss of appetite, diarrhea, dull eyes, dull coat, warm and/or runny nose, and *fever!*

Therefore, it is most advisable to have a thermometer on hand for checking temperature. There are several inexpensive metal rectal-type thermometers that are accurate, and safer than the glass variety that can be broken. This may happen either by dropping it, or perhaps by its breaking off in the dog because of improper insertion, or an aggravated condition with the dog that makes him violently resist the injection of the thermometer.

Whatever type you use, it should first be sterilized with alcohol and then lubricated with petroleum jelly to make the insertion as easy as possible.

The normal temperature for a dog is 101.5 degrees Fahrenheit, as compared to the human 98.6 degrees. Excitement as well as illness can cause this to vary a degree or two, but any sudden or extensive rise in body temperature must be considered as cause for alarm. Your first indication will be that your dog feels unduly "warm," and this is the time to take the temperature, *not* when the dog becomes very ill or manifests additional serious symptoms.

COPROPHAGY

Perhaps the most unpleasant of all phases of dog breeding is to come up with a dog that takes to eating stool. This practice, which is referred to politely as coprophagy, is one of the unsolved mysteries in the dog world. There simply is no confirmed explanation as to why some dogs do it.

However, there are several logical theories, all or any of which may be the cause. Some people cite nutritional deficiencies; others say that dogs that are inclined to gulp their food (which passes through them not entirely digested) find it still partially palatable. There is another theory that the preservatives used in some meat are responsible for an appealing odor that remains through the digestive process. Then again, poor quality meat can be so tough and unchewable that dogs swallow it whole and it passes through them in large undigested chunks.

There are others who believe the habit is strictly psychological, the result of a nervous condition or insecurity. Others believe the dog cleans up after itself because it is afraid of being punished as it was when it made a mistake on the carpet as a puppy. Some people claim boredom is the reason, or even spite. Others will tell you a dog does not want its personal odor on the premises for fear of attracting other hostile animals to itself or its home.

The most logical of all explanations, and the one veterinarians are inclined to accept, is that it is a deficiency of dietary enzymes. Too much dry food can be bad, and many veterinarians suggest trying meat tenderizers, monosodium glutamate, or garlic powder, all of which give the stool a bad odor and discourage the dog. Yeast or certain vitamins or a complete change of diet are even more often suggested. By the time you try each of the above you will probably discover that the dog has outgrown the habit anyway. However, the condition cannot be ignored if you are to enjoy your dog to the fullest.

There is no set length of time that the problem persists, and the only real cure is to walk the dog on leash, morning and night, and after every meal. In other words, set up a definite eating and exercising schedule before coprophagy is an established pattern.

MASTURBATION

A source of embarrassment to many dog owners, masturbation can be eliminated with a minimum of training.

The dog that is constantly breeding anything and everything, including the leg of the piano or perhaps the leg of your favorite guest, can be broken of the habit by stopping its cause.

The over-sexed dog—if truly that is what he is —which will never be used for breeding can be castrated. The kennel stud dog can be broken of the habit by removing any furniture from his quarters or by keeping him on leash and on verbal command when he is around people or in the house, where he might be tempted to breed pillows, people, etc.

Hormone imbalance may be another cause and your veterinarian may advise injections. Exercise can be of tremendous help. Keeping the dog's mind occupied by physical play when he is around people will also help relieve the situation.

Females might indulge in sexual abnormalities like masturbation during their heat cycle, or again, because of a hormone imbalance. But if they behave this way because of a more serious problem, a hysterectomy may be indicated.

A sharp "no!" command when you can anticipate the act, or a sharp "no!" when caught in the act will deter most dogs if you are consistent in your correction. Hitting or other physical abuse will only confuse a dog.

Denaire Joe Cool, bred by D. Paul Katzakian and owned by Joyce Watkins, Marcris Kennels, Miami, Florida.

No No Nanette is owned by Alyce E. Veazey of Charleston, West Virginia. Whelped in 1979, the sire was Ka-Doll's Wee Wun of Charo's ex Jessamine's Morning Glory.

RABIES

The greatest fear in the dog fancy today is still the great fear it has always been—rabies.

What has always held true about this dreadful disease still holds true today. The only way rabies can be contracted is through the saliva of a rabid dog entering the bloodstream of another animal or person. There is, of course, the Pasteur treatment for rabies which is very effective.

It should be administered immediately if there is any question of exposure. There was of late the incident of a little boy, who survived being bitten by a rabid bat. Even more than dogs being found to be rabid, we now know that the biggest carriers are bats, skunks, foxes, rabbits, and other warmblooded animals that pass it from one to another since they do not have the benefit of inoculation. Dogs that run free should be inoculated for protection against these animals. For city or house dogs that never leave their owner's side, it may not be as necessary.

For many years, Great Britain (because it is an island and because of the country's strictly enforced six-month quarantine) was entirely free of rabies. But in 1969, a British officer brought back his dog from foreign duty and the dog was found to have the disease soon after being released from quarantine. There was a great uproar about it, with Britain killing off wild and domestic animals in a great scare campaign, but the quarantine is once again down to six months, and things seem to have returned to a normal, sensible attitude.

Health departments in rural towns usually provide rabies inoculations free of charge. If your dog is outdoors a great deal, or exposed to other animals that are, you might wish to call the town hall and get information on the program in your area. One cannot be too cautious about this dread disease. While the number of cases diminishes each year, there are still thousands being reported and there is still the constant threat of an outbreak where animals roam free. Never forget, there is no cure.

Rabies is caused by a neurotropic virus which can be found in the saliva, brain, and sometimes the blood of the afficted warmblooded animal. The incubation period is usually two weeks or as long as six months, which means you can be exposed to it without any visible symptoms. As we have said, while there is still no known cure, it can be controlled.

You can help effect this control by reporting animal bites, educating the public to the dangers and symptoms, and prevention of it, so that we may reduce the fatalities.

There are two kinds of rabies; one form is called "furious" and the other is referred to as "dumb." The mad dog goes through several stages of the disease. His disposition and behavior change radically and suddenly; he becomes irritable and vicious. The eating habits alter, and he rejects food for things like stones and sticks; he becomes exhausted and drools saliva out of his mouth constantly. He may hide in corners, look glassy-eyed and suspicious, bite at the air as he races around snarling and attacking with his tongue hanging out. At this point paralysis sets in, starting at the throat so that he can no longer drink water though he desires it desperately; hence, the term hydrophobia is given. He begins to stagger and eventually convulse, and death is imminent.

In "dumb" rabies, paralysis is swift; the dog seeks dark, sheltered places and is abnormally quiet. Paralysis starts with the jaws, spreads down the body, and death is quick. Contact by humans or other animals with the drool from either of these types of rabies on open skin can produce the fatal disease, so extreme haste and proper diagnosis is essential. In other words, you do not have to be bitten by a rabid dog to have the virus enter your system. An open wound or cut that comes in touch with the saliva is all that is needed.

The incubation and degree of infection can vary. You usually contract the disease faster if the wound is near the head, since the virus travels to the brain through the spinal cord. The deeper the wound, the more saliva is injected into the body, and the more serious the infection. So, if bitten by a dog under any circumstances—or any warmblooded animal for that matter—immediately wash out the wound with soap and water, bleed it profusely, and see your doctor as soon as possible.

Also, be sure to keep track of the animal that bit, if at all possible. When rabies is suspected, the public health officer will need to send the animal's head away to be analyzed. If it is found to be rabies free, you will not need to undergo treatment. Otherwise, your doctor may advise that you have the Pasteur treatment, which is extremely painful. It is rather simple, however, to have the veterinarian examine a dog for rabies without having the dog sent away for positive diagnosis of the disease. A ten-day quarantine is usually all that is necessary for everyone's peace of mind.

Rabies is no respecter of age, sex, or geographical location. It is found all over the world from North Pole to South Pole, and has nothing to do with the old wives' tale of dogs going mad in the hot summer months. True, there is an increase in reported cases during summer, but only because that is the time of the year for animals to roam free in good weather and during the mating season when the battle of the sexes is taking place. Inoculation and a keen eye for symptoms and bites on our dogs and other pets will help control the disease until the cure is found.

VACCINATIONS

If you are to raise a puppy, or a litter of puppies, successfully, you must adhere to a realistic and strict schedule of vaccinations. Many puppyhood diseases can be fatal—all of them are debilitating. According to the latest statistics,

Sitting pretty is Gladys Jackson's Wittigen's Afternoon Delight.

ninety-eight per cent of all puppies are being inoculated after twelve weeks of age against the dread distemper, hepatitis, and leptospirosis, and manage to escape these horrible infections. Orphaned puppies should be vaccinated every two weeks until the age of twelve weeks. Distemper and hepatitis live virus vaccines should be used, since the puppies are not protected with the colostrum normally supplied to them through the mother's milk. Puppies weaned at six to seven weeks should also be inoculated repeatedly because they will no longer be receiving mother's milk. While not all will receive protection from the serum at this early age, it should be given and they should be vaccinated once again at both nine and twelve weeks of age.

Leptospirosis vaccination should be given at four months of age with thought given to booster shots if the disease is known in the area, or in the case of show dogs which are exposed on a regular basis to many dogs from far and wide. While animal boosters are in order for distemper and hepatitis, every two or three years is sufficient for leptospirosis, unless there is an outbreak in your immediate area. The one exception should be the pregnant bitch, since there is reason to believe that inoculation might cause damage to the fetus.

Strict observance of such a vaccination schedule will not only keep your dog free of these debilitating diseases, but will prevent an epidemic in your kennel, or in your locality, or to the dogs that are competing at the shows.

SNAKEBITE

As field trials and hunts and the like become more and more popular with dog enthusiasts, the incident of snakebite becomes more of a likelihood. Dogs that are kept outdoors in runs, or dogs that work the fields and roam on large estates are also likely victims.

Most veterinarians carry snakebite serum, and snakebite kits are sold to dog owners for just such a purpose. To catch a snakebite in time might mean the difference between life and death, and whether your area is populated with snakes or not, it behooves you to know what to do in case it happens to you or your dog.

Your primary concern should be to get to a doctor or veterinarian immediately. The victim should be kept as quiet as possible (excitement or activity spreads the venom through the body more quickly), and if possible the wound should be bled enough to clean it out before applying a tourniquet, if the bite is severe.

First of all, it must be determined if the bite is from a poisonous or non-poisonous snake. If the bite carries two horseshoe-shaped pinpoints of a double row of teeth, the bite can be assumed to be non-poisonous. If the bite leaves two punctures or holes—the result of the two fangs carrying venom—the bite is very definitely poisonous and time is of the essence.

Tuttles and Angel, both belonging to Sue Lively, North East, Maryland.

Recently, physicians have come up with an added help in the case of snakebite. A first aid treatment referred to as "hypothermia," which is the application of ice to the wound to lower body temperature to a point where the venom spreads less quickly, minimizes swelling, helps prevent infection, and has some influence on numbing the pain. If ice is not readily available, the bite may be soaked in ice-cold water. But even more urgent is the need to get the victim to a hospital or a veterinarian for additional treatment.

EMERGENCIES

No matter how well you run your kennel or keep an eye on an individual dog, there will almost invariably be some emergency at some time that will require quick treatment until you get the animal to the veterinarian. The first and most important thing to remember is to keep calm! You will think more clearly, and your animal will need to know he can depend on you to take care of him. However, he will be frightened and you must beware of fear-biting. Therefore, do not shower him with kisses and endearments at this time, no matter how sympathetic you feel. Comfort him reassuringly, but keep your wits about you. Before getting him to the veterinarian, try to alleviate the pain and the shock.

If you can take even a minor step in this direction it will be a help toward the final cure. Listed here are a few of the emergencies that might occur, and what you can do *after* you have called the vet and told him you are coming.

Ch. Zerox Copy of Lamplighter at 2½ years of age. Owned by Barb Beissel of Minneapolis, Minnesota.

276

Brok Arro Business Manager, Minted Mindy Blu of Cupoluv, and Anderleigh Rockin Robbie, C.D.— otherwise known as Gerry, Mindy, and Robbie—at the Silk N Satin Kennels in Wheeling, West Virginia.

BURNS

If you have been so foolish as to not turn your pot handles toward the back of the stove—for your children's sake as well as your dog's—and the dog is burned, apply ice or ice-cold water and treat for shock. Electrical or chemical burns are treated the same, but with an acid or alkali burn use, respectively, a bicarbonate of soda and a vinegar solution. Check the advisability of covering the burn when you call the veterinarian.

DROWNING

Most animals love the water but sometimes get in "over their heads." Should your dog take in too much water, hold him upside down and open his mouth so that water can empty from the lungs, then apply artificial respiration or mouth-to-mouth resuscitation. With a large dog, hang the head over a step or off the end of a table while you hoist the rear end in the air by the back feet. Then treat for shock by covering him with a blanket, administering a stimulant such as coffee with sugar, and soothing him with your voice and hands.

FITS AND CONVULSIONS

Prevent the dog from thrashing about and injuring himself, cover with a blanket, and hold down until you can get him to the veterinarian.

FROSTBITE

There is no excuse for an animal getting frostbite if you are "on your toes" and care for the animal; however, should frostbite set in, thaw out the affected area slowly by massaging with a circular motion and stimulation. Use petroleum jelly to help keep the skin from peeling off and/ or drying out.

HEART ATTACK

Be sure the animal keeps breathing by applying artificial respiration. A mild stimulant may be used, and give him plenty of air. Treat for shock as well, and get him to the veterinarian quickly.

SHOCK

Shock is a state of circulatory collapse that can be induced by a severe accident, loss of blood, heart failure, or any injury to the nervous system. Until you can get the dog to the veterinarian, keep him warm by covering him with a blanket, and administer a mild stimulant such as coffee or tea with sugar. Try to keep the dog quiet until the appropriate medication can be prescribed. Relapse is not uncommon, so the dog must be observed carefully for several days after initial shock.

SUFFOCATION

Administer artificial respiration and treat for shock with plenty of air.

Daiquiri of Carlen pictured in a beautiful portrait by Paula Wright. Owner is Helen Stern of Brooklyn, New York.

A charming trio of Estugo puppies.

SUN STROKE

Cooling the dog off immediately is essential. Ice packs, submersion in ice water, and plenty of cool air are needed.

WOUNDS

Open wounds or cuts that produce bleeding must be treated with hydrogen peroxide, and tourniquets should be used if bleeding is excessive. Also, shock treatment must be given, and the animal must be kept warm.

THE FIRST AID KIT

It would be sheer folly to try to operate a kennel or to keep a dog without providing for certain emergencies that are bound to crop up when there are active dogs around. Just as you would provide a first aid kit for people, you should also provide a first aid kit for the animals on the premises.

The first aid kit should contain the following items:

BFI or other medicated powder
jar of petroleum jelly
cotton swabs
bandage—1″ gauze
adhesive tape
bandaids
cotton gauze or cotton balls
boric acid powder

A trip to your veterinarian is always safest, but there are certain preliminaries for cuts and bruises of a minor nature that you can take care of yourself.

Cuts, for instance, should be washed out and medicated powder should be applied with a bandage. The lighter the bandage the better, so that the most air possible can reach the wound. Cotton-swabs can be used for removing debris from the eyes, after which a mild solution of boric acid wash can be applied. As for sores, use dry powder on wet sores, and petroleum jelly on dry sores. Use cotton for washing out wounds and drying them.

A particular caution must be given here on bandaging. Make sure that the bandage is not too tight to hamper the dog's circulation. Also, make sure the bandage is applied correctly so that the dog does not bite at it trying to remove it. A great deal of damage can be done to a wound by a dog tearing at a bandage to get it off. If you notice the dog is starting to bite at it, do it over or put something on the bandage that smells and tastes bad to him. Make sure, however, that the solution does not soak through the bandage and enter the wound. Sometimes, if it is a leg wound, a sock or stocking slipped on the dog's leg will cover the bandage edges and will also keep it clean.

This glorious Yorkshire Terrier is owned by Marcia A. Knudsen, Hiawatha Valley Yorkies, Lake City, Minnesota. Missy Yuhl was the photographer.

HOW NOT TO POISON YOUR DOG

Ever since the appearance of Rachel Carson's book *Silent Spring*, people have been asking, "Just how dangerous are chemicals?" In the animal fancy where disinfectants, room deodorants, parasitic sprays, solutions, and aerosols are so widely used, the question has taken on even more meaning. Veterinarians are beginning to ask, "What kind of disinfectant do you use?" "Have you any fruit trees that have been sprayed recently?" When animals are brought into their offices in a toxic condition, or for unexplained death, or when entire litters of puppies die mysteriously, there is good reason to ask such questions.

The popular practice of protecting animals against parasites has given way to their being exposed to an alarming number of commercial products, some of which are dangerous to their very lives. Even flea collars can be dangerous, especially if they get wet or somehow touch the genital regions or eyes. While some products are much more poisonous than others, great care must be taken that they be applied in proportion to the size of the dog and the area to be covered. Many a dog has been taken to the vet with an unusual skin problem that was a direct result of having been bathed with a detergent rather than a proper shampoo. Certain products that are safe for dogs may be fatal for cats. Extreme care must be taken to read all ingredients and instructions carefully before using the products on any animal.

The same caution must be given to outdoor chemicals. Dog owners must question the use of fertilizers on their lawns. Lime, for instance, can be harmful to a dog's feet. The unleashed dog

Elaine and George Nauman's Legagwann Suits Me.

that covers the neighborhood on his daily rounds is open to all sorts of tree and lawn sprays and insecticides that may prove harmful to him, if not as a poison, then as a producer of an allergy.

There are numerous products found around the house that can be lethal, such as rat poison, boric acid, hand soap, detergents, car anti-freeze, and insecticides. These are all available in the house or garage and can be tipped over easily and consumed. Many puppy fatalities are reported as a result of puppies eating mothballs. All poisons should be placed on high shelves out of the reach of *both* children and animals.

Perhaps the most readily available of all household poisons are plants. Household plants are almost all poisonous, even if taken in small quantities. Some of the most dangerous are the elephant ear, the narcissus bulb, any kind of ivy leaves, burning bush leaves, the jimson weed, the dumb cane weed, mock orange fruit, castor beans, Scottish broom seeds, the root or seed of the plant called "four o'clock," cyclamen, pimpernel, lily of the valley, the stem of the sweet pea, rhododendrons of any kind, spider lily bulbs, bayonet root, foxglove leaves, tulip bulbs, monkshood roots, azalea, wisteria, poinsettia leaves, mistletoe, hemlock, locoweed, and arrowglove. In all, there are over 500 poisonous plants in the United States. Peach, elderberry, and cherry trees can cause cyanide poisoning if the bark is consumed. Rhubarb leaves, either raw or cooked, can cause death or violent convulsions. Check out your closets, fields, and grounds around your home, and especially the dog runs, to see what should be eliminated to remove the danger to your dogs.

Mayfairs Katydid (owned by Virginia Bull) with Dachshund pal, Murilew Little Black Sambo.

SYMPTOMS OF POISONING

Be on the lookout for vomiting, hard or labored breathing, whimpering, stomach cramps, and trembling as a prelude to convulsions. Any delay in a visit to your veterinarian can mean death. Take along the bottle or package or a sample of the plant you suspect to be the cause to help the veterinarian determine the correct antidote.

The most common type of poisoning, which accounts for nearly one-fourth of all animal victims, is staphylococcic—infested food. Salmonella ranks third. These can be avoided by serving fresh food and not letting it lie around in hot weather.

There are also many insect poisonings caused by animals eating cockroaches, spiders, flies, butterflies, etc. Toads and some frogs give off a fluid that can make a dog foam at the mouth—and even kill him—if he bites just a little too hard!

Some misguided dog owners think it is "cute" to let their dogs enjoy a cocktail with them before dinner. There can be serious effects resulting from encouraging a dog to drink—sneezing fits, injuries as a result of intoxication, and heart stoppage are just a few. Whiskey for medicinal purposes, or beer for brood bitches should be administered only on the advice of your veterinarian.

Durrisdeer Blythe Spirit, owned and bred by Virginia Bull of Blairstown, New Jersey.

Marcris Legends Legacy. This lovely bitch was sired by Ch. Wildweir Respected Legend. Laurel, as she is called, was bred and owned by Joyce Watkins, Marcris Kennels, Miami, Florida.

There have been cases of severe damage and death when dogs have emptied ash trays and eaten cigarettes, resulting in nicotine poisoning. Leaving a dog alone all day in a house where there are cigarettes available on a coffee table is asking for trouble. Needless to say, the same applies to marijuana. The narcotic addict who takes his dog along with him on "a trip" does not deserve to have a dog. All the ghastly side effects are as possible for the dog as for the addict, and for a person to submit an animal to this indignity is indeed despicable. Don't think it doesn't happen. Unfortunately, in all our major cities the practice is becoming more and more a problem for the veterinarian.

Be on the alert and remember that in the case of any type of poisoning, the best treatment is prevention.

THE CURSE OF ALLERGY

The heartbreak of a child being forced to give up a beloved pet because he is suddenly found to be allergic to it is a sad but true story. Many families claim to be unable to have dogs at all; others seem to be able only to enjoy them on a restricted basis. Many children know animals only through occasional visits to a friend's house or the zoo.

Ch. Kesar's Lucky Star, bred and owned by Barbara Bedsted. The sire was Ch. Charbeth's Little Star ex Ch. Stardust's QT Cupcake.

While modern veterinary science has produced some brilliant allergists, the field is still working on a solution for those who suffer from exposure to their pets. There is no permanent cure as yet.

Over the last quarter of a century there have been many attempts at a permanent cure, but none has proven successful because the treatment was needed too frequently, or was too expensive to maintain over extended periods.

However, we find that most people who are allergic to their animals are also allergic to a variety of other things as well. By eliminating the other irritants, and by taking medication given for the control of allergies in general, many are able to keep pets on a restricted basis. This may necessitate the dog's living outside the house, being groomed at a professional grooming parlor instead of by the owner, or merely being kept out of the bedroom at night. A discussion of this "balance" factor with your medical and veterinary doctors may give new hope to those willing to try.

A paper presented by Mathilde M. Gould, M.D., a New York allergist, before the American Academy of Allergists in the 1960s, and reported in the September-October 1964 issue of the *National Humane Review* magazine, offered new hope to those who are allergic, by a method referred to as hyposensitization. You may wish to write to the magazine and request the article for discussion of your individual problem with your medical and veterinary doctors.

Surely, since the sixties, there have been additional advances in the field of allergy since so many people—and animals—are affected in so many ways.

ALLERGIES IN DOGS

It used to be that you recognized an allergy in your dog when he scratched out his coat and developed a large patch of raw skin, or sneezed himself almost to death on certain occasions. A trip to the veterinarian involved endless discussion as to why it might be, and an almost equally endless "hit and miss" cure of various salves and lotions with the hope that one of them would work. Many times the condition would correct itself before a definite cure was effected.

However, during the 1970s, through preliminary findings at the University of Pennsylvania Veterinary School, there evolved a diagnosis for allergies that eliminated the need for skin sensitivity tests. It is called RAST, and is a radioallergosobant test performed with a blood serum sample. It is not even necessary in all cases for the veterinarian to see the dog.

A cellulose disc laced with a suspected allergen is placed in the serum, and if the dog is allergic to that particular allergen, the serum will contain a specific antibody that adheres to the allergen on the disc. The disc is placed in a radioactively "labeled" antiserum that is attracted to that particular antibody. The antiserum binds with the antibody and can be detected with a radiation counter.

Furthermore, the scientists at the University of Pennsylvania also found that the RAST test has shown to be a more accurate diagnostic tool than skin testing because it measures the degree, and not merely the presence, of allergic reactions.

Durrisdeer Gingeralla, bred and owned by Virginia Bull of Blairstown, New Jersey.

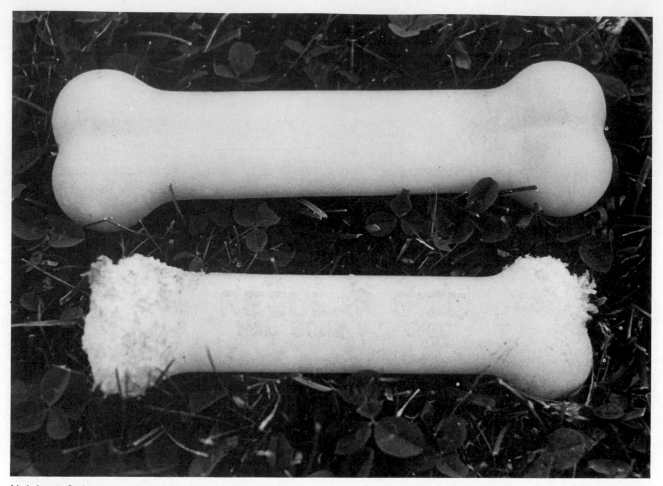

Nylabone® is the perfect chewing pacifier for young dogs in their teething stage and even for older dogs to help satisfy that occasional urge to chew. Unlike many other dog bones on the market today, Nylabone® does not splinter or fall apart; it will last indefinitely and as it is used it frills, becoming a doggie toothbrush that cleans teeth and massages gums.

DO ALL DOGS CHEW?

Chewing is the best possible method of cutting teeth and exercising gums. Every puppy goes through this teething process, and it can be destructive if the puppy uses shoes or table corners or rugs instead of the proper items. All dogs should have a Nylabone® available for chewing, not only to teethe on, but also for inducing growth of the permanent teeth, to assure normal jaw development, and to settle the permanent teeth solidly in the jaws. Chewing on a Nylabone® also has a cleaning effect and serves as a "massage" for the gums, keeping down the formation of tartar that erodes tooth enamel.

When you see a puppy pick up an object to chew, immediately remove it from his mouth with a sharp "No!" and replace the object with a Nylabone® Puppies take anything and every-

thing into their mouths so they should be provided with several Nylabones to prevent damage to the household. This same Nylabone® eliminates the need for the kind of "bone" which may chip your dog's mouth or stomach or intestinal walls. Cooked bones, soft enough to be powdered and added to the food, are also permissible if you have the patience to prepare them, but Nylabone® serves all the purposes of bones for chewing that your dog may require, so why take a chance on meat bones?

Electrical cords and wires of any kind present a special danger that must be eliminated during puppyhood, and glass dishes that can be broken and played with are also hazardous.

The answer to the question about whether all dogs chew is an emphatic *yes*, and the answer is even more emphatic in the case of puppies.

SOME REASONS FOR CHEWING

Chewing can also be a form of frustration or nervousness. Dogs sometimes chew for spite if owners leave them alone too long or too often. Bitches will sometimes chew if their puppies are taken away from them too soon; insecure puppies often chew thinking they're nursing. Puppies that chew wool, blankets, carpet corners, or certain other types of materials may have a nutritional deficiency or something lacking in their diet. Perhaps the articles have been near something that tastes good and they have retained the odor of food.

The act of chewing has no connection with particular breeds or ages. So we repeat, it is up to you to be on guard at all times until the need —or habit—passes.

So we repeat, it is up to you to be on guard at all times until the need—or habit—passes.

HIP DYSPLASIA

Hip dysplasia, or HD, is one of the most widely discussed of all animal afflictions, since it has appeared in varying degrees in just about every breed of dog. True, the larger breeds seem most susceptible, but it has hit the small breeds and is beginning to be recognized in cats as well.

While HD in man has been recorded as far back as 370 B.C., HD in dogs was more than likely referred to as rheumatism until veterinary

Silverwinds Ode To Love, owned by Elissa Taddle. The sire was Ch. Wildweir Fair N Square ex Wildweir Candytuft.

research came into the picture. In 1935, Dr. Otto Schales, at Angell Memorial Hospital in Boston, wrote a paper on hip dysplasia and classified the four degrees of dysplasia of the hip joints as follows:

Grade 1—slight (poor fit between ball socket)
Grade 2—moderate (moderate but obvious shallowness of the socket)
Grade 3—severe (socket quite flat)
Grade 4—very severe (complete displacement of head of femur at early age)

HD is an incurable, hereditary, though not congenital disease of the hip sockets. It is transmitted as a dominant trait with irregular manifestations. Puppies appear normal at birth but the constant wearing away of the socket means the animal moves more and more on muscle, thereby presenting a lameness, a difficulty in getting up, and severe pain in advanced cases.

The degree of severity can be determined around six months of age, but its presence can be noticed from two months of age. The problem is determined by x-ray, and if pain is present it can be relieved temporarily by medication. Exercise should be avoided since motion encourages the wearing away of the bone surfaces.

Dogs with HD should not be shown or bred, if quality in the breed is to be maintained. It is essential to check a pedigree for dogs known to be dysplastic before breeding, since this disease can be dormant for many generations.

Chelsea Nimar For Keeps takes some time out for a playful chew. "Bullet," bred and owned by Nina McIntire of Dallas, Texas, displays the need that all dogs have for chewing exercise.

ELBOW DYSPLASIA

The same condition can also affect the elbow joints and is known as elbow dysplasia. This also causes lameness, and dogs so affected should not be used for breeding.

PATELLAR DYSPLASIA

Some of the smaller breeds of dogs suffer from patellar dysplasia, or dislocation of the knee. This can be treated surgically, but the surgery by no means abolishes the hereditary factor; therefore, these dogs should not be used for breeding.

All dogs—in any breed—should be x-rayed before being used for breeding. The x-ray should be read by a competent veterinarian, and the dog declared free and clear.

THE UNITED STATES REGISTRY

In the United States we have a central Hip Dysplasia Foundation, known as the OFA (Orthopedic Foundation for Animals). This HD control registry was formed in 1966. X-rays are sent to the Foundation for expert evaluation by qualified radiologists.

All you need do for complete information on getting an x-ray for your dog is to write to the Orthopedic Foundation for Animals at 817 Virginia Ave., Columbia, Missouri 65201, and request their dysplasia packet. There is no charge for this kit. It contains an envelope large enough to hold your x-ray film (which you will have taken by your own veterinarian), and a drawing showing how to position the dog properly for x-rays. There is also an application card for proper identification of the dog. Then, hopefully, your dog will be certified "normal." You will be given a registry number which you can put on his pedigree, use in your advertising, and rest assured that your breeding program is in good order.

All x-rays should be sent to the address above. Any other information you might wish to have may be requested from Mrs. Robert Bower, OFA, Route 1, Constantine, Missouri 49042.

We cannot urge strongly enough the importance of doing this. While it involves time and effort, the reward in the long run will more than pay for your trouble. To see the heartbreak of

Fago Marigold's Michah, bred by Fay Gold and litter brother of Ch. Carlen's Jack Daniels, owned by Helen Stern.

Sun Sprite Cybele, bred by Sonya and Mary Lees, owned by the Troppers of Los Angeles, California.

parents and children when their beloved dog has to be put to sleep because of severe hip dysplasia as the result of bad breeding is a sad experience. Don't let this happen to you or to those who will purchase your puppies!

Additionally, we should mention that there is a method of palpation to determine the extent of affliction. This can be painful if the animal is not properly prepared for the examination. There have also been attempts to replace the animal's femur and socket. This is not only expensive, but the percentage of success is small.

For those who refuse to put their dog down, there is a new surgical technique that can relieve pain but in no way constitutes a cure. This technique involves the severing of the pectinius muscle which for some unknown reason brings relief from pain over a period of many months—even up to two years. Two veterinary colleges in the United States are performing this operation at the present time. However, the owner must also give permission to "de-sex" the dogs at the time of the muscle severance. This is a safety measure to help stamp out hip dysplasia, since obviously the condition itself remains and can be passed on through generations.

HD PROGRAM IN GREAT BRITAIN

The British Veterinary Association (BVA) has made an attempt to control the spread of HD by appointing a panel of members of their profession who have made a special study of the disease to read x-rays. Dogs over one year of age may be x-rayed and certified as free. Forms are completed in triplicate to verify the tests. One copy remains with the panel, one copy is for the owner's veterinarian, and one for the owner. A record is also sent to the British Kennel Club for those wishing to check on a particular dog for breeding purposes.

GERIATRICS

If you originally purchased good healthy stock and cared for your dog throughout his life, there is no reason why you cannot expect your dog to live to a ripe old age. With research and the remarkable foods produced for dogs, especially in this past decade or so, his chances of longevity have increased considerably. If you have cared for him well, your dog will be a sheer delight in his old age, just as he was while in his prime.

We can assume you have fed him properly if he is not too fat. If there has been no great illness, then you will find that very little additional care and attention are needed to keep him well. Exercise is still essential, as is proper food, booster shots, and tender loving care.

Ch. Dot's Penny Poo Bear is pictured winning at 11½ years of age at a recent show. The sire was Beholda Blueprint ex Jim's Pollyanna. Owned by Dorothy Gaunt of West Covina, California. Missy Yuhl photo.

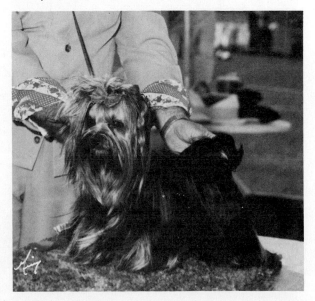

American and Canadian Ch. Wildweir Candytuft, owned by Elissa Taddie. Candy is still alive at 16 years of age and has all her teeth! Her sire was Ch. Wildweir Pomp N' Circumstance, a top sire, and Wildweir Scarlet Ribbons, a top dam.

When discussing geriatrics, the question of when a dog becomes old or aged usually is asked. We have all heard the old saying that one year of a dog's life is equal to seven years in a human. This theory is strictly a matter of opinion, and must remain so, since so many outside factors enter into how quickly each individual dog "ages." Recently, a new chart was devised that is more realistically equivalent:

DOG	HUMAN
6 months	10 years
1 year	15 years
2 years	24 years
3 years	28 years
4 years	32 years
5 years	36 years
6 years	40 years
7 years	44 years
8 years	48 years
9 years	52 years
10 years	56 years
15 years	76 years
21 years	100 years

It must be remembered that such things as serious illnesses, poor food and housing, general neglect, and poor beginnings as puppies will take their toll of a dog's general health and age him more quickly than a dog that has led a normal, healthy life. Let your veterinarian help you determine an age bracket for your dog in his later years.

While good care should prolong your dog's life, there are several "old age" disorders to watch for no matter how well he may be doing. The tendency toward obesity is the most common, but constipation is another. Aging teeth and a slowing down of the digestive processes may hinder digestion and cause constipation, just as any major change in diet can bring on diarrhea. There is also the possibility of loss or impairment of hearing or eyesight which will also tend to make the dog wary and distrustful. Other behavioral changes may result as well, such as crankiness, loss of patience, and lack of interest; these are the most obvious changes. Other ailments may manifest themselves in the form of rheumatism, arthritis, tumors and warts, heart disease, kidney infections, male prostatism, and female disorders. Of course, all these require a veterinarian's checking the degree of seriousness and proper treatment.

Even if a heart condition develops, there is still no reason to believe your dog cannot live to an old age. A diet may be necessary, along with medication and limited exercise, to keep the condition under control. In the case of deafness, or partial blindness, additional care must be taken to protect the dog, but neither infirmity will in any way shorten his life. Prolonged exposure to temperature variances; overeating; excessive exercise; lack of sleep; or being housed with younger, more active dogs, may take an unnecessary toll on the dog's energies and induce serious trouble. Good judgment, periodic veterinary checkups, and individual attention will keep your dog with you for many added years.

DOG INSURANCE

Much has been said for and against canine insurance, and much more will be said before this kind of protection for a dog becomes universal and/or practical. There has been talk of establishing a Blue Cross-type plan similar to the one now existing for humans. However, the best insurance for your dog is *you*! Nothing compensates for tender, loving care. Like the insurance policies for humans, there will be a lot of fine print in the contracts revealing that the dog is not covered after all. These limited conditions usually make the acquisition of dog insurance expensive and virtually worthless.

Blanket coverage policies for kennels or establishments that board or groom dogs can be an advantage, especially in transporting dogs to and from their premises. For the one-dog owner, however, whose dog is a constant companion, the cost for limited coverage is not necessary.

THE HIGH COST OF BURIAL

Pet cemeteries are mushrooming across the nation. Here, as with humans, the sky can be the limit for those who wish to bury their pets ceremoniously. The costs of plots and satin-lined caskets, grave stones, flowers, and so on run the gamut of prices to match the emotions and means of the owner.

IN THE EVENT OF YOUR DEATH

This is a morbid thought perhaps, but ask yourself the question, "If death were to strike at this moment, what would become of my dogs?"

Perhaps you are fortunate enough to have a relative, child, spouse, or friend who would take over immediately, if only on a temporary basis. Perhaps you have already left instructions in your last will and testament for your pet's housing, as well as a stipend for its care.

Provide definite instructions before a disaster occurs or your dogs are carted off to the pound to be destroyed, or stolen by commercially inclined neighbors with "resale" in mind. It is a simple thing to instruct your lawyer about your wishes in the event of sickness or death. Leave instructions as to feeding and care, posted on your kennel room or kitchen bulletin board, or wherever your kennel records are kept. Also, tell several people what you are doing and why. If you prefer to keep such instructions private, merely place them in sealed envelopes in a known place with directions that they are to be

Yorkholm's Tiny Teazer, whelped in 1982, is a puppy hopeful at the Livonia, Michigan, kennels of Muriel Holman.

opened only in the event of your death. Eliminate the danger of your animals suffering in the event of an emergency that prevents your personal care of them.

KEEPING RECORDS

Whether you have one dog or a kennel full of them, it is wise to keep written records. It takes only a few moments to record dates of inoculations, trips to the vet, tests for worms, etc. It can avoid confusion or mistakes such as having your dog not covered by immunization if too much time elapses between shots because you have to guess at the date of the last shot.

Make the effort to keep all dates in writing rather than trying to commit them to memory. A rabies injection date can be a problem if you have to recall that "Fido had the shot the day Aunt Mary got back from her trip abroad, and let's see, I guess that was around the end of June."

In an emergency, these records may prove their value if your veterinarian cannot be reached and you have to call on another, or if you move and have no case history on your dog for the new veterinarian. In emergencies, one does not always think clearly or accurately, and if dates, types of serums used, and other information are a matter of record, the veterinarian can act more quickly and with more confidence.

TATTOOING

Ninety percent success has been reported on the return of stolen or lost dogs that have been tattooed. More and more this simple, painless, inexpensive method of positive identification for dogs is being reported all over the United States. Long popular in Canada, along with nose prints, the idea gained interest in this country when dognapping started to soar as unscrupulous people began stealing dogs for resale to research laboratories. Pet dogs that wander off and lost hunting dogs have always been a problem. The success of tattooing has been significant.

Tattooing can be done by the veterinarian for a minor fee. There are several dog "registries" that will record your dog's number and help you locate it should it be lost or stolen. The number of the dog's American Kennel Club registration is most often used on thoroughbred dogs, or the owner's Social Security number in the case of mixed breeds. The best place for the tattoo is the groin. Some prefer the inside of an ear, and the American Kennel Club has ruled that the judges officiating at the AKC dog shows not penalize the dog for the tattoo mark.

The tattoo mark serves not only to identify your dog should it be lost or stolen, but offers positive identification in large kennels where several litters of the same approximate age are on the premises. It is a safety measure against unscrupulous breeders "switching" puppies. Any age is a proper age to tattoo, but for safety's sake, the sooner the better.

The buzz of the needle might cause your dog to be apprehensive, but the pricking of the needle is virtually painless. The risk of infection is negligible when done properly, and the return of your beloved pet may be the reward for taking the time to insure positive identification for your dog.

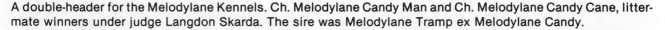

A double-header for the Melodylane Kennels. Ch. Melodylane Candy Man and Ch. Melodylane Candy Cane, littermate winners under judge Langdon Skarda. The sire was Melodylane Tramp ex Melodylane Candy.

A beautiful shot of one of Maybelle Neuguth's Yorkshire Terriers, photographed in the 1960s.

Ch. Kesar's Teddie Bear and Kesar's Barbie Doll, bred by Barbara Bedsted, are pictured here winning at a recent show. The sire was Best in Show Ch. Shadomountin Sparrow Hawk ex Ch. Stardust's Qt Cupcake.

Ch. Tiffany's Hope For Two, the first champion finished by the Estugo Kennels of Hugo J. Ibanez and Stephen B. Maggard. This charming photograph was taken of Hope in 1978.

CHAPTER SIXTEEN

Pursuing a Career in Dogs

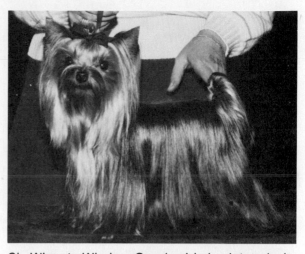

Ch. Wingate Windsor Gayelyn Iris is pictured winning at the 1982 National Specialty Show in New York City. Bred, owned, and handled by Suzanne Jones of New York Mills, New York.

One of the biggest joys for those of us who love dogs is to see someone we know or someone in our family grow up in the fancy and go on to enjoy the sport of dogs in later life. Many dog lovers, in addition to leaving codicils in their wills, are providing in other ways for veterinary scholarships for deserving youngsters who wish to make their association with dogs their profession.

Unfortunately, many children who have this earnest desire are not always able to afford the expense of an education that will take them through veterinary school, and they are not eligible for scholarships. In the 1960s, during my tenure as editor of *Popular Dogs* magazine, I am happy to say I had something to do with the publicizing of college courses, whereby those who could not go all the way to a veterinary degree could earn an Animal Science degree and thus still serve the fancy in a significant way. The Animal Science courses cost less than half of what it would take to become a veterinarian, and those achieving these titles have become a tremendous assistance to the veterinarian.

We all have experienced the more and more crowded waiting rooms at the veterinary offices, and are aware of the demands on the doctor's time, not just for office hours, but for his research, consultation, surgery, and other expertise. The tremendous increase in the number of dogs and cats and other domestic animals, both in cities and the suburbs, has resulted in an almost overwhelming consumption of veterinarians' time.

Until recently, most veterinary assistance was made up of kennel men or women who were restricted to services more properly classified as office maintenance, rather than actual veterinary aid. Needless to say, their part in the operation of a veterinary office is both essential and appreciated, as are the endless details and volumes of paperwork capably handled by office secretaries and receptionists. However, still more of a veterinarian's duties could be handled by properly trained semi-professionals.

With exactly this additional service in mind, many colleges are now conducting two-year courses in animal science for the training of such para-professionals, thereby opening a new field for animal technologists. The time saved by the assistance of these trained technicians, who now relieve the veterinarians of the more mechanical chores and allow them additional time for diagnosing and general servicing of their clients, will be beneficial to all involved.

"Delhi Tech," the State University Agricultural and Technical College at Delhi, New York, was one of the first to offer the required courses for this degree. Now, many other institutions of learning are offering comparable courses at the college level. Entry requirements are usually that each applicant must be a graduate of an approved high school or have taken the State University admissions examination. In addition, each applicant for the Animal Science Technology program must have some previous credits in mathematics and science, with chemistry an important part of the science background.

Vale Yorkshire Terriers, photographed in the 1950s.

The program at Delhi was a new educational venture dedicated to the training of competent technicians for employment in the biochemical field, and has been generously supported by a five-year grant, designated as a "Pilot Development Program in Animal Science." This grant provided both personal and scientific equipment with obvious good results when it was done originally pursuant to a contract with the United States Department of Health, Education, and Welfare. Delhi is a unit of the State University of New York and is accredited by the Middle States Association of Colleges and Secondary Schools. The campus provides offices, laboratories, and animal quarters, and is equipped with modern instruments to train technicians in laboratory animal care, physiology, pathology, microbiology, anesthesia, X-ray, and germ-free techniques. Sizable animal colonies are maintained in air-conditioned quarters: animals housed include mice, rats, hamsters, guinea pigs, gerbils, and rabbits, as well as dogs and cats.

First-year students are given such courses as livestock production, dairy food science, general, organic and biological chemistry, mammalian anatomy, histology and physiology, pathogenic microbiology, and quantitative and instrumental analysis, to name a few. Second year students matriculate in general pathology, animal parasitology, animal care and anesthesia, introductory psychology, animal breeding, animal nutrition, hematology and urinalysis, radiology, genetics, food sanitation and meat inspection, histological techniques, animal laboratory practices, and axenic techniques. These, of course, may be supplemented by electives that prepare the student for contact with the public in the administration of these duties. Such recommended electives include public speaking, botany, animal reproduction, and other related subjects.

In addition to Delhi, one of the first to offer this program was the State University of Maine. Part of their program offered some practical training for the students at the Animal Medical Center in New York City. Often after this initial "in the field" experience, the students could perform professionally, immediately upon entering a veterinarian's employ, as personnel to do laboratory tests, x-rays, blood work, fecal examinations, and general animal care. After the courses at college, they were equipped to perform all of the following procedures as para-professionals:

* Recording of vital information relative to a case. This would include such information as the client's name, address, telephone number, and other facts pertinent to the visit. The case history would include the breed, age of animal, its sex, temperature, etc.
* Preparation of the animal for surgery.
* Preparation of equipment and medicaments to be used in surgery.
* Preparation of medicaments for dispensing to clients on prescription of the attending veterinarian.
* Administration and application of certain medicines.
* Administration of colonic irrigations.
* Application or changing of wound dressings.
* Cleaning of kennels, exercise runs, and kitchen utensils.
* Preparation of food and the feeding of patients.
* Explanation to clients on the handling and restraint of their pets, including needs for exercise, house training, and elementary obedience training.

The Yorkie is Sun Sprite Jadestone Doll, photographed in 1981. Bred by Elda and Nathan Tropper, owned by Janice Williams.

* First-aid treatment for hemorrhage, including the proper use of tourniquets.
* Preservation of blood, urine, and pathologic material for the purpose of laboratory examination.
* General care and supervision of the hospital or clinic patients to insure their comfort. Nail trimming and grooming of patients.

Credits are necessary, of course, to qualify for this program. Many courses of study include biology, zoology, anatomy, genetics, and animal diseases, and along with the abovementioned courses, the fields of client and public relations are touched upon, as well as a general study of the veterinary medical profession.

By the mid-seventies there were a reported 30,000 veterinarians practicing in the United States. It is estimated that within the following decade more than twice that number will be needed to take proper care of the domestic animal population in this country. While veterinarians are graduated from twenty-two accredited veterinary colleges in this country and Canada, recent figures released by the Veterinary Medical Society inform us that only one out of every seven applicants is admitted to these colleges. It becomes more and more obvious that the para-professional person will be needed to back up the doctor.

Students having the desire and qualifications to become veterinarians, however, may suffer financial restrictions that preclude their education and licensing as full-fledged veterinarians. The Animal Science Technologist with an Associate degree in Applied Science may very well become the answer as a profession in an area close to their actual desire.

Their assistance in the pharmaceutical field, where drug concerns deal with laboratory animals, covers another wide area for trained assistants. The career opportunities are varied and reach into job opportunities in medical centers, research institutions, and government health agencies; at present, the demand for graduates far exceeds the current supply of trained personnel.

Kelli, owned by Charlene Roland of Charleston, West Virginia.

As to financial remuneration, beginning yearly salaries are relatively low and estimated costs of basic college expenses relatively high, but the latter include tuition, room and board, college fees, essential textbooks, and limited personal expenses. These personal expenses, of course, will vary with individual students, as well as their other expenses, though the costs are about half of those involved in becoming a full-fledged veterinarian.

Those interested in pursuing a career of this nature might obtain the most current list of accredited colleges and universities offering these programs by consulting the American Veterinary Medical College, 600 S. Michigan Avenue, Chicago, Illinois 60605.

As the popularity of this profession increased, additional attention was given to the list of services, and the degrees to which one could aspire was expanded. There are para-professionals with Associate of Science degrees, and some colleges and universities have extended the courses to four years' duration which lead to Bachelor of Science degrees.

Yorkholms Chantilly Lace, owned by Muriel Holman of Livonia, Michigan. The sire was Trivar's Wee Master Ashley ex Dandy's Sweet Candy.

Barbara Humphries, handler for the Nikko Kennels, enjoys an afternoon with some of the Nikko Yorkies, owned by Gloria and Stanley Lipman in Escondido, California.

At the University of Minnesota Technical College, a two year course offers a degree of Associate in Applied Science after the successful completion of 108 credit hours. This Animal Health Technology course prepares the students for future careers in the following fields:
* Laboratory Animal Technician (Junior)
* Experimental Animal Technician
* Clinical Laboratory Animal Assistant
* Laboratory Animal Assistant in Radiology
* Laboratory Animal Research Assistant
* Small Animal Technician (General)
* Small Animal Veterinarian's Assistant
* Small Animal Veterinarian's Receptionist
* Animal Hospital Technician
* Zoo Technician
* Large Animal Technician (General)
* Large Animal Veterinarian's Receptionist
* Large Animal Clinic Assistant
* Meat Animal Inspection Technician

PART-TIME KENNEL WORK

Youngsters who do not wish to go on to become veterinarians or animal technicians can get valuable experience and extra money by working part-time after school and on weekends, or full-time during summer vacations, in a veterinarian's office. The exposure to animals and office procedure will be time well spent.

Kennel help is also an area that is wide open for retired men and women. They are able to help out in many areas where they can learn and stay active, and most of the work allows them to set their own pace. The understanding and patience that age and experience brings is also beneficial to the animals they will deal with; for their part, these people find great reward in their contribution to animals and in keeping active in the business world as well.

PROFESSIONAL HANDLING

For those who wish to participate in the sport of dogs and whose interests or abilities do not center around the clinical aspects of the fancy, there is yet another avenue of involvement.

For those who excel in the show ring, who enjoy being in the limelight and putting their dogs through their paces, a career in professional handling may be the answer. Handling may include a weekend of showing a few dogs for special clients, or it may be a full-time career that can also include boarding, training, conditioning, breeding, and showing dogs for several clients.

Depending on how deep is your interest, the issue can be solved by a lot of preliminary consideration before it becomes necessary to make a decision. The first move would be to have a long, serious talk with a successful professional

Ch. Nikko's Pettising, owned by Gloria Lipman, is pictured winning under judge Tom Stevenson at a 1980 show. Handled here by Allan Chambers, assistant to Barbara Humphries, who usually handled Pettising during her show ring career.

Park Royal Bundle of Joy, handled by Jo Ann Noffsinger for owner Kathy Park of Hacienda Heights, California. Judge Robert Wills gave Joy this 3-point major win at a recent Las Vegas show.

handler to learn the pros and cons of such a profession. Watching handlers in action from ringside as they perform their duties can be revealing. A visit to their kennels for an on-the-spot revelation of the behind-the-scenes responsibilities is essential. Working for them full or parttime would be the best way of all.

Professional handling is not all glamour in the show ring. There is plenty of "dirty work" behind the scenes twenty-four hours of every day. You must have the necessary ability and patience for this work, as well as the ability and patience to deal with the *clients*—the dog owners who value their animals above almost anything else and would expect a great deal from you in the way of care and handling.

DOG JUDGING

There are also those whose professions, age, or health prevent them from owning, breeding, or showing dogs, and who turn to judging at dog shows after their active years in the show ring are no longer possible. Breeder-judges make a valuable contribution to the fancy by judging in accordance with their years of experience in the fancy, and the assignments are enjoyable. Judging requires experience, a good eye for dogs, and an appreciation of a good animal.

296

DOG TRAINING

Like the professional handler, the professional dog trainer has a most responsible job. You need not only to be thoroughly familiar with the correct and successful methods of training a dog, but must also have the ability to communicate with dogs. True, it is very rewarding work, but training for the show ring, obedience, or guard dog work must be performed exactly right for successful results, and to maintain a good business reputation.

Wildweir Briefcase, handled by Merrill Cohen at a 1969 show. Earl Graham photo.

Training schools are quite the vogue nowadays, with all of them claiming success. Careful investigation should be made before enrolling a dog, and even more careful investigation should be made of their methods and of their actual successes before becoming associated with them.

GROOMING PARLORS

If you do not wish the twenty-four-hour a day job that is required by a professional handler or professional trainer, but still love working with and caring for dogs, there is always the very profitable grooming business. Poodles started the ball rolling for the swanky, plush grooming establishments that sprang up all over the major cities, many of which seem to be doing very well. Here again, handling dogs and the public well is necessary for a successful operation, in addition to skill in the actual grooming of dogs of all breeds.

While shops flourish in the cities, some of the suburban areas are now featuring mobile units which by appointment will visit your home with a completely equipped shop on wheels, and will groom your dog right in your own driveway.

Ch. Johnstoy Ridin' High, pictured winning under judge Merrill Cohen. Owners are Dick and Bronya Johnston of Tyler, Texas.

Ready for bed is Sun Sprite's Devonshire Doll, owned by Cheryl Seney. Doll was bred by Elda and Nathan Tropper of Los Angeles, California.

THE PET SHOP

Part-time or full-time work in a pet shop can help you make up your mind rather quickly as to whether you would like to have a shop of your own. For those who love animals and are concerned with their care and feeding, the pet shop can be a profitable and satisfying association.

Ed and Gert Molik, owners of the Tyrone Hills Kennels in Fenton, Michigan, with judge Nancy Donovan claiming a recent win with one of their champion Yorkies.

297

American, Mexican, and Canadian Ch. Wildweir Ten O'Clock Scholar, owned by Kay Radcliffe.

Wildweir Cover Girl poses prettily for this Frasie Studio photograph. Cover Girl is owned by Mrs. Leslie Gordon, Jr. and Miss Janet Bennett.

Dot's Lucky Strike, owned by Dorothy Gaunt. The sire was Viclar's Sir Midgen.

Ch. Dot's Wish Upon A Star, bred by Dorothy Gaunt and owned by Kathleen Park, Park Royal Yorkies, Hacienda Heights, California.

Ch. Melodylane Oh Susannah, by Ch. Melodylane Mini Trail ex Melodylane Peppermint Candy, bred by Mary Purvis and co-owned by her and Lois Phelan.

Ch. Melodylane Sweet Stuff, by Gayman's Tom Thumb ex Stacy Peppy, handled by Mary Purvis, her breeder.

Ch. Hampshire Flamboyant, owned and handled by Bonnie Jean James of Oak Ridge, New Jersey.

Ch. Hampshire The Editor scoring a win under breeder-judge Morris Howard of Trivar Kennels fame. The Editor is co-owned by Bonnie Jean James (shown handling) and Mary Ressler of Oak Ridge, New Jersey.

BEST OF WINNERS

ASHBEY PHOTO

Canadian Ch. Tyrone Hills Sweet Lollipop, owned by Ed and Gert Molik of Fenton, Michigan.

Barb Heckerman handles Tyrone Hills Crystal Bleu on the way toward winning his championship title. Breeder-owners are Ed and Gert Molik.

BEST OF BREED OR VARIETY

PHOTO BY K. BOOTH

(Left) The magnificently coated Ch. Mayfair Barban Mocha Mousse. Co-owners and breeders are Ann Seranne and Barbara Wolferman, Newton, New Jersey. (Below) American and Canadian Ch. Juana and Jentres Blue Jeans, a top-producing bitch from the Northwest with seven champions to her credit and several pointed. Owner is Juana Phillips, Vancouver, Washington.

Ch. Windsor Gayelyn Treemonisha, owned and shown by Kathleen B. Kolbert of Oxford, Connectticut. This lovely daughter of Ch. Windsor Gayelyn Gilded Lilly was bred by Kathleen B. Kolbert and Marilyn J. Koenig.

(Above) Ch. Maybelle's Snoopy Mardi Gras, owned by Helen Stern of Brooklyn, New York. (Below) Trail West Dixie's Debut with her owner, Dixie Bletch of Clackamas, Oregon.

Ch. Gloamin Christmas Cracker, imported from England and shown during the 1958-1959 show season by owner-handlers Mrs. Leslie Gordon and Miss Janet Bennett of Wildweir Kennels, Glenview, Illinois. His show record included 3 Bests in Show, 1 Specialty win, 11 Toy Groups, 12 Group Placings and 28 Breed wins.

Ch. Trivar's Suds Sipper, top-winning Yorkie for 1978 and 1979, winner of 23 Bests in Show including the national specialty in New York and the Delaware Valley specialty twice. Bred and owned by Johnny Robinson and Morris Howard, Trivar Kennels, Potomac, Maryland.

Ch. Wright's Wee Willie is pictured "winning big" for a four-point major on the way to his championship at the Yorkshire Terrier Club of America supported entry at the Beverly Hills Kennel Club show under breeder-judge Jim Nickerson. Willie was handled by Jan Bridgeforth for owner and breeder Florence Wright.

Ch. Rockin Robyn is pictured winning at the Fort Worth Kennel Club show. Robyn was Winners Bitch and Best of Opposite Sex over top-winning Specials for a five-point major at the Yorkshire Terrier Club of America supported entry show. Owner is Charlene Malcangi of DeWitt, Michigan.

Ch. Broomhill's Jethro, owned by Eugene Hauff of Anoka, Minnesota, is pictured winning the Toy Group under respected Toy breeder Joseph Rowe. Jethro's sire was Ch. Trivar's Tycoon ex Trivar's Hanky Panky.

Ch. Sun Sprite Gemstone, bred by Elda and Nathan Tropper, co-owned by Elda Tropper and Barbara Bedsted. The sire was American and Canadian Ch. Clarkwyn Jubilee Eagle ex Sun Sprite Cybele. Juding was Lois Wolff McManus; handling was Barbara Bedsted.

Ch. Sun Sprite Gemstone, co-owned by Sun Sprite and Kesar Kennels, was sired by Ch. Clarkwyn Jubilee Eagle ex Sun Sprite Cybele. Photo by Lloyd W. Olson Studio.

Ch. Dot's Top Banana, photographed by Missy Yuhl for owner-breeder Dorothy Gaunt.

These winners at a recent show are Ch. Dot's Wish Upon a Star, 2 years old; Ch. Dot's Blue Calico Patches, 11 months old; and Ch. Dot's Bubble Dancer of Rohndon, 11 months old. The breeder was Dorothy Gaunt of West Covina, California.

While shown only a dozen times, wins for Ch. Indigo Night Music included Best Puppy in Match at the Yorkshire Terrier Club of Greater New York Specialty at nine months of age, as well as Best of Breed over 69 entries at the annual Yorkshire Terrier Club of America supported entry event at Riverhead Kennel Club. Music was finished from the Bred-by-Exhibitor Class by owner-handler-breeder Grace Stanton, Indigo Yorkies, Wayne, New Jersey.

Grand Sweepstakes Winner at the 1981 Yorkshire Terrier Club of America Specialty in New York City was Nicole of Les Filles. Breeder-owners of Nicole are D. M. Miles, L. H. Lasiter, and B. J. Fritch; handler-agent is Kathy Bucher of Claremore, Oklahoma. Judge, Dorothy Truitt.

Specialty Best in Show and multiple Group winner Ch. Loveland's Good Buddy was bred by Mary Ann Paul and Bruce Paul, co-owned by them and the Melodylane Kennels, Centerville, Iowa. Handled here by Mary Purvis under judge Mrs. Bettie Krause. The sire was Ch. Fardust's Fury ex Ch. Melodylane Darlin Daisy Mae.

Yorkfold Satin Lady is owned by Clara Powanda of Wheeling, West Virginia.

Silk N Satin Talk of the Town is pictured winning at the prestigious International Kennel Club of Chicago show in 1982 under judge KeKe Blumberg. Bobbi Rothenbach handled for owner Clara Powanda, Silk N Satin Kennels, Wheeling, West Virginia.

Ch. Cupoluv's Fair LeGrand tied for top-producing stud dog in the United States for 1981. This 4½ pound bundle of energy is owned by Zinaida Daricek of Avondale, Pennsylvania.

Ch. Mayfair Barban Verikoko, Number 10 Toy Dog and Number 1 Yorkshire Terrier in the nation for 1981, Kennel Review System. He is pictured here winning the breed at the 1981 Westminster Kennel Club show under judge Frank Sabella. Wendell Sammett handled for owners Ann Seranne and Barbara Wolferman, Mayfair Yorkie House, Newton, New Jersey.

The multiple Group winner, Ch. Melodylane Right On Man, bred by Mary Purvis and owned by her and Freeman Purvis, is pictured winning the Toy Group under judge Charles Hamilton. Right On was one of the Top Ten Yorkies during the 1970s.

Ch. Windsor Gayelyn Show N Tell, bred by Kathleen Kolbert and co-owned by her and Suzanne M. Jones, was whelped in 1976 and is pictured winning the breed under judge Henry Stoecker. The sire was Windsor Gayelyn Jingle Bell ex Windsor Gayelyn.

Ch. Bow Bellsthree Penny Bit, owned by Dorothy Carr and pictured winning a five-point major under judge Kathleen Kolbert at a Yorkshire Terrier Club of America supported entry show.

Dr. and Mrs. Robert Leibling's Ch. Carnaby Piece of the Rock is pictured winning under judge Kathleen Kolbert. One of the Top Ten Yorkshire Terriers for 1981, "Billy" was sired by Ch. Carnaby Rock N Roll ex Ch. Carnaby Celebration; bred and handled by Terence Childs.

Best of Breed at the 1977 Westminster Kennel Club show is American and Canadian Ch. Carnaby Rock N Roll, owned by the Barnhill Kennels in Woodbury, Connecticut. Carnaby dogs were also Winners Dog and Winners Bitch at this show. "Rocky" was also Best of Breed at the Yorkshire Terrier Club of America Specialty Show the day before this win, which was under judge Edna Ackerman. Terence Childs is handling.

Ch. Niki Birth of the Blues, Best of Winners at the 1981 Westminster Kennel Club show in New York City. Judge Frank Sabella gave the fourteen-month-old dog the nod with owner Mary Bratschi of Grand Ledge, Michigan, handling.

Ch. Dot's Call Me Melanie took Best of Breed three times from the classes on the way to her championship. This win was under Irene Phillips Schlintz, creator of the Phillips System ratings for show dogs.

CHAPTER SEVENTEEN

Yorkshire Terrier Statistics and the Phillips System

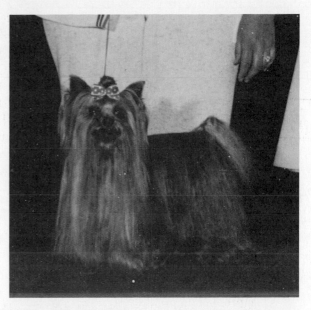

Ch. Melodylane Mini Trail, a multiple Group and Specialty Show winner, was among the Top Ten winners for three years. Owned by Freeman and Mary Purvis of Centerville, Iowa, and bred by Mary Purvis, his sire is Ch. Northshire's Mazel Tov ex Melodylane Patti Marle.

As Yorkshire Terriers continued to grow in popularity, it was only natural that their entries at dog shows continued to swell and competition became steadily keener. The larger the entries, however, the more coveted the wins. In 1956, when Irene Phillips created her Phillips System for evaluating show dogs, Yorkshire Terrier fanciers fell right in line with her point system and began keeping records of their dogs' wins to compare them not only with other Yorkshires, but with other Toy dogs and even other dogs of all breeds.

By the 1980s, a quarter of a century later, dog fanciers are still keeping score on the top winners in the breeds. Although many a "system" of making it to the top of a winner's list has been recorded and publicized (or come and gone), there is no denying that they are all based on the most popular, fairest, and most remembered of all systems for naming the top winning dogs in the country.

We may all be proud of the remarkable list of sensational little Yorkies that have already "made their claim to fame." This book would be less than complete if it did not pay tribute in both words and pictures to those Yorkies that have earned their titles by accumulation of Phillips System points, the first compiled system of achievement for the nation's top show dogs.

WHAT IS THE PHILLIPS SYSTEM?

In the mid-fifties Mrs. John Phillips, a woman famous for her Haggiswood Irish Setter Kennels and a judge of many breeds, devised a point system based on the show records published in the *American Kennel Gazette* to record the wins of dogs competing at the dog shows.

As in all sports, competition and enthusiasm in the dog fancy run high, and Irene Phillips—now Mrs. Harold Schlintz—came up with a simple, yet certainly true, method of tallying wins for this competition.

HOW THE SYSTEM WORKS

The Phillips System was designed to measure, with fairness, the difference between a dog show win scored over many dogs and one scored over just a few dogs. For example, a Best in Show win over 1000 dogs should obviously have more significance than a Best in Show scored over 200 dogs. The Phillips System acknowledged this difference by awarding points in accordance with the number of dogs over which a win was scored. Points were awarded for Best in Show and Group Placings only; Best of Breed wins did not count.

The Best in Show dog earned a point for each dog in actual competition; absentees or obedience dogs were not counted. The first place

Ch. Coulgorm Gay Lady, owned by the Wildweir Kennels.

winner in each of the six groups earned a point for each dog defeated in his group. The dog that placed second earned a point for each dog in the group minus the total dogs in the breed that were first. Third in the group earned a point for each dog in the group minus the total of the breeds that were first and second. Fourth in the group earned a point for each dog in the group minus the total of the breeds that were first, second, and third.

Sources for the count were taken from the official records for each dog show as published each month in the *American Kennel Gazette*, the official publication for the American Kennel Club. An individual card was kept on each dog, and on every dog that placed in the Group or won a Best in Show during the entire year. Figures were tallied for publication at the end of each twelve-month period, and a special issue of *Popular Dogs* magazine was devoted each year to presenting the Top Ten Winners in each breed.

The published figures included the total number of points (or number of dogs defeated), the number of Bests in Show, and the numbers of Group Placements. It is extremely interesting to note that as each year passed there was a tremendous increase in the amount of points ac-

crued by the big winners. This fact is proof positive of the amazing success and increase in the number of entries at the dog shows from the mid-fifties, when the system was first created by Mrs. Phillips, to the mid-seventies, when it became a matter of record that the Number One dog in the nation amassed over 50,000 points to claim the title of Top Show Dog in the United States that year. You will recall that each point represented a competitor defeated!

The Phillips System, which Mrs. Phillips not only devised but also compiled during those early years, was sold as an annual feature to *Popular Dogs* magazine, whose editor at that time, Mrs. Alice Wagner, did much to make it the most important rule of success for a show dog. Later, when I took over as editor of *Popular Dogs* in 1967, I carried on the tradition and did the compilation of the figures as well. For the five years during which I tallied the finals for the Phillips System, it was a constant source of enjoyment for me to watch the leading dogs in this country, in all breeds, climb to the top. Because I knew so many others who felt the same way, and since the competition increased with each passing year, I felt that a healthy sampling of the Yorkshire Terriers which have achieved honors in this System should be represented in this book so that they may become a matter of permanent record in the history of the breed.

YORKIES IN 1956—THE SYSTEM'S FIRST YEAR

Our Yorkshire Terriers did well for themselves in the very first year the Phillips System was introduced. Not only did Champion Star Twilight of Clu-Mor top the list of Yorkshires, but it was Number Five on the list of Top Ten Toys with 2,552 points. These points represented three Best in Show wins, eleven Group Firsts, and two Group Seconds. Mrs. Leslie S. Gordon and Miss Janet Bennett, who imported and owned this marvelous little Yorkie, could afford to be proud of their dog.

That was the year that Champion Star Twilight of Clu-Mor was the only Yorkie to win a Best in Show, and his record becomes even more admirable when one considers that of all Yorkshire Terrier entries in the shows, there were only twenty-three Group First wins, nineteen Group Seconds, twenty-three Group Thirds, and twelve Group Fourths for which Yorkies could account.

Champion Blue Velvet of Soham, another import owned by Miss Janet Bennett and Mrs. Leslie Gordon, accounted for four of the Group Firsts. Betty Trudgian's Abon Hassan's Lady Iris came in with two Group Firsts, as did the Gordon-Bennett team's Champion Coulgorm Gay Lady. Our little Yorkshires were off to a good start during the first year in which the Phillips System called attention to show winners.

THE PHILLIPS SYSTEM THROUGH THE FIFTIES

1957

Champion Blue Velvet of Soham moved up to the Top Ten Toy list this second year of the Phillips System by taking the Number Six position. His Best in Show at Somerset Hills under famous dog man Percy Roberts, along with his nine Group Firsts, twelve Group Seconds, three Group Thirds and two Group Fourths, brought his total wins to that date to one Best in Show, fifteen Group Firsts, twenty-seven Placings, and forty-four Bests of Breed. This little dog was a half brother to his kennel-mate, the all-time great in the breed, Champion Star Twilight of Clu-Mor, that ranked Number Five the year before. Though Star Twilight was the only other Yorkshire Terrier to win a Best in Show that year, Yorkies in general accounted for a total of two Bests in Show, nineteen Group Firsts, twenty-five Group Seconds, twenty-two Group Thirds, and twenty-four Group Fourths.

1958

No Yorkshire Terrier placed in the Top Ten Toy Group in 1958, but Champion Star Twilight of Clu-Mor distinguished himself by making the list of Toy dogs with three or more champion offspring for that year. He sired seven champions in 1958, establishing himself as a potent stud in our breed.

Best In Show winner over 932 dogs at the 1954 Wisconsin Kennel Club show was Ch. Star Twilight of Clu-Mor, pictured here with his handler Mrs. Leslie Gordon, Jr. Star Twilight is co-owned by Mrs. Gordon and Miss Janet E. Bennett of the Wildweir Kennels.

1959

No Yorkshire Terrier made the list of Top Ten Toy Dogs for 1959 either, but a newcomer to the scene, Champion Gloamin' Christmas Cracker did make the list as winner for each Toy breed placing in group. This was accomplished by accumulating 1,250 points with one Best in Show, five Firsts in Group, four Group Seconds, one Group Third, and one Group Fourth.

Champion Star Twilight once again produced seven champions during that year, and made the list of producers of five or more champions.

Ch. Buranthea's Doutelle, pictured winning Best in Show at a 1962 dog show. Owned by the Wildweir Kennels of Mrs. Leslie Gordon and Miss Janet Bennett.

THE DECADE OF THE SIXTIES

No Yorkshire Terrier made the list of the Top Ten Toys in 1960, but that is not to say that they were not continuing to climb the lists in number of registrations with the American Kennel Club. Entries were up also, and the breed's popularity continued to grow—in and out of the show ring. At the beginning of this decade, Champion Star Twilight of Clu-Mor was known as the all-time greatest winner and sire of Yorkshire Terriers. Star Twilight was shown 104 times, and won the breed every time out. His total score was twenty-six Bests in Show, eighty-one Group Firsts, and twenty-two Group Placements. He claimed American and Canadian champions as his get, and continued to be a stud force at the kennels of his owners, Mrs. Leslie Gordon and her sister, Miss Janet Bennett.

1960

It was in 1960 that Champion Gloamin' Christmas Cracker won a Best in Show at Land O Lakes under the famous and great dog man, Alva Rosenberg. Cracker also had six Group Firsts to his credit.

In addition, 1960 was the year that the Wildweir Kennels' Champion All Star of Wildweir captured three Group wins, as did Betty Trudgian's Champion Sir Michael of Astolat. The Prizer-Nickerson Yorkie, Champion Grenbar Tippacanoe, won two Group Firsts, and so did the Davis dog, Champion Little Sir Chuck of Ramon.

Champion Little Tim of Nottingham, Stirkean's Springstar, Champion Tid Le Wink, and two Wildweir entries, Wildweir Queen of Hearts and Wildweir Ticket to the Moon, each won a Group First.

1961

The year 1961 saw a Yorkshire Terrier back on the list of Top Ten Toy dogs. In the Number Six spot, Champion Buranthea's Doutelle racked up a total of 4,090 points by winning two Bests in Show, fifteen Group Firsts, twelve Group Seconds, five Group Thirds, and one Group Fourth. Once again, Mrs. Leslie Gordon and sister Janet Bennett had the leading entry, and had won two more Bests in Show by the first month of 1962 with their little Yorkie, handled by Mrs. Gordon, on the Florida Circuit.

This was also the year that *Popular Dogs* featured a statistical survey compiled by Robert Graham, Jr., on the Top Producers for the year. While no Yorkshire Terrier made the list of Top Twelve Sires All-Breeds, a total of thirty-eight Yorkshires were responsible for forty-four champions.

1962

By 1962, the Phillips System ratings were considered so prestigious that *Popular Dogs* that year featured the Top Fifty leaders in all-breed competition. (By this time, the ratings were being compiled by Mrs. Evelyn P. Sidewater.) That article also presented the Top Winner in each individual breed. The Top Yorkshire Terrier was Champion Buranthea's Doutelle, amassing 2,197 points and ranking as Number Nine in the Top Ten Toy Group. Doutelle had won two Bests in Show, four Group Firsts, nine Group Seconds, four Group Thirds, and two Group Fourths.

In 1962, forty-one Yorkshire Terriers sired forty-three champions for the breed, and the breed won three Bests in Show. It was the year that the Gordon-Bennett winning team came up with another Best in Show winner with their Champion Yorkfold's Chocolate Boy, and their Champion Buranthea's Doutelle garnered four Group Firsts during the show season. Their Chocolate Boy won three Group Firsts and Champion Progress of Progresso also won three Group Firsts. Progress and Champion Mr. Kipps of Grenbar were both owned by the Prizer-Nickerson partnership, with Mr. Kipps the winner that year of a single Group First. The Gordon-Bennett's Champion Proud Girl of Clu-Mor also won a Group, as did the Davis dog, Champion Tabordale Pepper Pot, Nancy and David Lerner's Champion Topsy of Tolestar, the Flietinghoff's Champion Kirnels Yum Yum, the Hermel's Champion Lilly of Ramon, the Clark's Champion Toy Clown of Rusklyn, and the Johnson's Champion Pop N Jay Fly By Night.

It was obvious that by the end of 1962 many new names and bloodlines were beginning to appear to further ensure the future of our breed.

1963

The darling little bitch, Champion Proud Girl of Clu-Mor, made it to Number Seven on the list of Top Ten Toys for the year 1963. With 3,150 points, a Best in Show, nineteen Group Firsts, and fourteen Group Placements, Proud Girl was followed by Champion Progress of Progresso and Champion Kirnel's Yum Yum at the top of the breed.

Yorkshire Terriers had reached thirtieth in breed population as determined by individual registrations with the American Kennel Club, which was up from fortieth less than a decade earlier. Registrations were over 2,500 this year.

1964

This is the year that Champion Wildweir Moon Rose was "lucky" Number Seven for Mrs. Leslie Gordon and Miss Janet Bennett. It was their first dog that made the list bearing their own kennel name of Wildweir, and she won a total of 3,650 points to get there. Her record for the show season was three Bests in Show, nineteen Group Firsts, ten Group Seconds, and three Group Thirds. Moon Rose was

Ch. Wildweir Moonrose, bred and owned by Mrs. Leslie Gordon and Janet Bennett, was the winner of 3 Bests in Show, 26 Toy Groups, and 2 Yorkshire Terrier Club of America Specialties. Her sire was Ch. Prince Moon of Clu Mor ex Ch. Rose Petal of Clu-Mor. Whelped in 1961, Moonrose was the dam of a Group-winning champion.

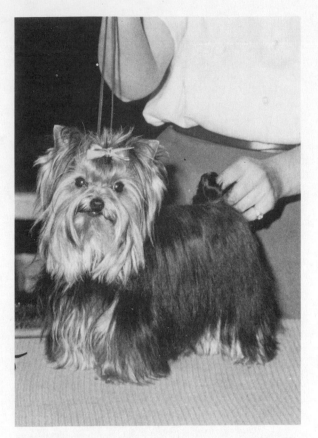

The incredible Ch. Wildweir Pomp N Circumstance, a sire of 95 champions, 4 Best in Show winners and 14 Group winners (including the 4 that went on to Bests in Show). Whelped in 1959, the sire was Ch. Wildweir Cock of the Walk ex Capri Venus. He is the great-great grandsire of Ch. Wildweir Bumper Sticker and the Westminster Best in Show winner, Ch. CeDe Higgens. Bred and owned by Mrs. Leslie Gordon and Miss Janet E. Bennett.

followed by their Champion Wildweirs Skaters Waltz with 2,480 points, four Group Firsts, eight Group Seconds, ten Group Thirds, and six Group Fourths. Their Champion Proud Girl of Clu-Mor was also a winner in the Top Three Yorkshire Terriers published in *Popular Dogs* with 798 points, two Group Firsts, three Group Seconds, and three Group Fourths.

Champion Gayfold Lorelai also won four Groups in 1964. Those winning a single Group First were Champion Hampark Golden Choice, Jeremey's Mr. Impresario, Champion Kirnels Yum Yum, Champion Lilly of Ramon, Champion Pequa De Lovely, Champion Toy Clown of Rusklyn, Champion Yorkfold Jackanapes, Champion Yorkfold Brunobear, and another entry from Wildweir, their up-and-coming Wildweir Darktown Strutter.

1965

Again in 1965, *Popular Dogs* published only the Top Three in each breed, along with the Top Ten in each group, and the Top Ten in all breeds.

No Yorkshire Terrier made the list of Top Ten Toys, but Champion Wildweir Moon Rose again headed the list of Top Ten Yorkshires. For this year, her points added up to 2,305. There was no Best in Show win, but she did manage to rack up seven Group Firsts, twelve Group Seconds, three Group Thirds, and one Group Fourth to get her the top spot. Champion Yorkfold Brunobear was second with an even 2,000 points and a Best in Show. Brunobear also had eight Group Firsts, six Group Seconds, six Group Thirds, and two Group Fourths. Number three on the list of Top Ten Yorkshires was Champion Wildweir Skaters Waltz with 1,087 points, two Group Firsts, four Group Seconds, five Group Thirds, and five Group Fourths.

Champion Wildweir Pomp N' Circumstance headed the list of Top Producing Sires for 1965, having sired fourteen champions for that year. He also shared the Number One spot in the Toy Group with a Pomeranian, Champion Sungold's Gay Cavilier, who also sired fourteen champions.

1966

There were no Yorkshire Terriers in the Top Ten All-breed Winners, nor in the Top Ten Toys in 1966. Many of the breed winners were repeaters, and once again a few newcomers came on the scene.

1966 was also the year that the journal *Dogs In Canada* presented what was called their "Blue Book of Top Winning Dogs." It featured the Top Ten dogs in all-breed competition, the Top Ten in each group, the Top Three Dogs in each breed, and a pictorial gallery of many of the winners.

The "Blue Book's" only difference from the Phillips System was that it gave one point for each dog defeated from Best of Breed to Best in Show. It also issued a certificate to the owner of each of the top winning dogs.

There were no Yorkshire Terriers in the Top Ten All-breed category, but Number Eight in the Toy Group was a dog named Champion Cedarlane Rum N Coke, who had 596 points. The Top Three list was headed, of course, by Rum N Coke, with American and Canadian Champion Leprechauns Fancy at Number Two with 131 points, and Champion Devandales Elizabeth at Number Three with 117.

Ch. Mayfair's Odd Fella is pictured winning Best in Show at the 1968 Progressive Dog Show under Mrs. Merle Smith. The late Mrs. E. Blamey, president of the club, presented the trophy. Wendell Sammet handled for owners-breeders Ann Seranne and Barbara Wolferman, Mayfair Yorkie House, Newton, New Jersey.

1967

My first year as editor of *Popular Dogs* magazine and my first year as compiler of the Phillips System was 1967. There was such interest in the Phillips System at this time that I published the Top Fifty Dogs for that year. As proof of how much the dog fancy had grown in ten years, it should be noted that Number One that year, Champion Salilyns Aristocrat, an English Springer Spaniel owned by Mrs. F. H. Gasow, had tallied 42,364 points, as compared to the 11,029 points won by the Toy Poodle, Champion Blakeen Ding Ding, the Number One winner in 1956, the first year of the Phillips System.

Unfortunately, no Yorkshire Terrier was in the Top Fifty Dogs, but yet another Wildweir dog did make Number Six on the list of Top Ten Toys. Champion Wildweir Fair N Square managed to garner 4,527 points, with three Bests in Show, seventeen Group Firsts, ten Group Seconds, and five Group Thirds. Once again Mrs. Leslie Gordon and her sister Janet Bennett were victorious.

1968

Yorkshire Terriers once again were conspicuous by their absence from the Top Ten All-breed and Top Ten Toys lists.

Mrs. Leslie Gordon and Janet Bennett had the top two Yorkshires in the Top Ten in 1968. They were campaigning their Champion Royal Picador to the Number One Yorkshire Terrier position, while Merrill and Helen Cohen were campaigning their Champion Wildweir Prim N Proper to the Number Two spot. Picador won the Breed at Westchester that year, and took the Yorkshire Terrier Club of America Specialty as well. He was the winner of thirty-five Bests of Breed, fourteen Toy Groups, and eighteen Group Placements. Prim N Proper was the top-winning bitch that year, the top-winning American-bred Yorkshire Terrier, and the top-winning Yorkshire Terrier in the East. She had a total of thirty-nine Bests of Breed, six Toy Groups, and twenty-two Group Placements.

1968 was also the year in which Ann Seranne and Barbara Wolferman saw their Champion

327

Mayfairs Oddfella go all the way to the Number Three spot in the Top Ten Yorkshire Terriers, and became the only Yorkie to win a Best in Show.

Ann Goldman's Champion Starfire Gold Bangle was Number Four, M. Davis' Champion Darn Toot'N of Gayelyn was Number Five, R. and H. Fields' Champion Ru Genes King Corky-Son was Number Six, and F. Cohen's Champion Wildweir Sandwich Man was Number Seven. All scored more than 1000 points. Numbers Eight, Nine, and Ten were Mrs. Geraghty's Champion Bella Donna of Winpal, Mrs. D. Roth's Champion Templevale Pukka-Sahib, and V. Knoche's Champion Ginny K's Little Miss Muffet.

Ch. Starfire Gold Bangle, pictured with handler Evonne Chashoudian, is owned by Mrs. Anne Herzberg Goldman of Santa Monica, California.

1969

Irish and American Champion Continuation of Gleno was the Wildweir Kennels entry in the Top Ten Toy Dogs finals for 1969. He earned over 5000 points for his four Bests in Show, fifteen Group Firsts, eight Group Seconds, two Group Thirds, and two Group Fourths. This charming little import had also won Specialties and Bests in Show in Ireland before being imported to this country by his handler, Mrs. Leslie Gordon, and her sister, Miss Janet Bennett.

Wildweir was responsible for four of the Top Ten Yorkshires of 1969. Merrill Cohen's Champion Wildweir Prim N Proper was Number Three, F. Cohen's Champion Wildweir Sandwich Man was Number Four, and K. Radcliffe's Champion Wildweir Ten O'clock Scholar was Number Seven. The Number Two Yorkie, Champion Ru Gene's King Corky-Son, owned by Ruth and Gene Fields, was the Number One American-bred Yorkshire Terrier, the Number One Western Yorkie, and winner of Best of Breed at the Yorkshire Terrier Club of America Specialty Show, held in conjunction with the Kennel Club of Beverly Hills.

1969 was also the year that Ann Seranne and Barbara Wolferman had two dogs on the list of Top Ten Yorkies. Their Champion Mayfair's Oddfella was Number Five, and their Champion Gaytonglen's Teddy of Mayfair was Number Eight.

F. Geraghty's Champion Yorkfold Jezebel was Number Six, L. Barry's Champion Precious Posy was Number Nine, and J. and D. Scott's Champion Pete's Tiger was Number Ten.

THE SYSTEM IN THE SEVENTIES

As we began the decade of the 1970s that was to herald an even greater popularity for the Yorkshire Terrier, the Phillips System Top Ten Toys found Champion Continuation of Gleno at Number Nine on the list. Gleno had won two Bests in Show during that first year, with eight Group Firsts, six Group Seconds, eight Group Thirds, and two Group Fourths for a total of 4,479 points.

1970

The Number One Yorkshire in 1970, and the Number Three dog in the Top Ten of all Toy breeds went to American and Mexican Champion Camelot's Little Pixie. Bred and owned by Mrs. Lee Sakal of Orange, California, and co-owned and handled by Richard M. Sakal, Pixie was also the Number One Western Yorkshire and Number Thirty-four of all Toys nationwide. He defeated over 9,000 dogs in this one year of campaigning, and became the first Yorkshire to place as high as Number Three in the Top Ten Toys list.

Pixie's year-end total was three Bests in Show, sixteen Group Firsts, four Group Seconds, four Group Thirds, and one Group Fourth—for a total of 9,178 points.

Other 1970 Top Ten Yorkshire Terrier winners were Champion Wenscoes Whynot of Shauma, owned by B. Conaty, at Number Three; Ann Seranne and Barbara Wolferman's Champion Gaytonglen Teddy of Mayfair, at Number Four; the Cohen's Champion Wildweir Prim N Proper and Champion Wildweir Sandwich Man, at Numbers Five and Six; Champion Shareen Mr. Tee See, owned by T. and M. Spilling, at Number Seven; Champion Heart G's Spunky Sparky, owned by C. and J. Mansfield, at Number Eight; F. Geraghty's Champion Yorkfold Jezebel, at Number Nine; and K. Radcliffe's Champion Kajimanor Olde Blue, at Number Ten.

1971

Champion Gaytonglen Teddy of Mayfair went to the top of the Top Ten Yorkshire Terriers list for owners Ann Seranne and Barbara Wolferman by winning 3,804 points in the Phillips System. T. and M. Spilling's Champion Shareen Mr. Tee See moved from the Number Seven spot the year before up to Number Two for this year, followed by Morris Howard's Champion Trivars Tycoon, M. Geraghty's Champion Yorkfold the Witch

Ch. Wildweir Sandwich Man is pictured winning Best In Show under judge William Henry at the 1970 Lancaster Kennel Club show. Owned by Frances Cohen.

Ch. Shareen Mr. Tee See, owned by Thomas and Margaret Spilling, pictured taking Best in Show at the 1970 Columbus Kennel Club show under judge Phil Marsh with Mrs. Spilling handling. Mr. J.R. Allen, mayor of the city of Columbus, presented the trophy. Earl Graham photo.

Hunter, Mrs. Sakal's Champion Camelots Little Sir Hector, F. Cohen's Champion Wildweir Sandwich Man, R.L. Cooper's Champion Cattlestone Chalk Talk, Champion Yot Club's Jiminy Cricket, Champion Heart G's Spunky Sparky, and the Gordon-Bennett entry Champion Continuation of Gleno.

1972

1972 saw all but three of the 1971 contenders back on the charts. True, no Yorkshire Terrier made it to the Top Ten All-breed ratings, nor the Top Ten Toys, but once again Champion Gaytonglen Teddy of Mayfair distinguished himself by garnering 3,799 points and making it to the Number One Yorkshire Terrier for the year.

Champion Wildweir Contrail was Number Two in 1972 with one Best in Show, six Group Firsts, six Group Seconds, and three Group Thirds. Morris Howard's Champion Trivar's Tycoon was once again Number Three. Number Four was a newcomer to the list, W. and D. Naegele's Champion Northshire's Mazel Tov. Numbers Five through Nine were Champion Shareen Mr. Tee See, Champion Yorkfold the Witch Hunter, Champion Heart G's Spunky Sparky, Champion Yot Clubs Jiminy Cricket, and Champion Continuation of Gleno (up one notch from 1971). The Number Ten position went to Commander and Mrs. Leonard's Champion Arriba of Arriso, another newcomer on the list of Top Ten Yorkies.

1973

By the time of the final tabulation for the Phillips System in 1973, Champion Wildweir Contrail had moved up to Number One for the year. The magazine did not feature a Top Ten in Toys for 1973, nor did it feature a Top Ten in All-breeds. But the Top Ten Yorkies were listed, and showed that Champion Mayfair Barban Loup De Mer was Number Two. This homebred entered by Ann Seranne and Barbara Wolferman found his kennelmate, Champion Mayfair Barban Yam N Yelly, in the Number Four spot, and their other kennelmate, Champion Gaytonglen Teddy of Mayfair, took the Number Five position. Number Three went to Morris Howard and Johnny Robinson's Champion Trivars Tycoon for the third year in a row.

Two Yorkies bred by the Clarkwyn Kennels' breeding made the list. Number Six was R. S. Jenkins' Champion Clarkwyn Jubilee Eagle, while Number Seven was Champion Clarkwyn *Jamboree* Eagle, owned by A. C. and F. H. Hattori. Champion Kirnels Buckaroo owned by Mr. and Mrs. K. S. Fietinghoff was Number Eight, and the Wildweir Kennels entry, Champion Continuation of Gleno, was Number Nine, followed by F. C. Geraghty's Champion Yorkfold the Witch Hunter at Number Ten.

Irish and American Ch. Continuation of Gleno, shown in 1969 through 1973, had a total of 5 Bests in Show, 2 Specialty Bests in Show, and 28 Group Placings to his credit. Whelped in 1966 and bred by Mrs. Eugene Weir, he was imported by his owner-handlers Mrs. Leslie Gordon and Miss Janet Benett. The sire was English, Irish, Japanese Ch. Wedgwood's Starmist Joybelle of Gleno.

American and Canadian Ch. Carnaby Rock N Roll is pictured winning the Veteran Dog Class at nine years of age. This was Rocky's last appearance in the show ring, and wound up his record with 6 Bests in Show, 40 Group Firsts, and 150 Bests of Breed. He won the Breed at Westminster in 1975 and 1977, and is the sire of at least 25 champions. Always breeder-owner-handled by Terence Childs, of Barnhill Kennels, Woodbury, Connecticut, Rocky is co-owned by Joseph R. Champagne.

A NEW RATING SYSTEM IN 1975

By 1975, *Popular Dogs* magazine was no longer in the business of rating dogs, and a new rating system had been established in a magazine called *Showdogs*. Their rating system was featured in the April 1976 issue, and listed the 1975 Top Twenty in the all-breed category. There were no Yorkshire Terriers listed in the Top Twenty, but it is interesting to note that within the two decades from the time the Phillips System had started, the top-winning dog for this year had earned 72,818 points to be Number One—more than a slight indication that dog show entries were still skyrocketing, and that competition was keener than even for these top awards.

Showdogs also listed the Top Ten in each Group, and Ann Seranne and Barbara Wolferman's Champion Mayfair Barban Loup De Mer was Number Nine in the Group listing and the Number One Yorkie with 5,963 points, Trivar Kennels had a new entry this year that took them to the Number Two spot among Yorkies; Trivar's Gold Digger had 3,760 points representing that many dogs defeated for the year. Numbers Three through Eight were Carnaby Rock and Roll, Champion Melody Lane Mini Trail, Champion Doodletown Counterpoint, Champion Judabobs I'm A Tiger, Champion Mayfair Barban Marzipan, and Gait Moor Little Big Man. Number Nine went to a little dog destined to reach the pinnacle of success in the show world, as Champion CeDe Higgens was within a few years to go on to a Best in Show at Westminster after a fantastic success in the show rings. The Number Ten winner was Champion Arslan Darwin Darby.

1977 BRINGS ANOTHER CHANGE

By 1977, the rating system had once again shifted to yet another magazine, and this year appeared in *Shows & Dogs*. It listed Champion CeDe Higgens as Number Four All-breeds with a total of 37,467 points. This made him Number One Toy Dog and, naturally, Number One Yorkshire Terrier as well. He was the first Yorkshire Terrier ever to make the Top Ten in an All-breed listing in the history of our rating systems; truly an accomplishment of which to be proud.

It was also at this point in time that it became evident that magazines were "coming and going" and that individual breed publications were featuring their own rating systems with variations on a theme. None could actually use the title of Phillips System, but each changed the scoring just enough to warrant their own claim to tallying the score. It is proof positive that competition in the dog fancy was incentive enough to keep interest high, in spite of the

Stud Dog Class winners at a recent Yorkshire Terrier Club of St. Louis were Melodylane Blu Miss, handled by owner Tim Lehmann; Melodylane Forever Amber, handled by owner Mary Ann Paul; Ch. Melodylane Mini Trail, handled by Mary Purvis; Melodylane Right On Man, handled by Freeman Purvis; and Melodylane Oh Susannah, handled by Lois Phelan. The judge was Stanley Hansen. All these little dogs finished for their championships at a later date. This was a truly memorable day for Mary Purvis and her Melodylane Kennels, where all were bred.

many differences and requirements, to the point where one almost needed a book of instructions to follow each breed listing.

There was so much interest, as a matter of fact, that Irene Phillips, now Mrs. Harold Schlintz, took on the tremendous task of compiling a list of the Great Show Dogs of America, 1955-1966, which was then featured in consecutive issues of *Show Dogs* magazine. In the January 1977 issue, she presented the Top Producers for the Yorkshire breed during this period, and all in the Top Five were owned or bred by the Wildweir Kennels. Champion Star Twilight of Clu-Mor was Number One, followed by American and English Champion Buranthea's Doutelle, Champion Blue Velvet of Soham, Champion Proud Girl of Clu-Mor, and Champion Wildweir Moon Rose.

1978

In 1978, Champion Trivar's Suds Sipper was the Number One winner for the year. Champion CeDe Higgens, owned by the Switzers, was Number Two, and Champion Wildweir Bumper Sticker was Number Three. Champion Robtell Sting, also owned by the Switzers, was Number Four, and D. E. Lascoutx and J. F. Joly III's Champion Andora's El Bandido was Number Five. In sixth place was Champion Mayfair Barban Quinnat, and Champion Mayfair Barban Yohoo was tenth, both dogs owned by Ann Seranne and Barbara Wolferman. Number Seven was Champion Jofre's Mister Ramblin Man, owned by J. M. and D. French; Number Eight was K. M. and E. L. Bucher's Champion Shadomountin Sparrow Hawk. C. J. Fencl's Champion Kajo's Sassafras was Number Nine.

Ch. Wildweir Bumper Sticker, winner of 12 Bests in Show, 9 Specialties, 62 Toy Group Firsts, 87 Group Placings, and 151 Bests of Breed. This grandson of Ch. Wildweir Fair N Square was born in 1975 and was sired by Ch. Doodletown Counterpoint ex Wildweir Date-Line. Bred, owned, and shown by Mrs. Leslie Gordon, Jr., and Miss Janet E. Bennett, Wildweir Kennels.

Top-winning Yorkshire Terrier for 1978 and 1979 was Ch. Trivar's Suds Sipper. Bred and owned by Johnny Robinson and Morris Howard of the Trivar Kennels in Potomac, Maryland. This Best of Breed win was under judge Ken Miller.

1979

At the end of 1979, Champion Mayfair Barban Quinnat had moved up to the Number One position, and Champion Trivar's Suds Sipper was Number Two. Champion Wildweir Bumper Sticker repeated in the Number Three spot, with Champion Shadomountin Sparrow Hawk as Number Four. Champion Robtell Sting was Number Five; Champion Kajo's Sassafras was Number Six; and a newcomer to the ranks, Champion Siresis Delta Tee, owned by S. and R. Iseri, was Number Seven. Number Eight also went to a newcomer to the list, A. M. Johnson's Champion Pegmates' Man About Town. Number Nine was Kathleen Kolbert's Champion Wynsipp's Mr. Dinks, and Number Ten was Champion Loveland's Good Buddy, owned by B. and M. A. Paul, and F. and M. Purvis.

1980

Champion Wildweir Bumper Sticker was Number One on the charts in 1980, with Champion Mayfair Barban Quinnat in the Number

Two spot. Numbers Three through Ten were Champion Barban Verikoko, Champion Trivar's Suds Sipper, Champion Shadomountin Sparrow Hawk, Champion Lovelands Good Buddy, Champion Wynsippis Mr. Dinks, Champion Pegmate's Man About Town, Champion Robtells Sting, and Champion Kajo's Sassafras.

Ch. Mayfair Barban Quinnat wins one of his many Bests in Show. Wendell Sammet handled for owners Ann Seranne and Barbara Wolferman, Mayfair Yorkie House, Newton, New Jersey. Judge at this 1979 show was E. Irving Eldredge. Ashbey photo.

Stepping out in the Toy Group at the 1981 Westminster Kennel Club show is Ch. Mayfair Barban Verikoko with handler Wendell Sammet. "Koko" is co-owned by Ann Seranne and Babara Wolferman of the Mayfair Yorkie House. They are also co-breeders of this excellent showman.

1981

Champion Mayfair Barban Verikoko climbed into the Number One spot for 1981, and another Trivar entry, Champion Trivar's Cookie Monster, went all the way to the Number Two position in his first appearance among the Top Ten. Champion Wildweir Bumper Sticker reverted to his Number Three spot, while Champion Pegmates Man About Town came in at Number Four. There were two Barbee dogs on the chart for Top honors: Number Five went to Champion Barbee Good Time Charlie, and Number Eight was the Switzers' Champion Barbee Denaire Dickens. Number Six was A. Walsh's Champion Penney's Touch of Class, and Number Seven was J. Ashe's Champion Jen's Chiquita. Number Nine was J. Hathhorn's Champion Carousel's The Show Biz Kid, and Number Ten was A. M. Walkmaster's Champion Amwalk's Tigre De Oro.

At the time this book went to press the 1982 lists were not yet published. However, it is plain to see from the lists already presented that many of the good dogs are repeaters and deserve credit for the consistent winning they do during their show ring careers.

STATISTICS TODAY AND IN THE FUTURE

In the 1980s the leading source for Yorkshire Terrier statistics is unquestionably the *Yorkie Tales* magazine, a monthly publication devoted exclusively to the goings-on in the Yorkie world. It not only lists the Top Twenty Yorkshire Terriers based on the results recorded in the *American Kennel Club Gazette*, but also includes Specialty wins and Best of Breed wins. It also features the Top Winners in Obedience.

There is no doubt that Yorkshire Terriers are at the top of the list of favorite breeds as this book goes to press. "Pet-crazy" America owned over forty-nine million dogs by 1982, not to mention forty-two million cats, twenty-five million birds, and hundreds of millions of other animals, according to the Pet Food Institute statistics, which further report that over four billion dollars a year is spent on pet food, over two billion for veterinary services, and many other millions for shelters, obedience training, and so on.

Much money is spent in pet shops for dog accessories and related items to add to the pleasure of our pets.

Phydeau learns to play Christmas carols. Bred and owned by Virginia Bull, Durrisdeer Kennels, Blairstown, New Jersey.

Ch. Cinderella of Chelsea Beach, owned by Ilse Horvath of Pasadena, Maryland.

Ch. Tiffany's Hope For Two, owned by Hugo J. Ibanez and Stephen B. Maggard Estugo Kennels, Charlotte, North Carolina. She is the dam of International Ch. Estugo's Stargazer.

336

Sun Sprite Miss Twiggy, owned by Clarissa Bronzene, bred by the Sun Sprite Kennels in Los Angeles, California.

Eden Valley Matcho Man, bred by Dolores Kauffman and owned by Jan Chisholm.

Lady Godiva of S. Woodland, bred by V. Miller and owned by Arlene Schwartz of Beachwood, Ohio.

A lovely headstudy of Minted Mindy Blue of Cupoluv, owned by Clara Powanda of Wheeling, West Virginia.

Ch. Estugo's Stella Star, photographed at nine months of age. Co-owned by Hugo Ibanez and Stephen Maggard, Estugo's Kennels, Charlotte, North Carolina. This charming photograph was a cover on a recent issue of a Yorkshire Terrier magazine.

Glossary of Dog Terms

Achilles heel. The major tendon attaching the muscles of the calf from the thigh to the hock.

AKC. The American Kennel Club. Address: 51 Madison Avenue, New York, NY 10010.

Albino. Pigment deficiency, usually a congenital fault, which renders skin, hair, and eyes pink.

Almond eye. The shape of the eye opening, rather than the eye itself, which slants upwards at the outer edge, hence giving it an almond shape.

American Kennel Club. Registering body for canine world in the United States. Headquarters for the stud book, dog registrations, and federation of kennel clubs. It also creates and enforces rules and regulations governing dog shows.

Angulation. The angles formed by the meeting of the bones.

Anus. Anterior opening found under the tail for purposes of alimentary canal elimination.

Apple-head. An irregular roundness of top-skull. A domed skull.

Apron. On long-coated dogs, the longer hair that frills outward from the neck and chest.

Babbler. Hunting dog that barks or howls while out on scent.

Balanced. A symmetrical, correctly proportioned animal; one having correct balance of one part in regard to another.

Barrel. Rounded rib section; thorax, chest.

Bat ear. An erect ear, broad at base, rounded or semi-circular at top, with opening directly in front.

Bay. The howl or bark of the hunting dog.

Beard. Profuse whisker growth.

Beauty spot. Usually roundish colored hair on a blaze of another color. Found mostly between the ears.

Beefy. Overdevelopment or overweight in a dog, particularly hindquarters.

Bitch. The female dog.

Blaze. A type of marking; white stripe running up the center of the face between the eyes.

Blocky. Square head.

Bloom. Dogs in top condition are said to be "in full bloom."

Blue merle. A color designation. Blue and gray mixed with black; marbled-like appearance.

Bossy. Overdevelopment of the shoulder muscles.

Brace. Two dogs (a matched pair) that move in unison.

Breeching. Tan-colored hair on inside of the thighs.

Brindle. Even mixture of black hairs with brown, tan, or gray.

Brisket. The forepart of the body below the chest.

Broken color. A color broken by white or another color.

Broken-haired. A wiry coat.

Broken-up face. Receding nose together with deep stop, wrinkle, and undershot jaw.

Brood bitch. A female used for breeding.

Brush. A bushy tail.

Burr. Inside part of the ear which is visible to the eye.

Butterfly nose. Parti-colored nose or entirely flesh color.

Button ear. The edge of the ear which folds to cover the opening of the ear.

C.A.C.I.B. Award made in European countries to international champion dogs.

Canine. Animals of the Canidae family which includes not only dogs, but foxes, wolves, and jackals.

Canines. The four large teeth in the front of the mouth often referred to as fangs.

Castrate. To surgically remove the testicles on the male dog.

Cat-foot. Round, tight, high-arched feet said to resemble those of a cat.

Character. The general appearance or expression said to be typical of the breed.

Cheeky. Fat cheeks or protruding cheeks.

Chest. Forepart of the body between the shoulder blades and above the brisket.

China eye. A clear blue wall-eye.

Chiseled. A clean-cut head, especially when chiseled out below the eye.

Chops. Jowls or pendulous lips.

Clip. Method of trimming coats according to an individual breed standard.

Cloddy. Thick set or plodding dog.

Close-coupled. A dog short in loins; comparatively short from withers to hipbones.

Cobby. Short-bodied; compact.

Collar. Usually a white marking, resembling a collar, around the neck.

Condition. General appearance of a dog showing good health, grooming, and good care.

Conformation. The form and structure of the bone or framework of the dog in comparison with requirements of the standard for the breed.

Corky. Active and alert dog.

Couple. Two dogs.

Coupling. Leash or collar-ring for a brace of dogs.

Couplings. Body between the withers and the hipbones.

Cowhocked. When the hocks turn toward each other and sometimes touch.

Crank tail. Tail carried down.

Crest. Arched portion of the back of the neck.

Cropping. Cutting or trimming of the ear leather to get ears to stand erect.

Crossbred. A dog whose sire and dam are of two different breeds.

Croup. The back part of the back above the hind legs. Area from hips to tail.

Crown. The highest part of the head; the topskull.

Cryptorchid. Male dog with neither testicle visible.

Culotte. The long hair on the back of the thighs.

Cushion. Fullness of upper lips.

Dappled. Mottled marking of different colors with none predominating.

Deadgrass. Dull tan color.

Dentition. Arrangement of the teeth.

Dewclaws. Extra claws, or functionless digits on the inside of the front and/or rear legs.

Dewlap. Loose, pendulous skin under the throat.

Dish-faced. When nasal bone is so formed that nose is higher at the end than in the middle or at the stop.

Disqualification. A dog that has a fault making it ineligible to compete in dog show competitions.

Distemper teeth. Discolored or pitted teeth as a result of having had distemper.

Dock. To shorten the tail by cutting.

Dog. A male dog, though used freely to indicate either sex.

Domed. Evenly rounded in topskull; not flat but curved upward.

Down-faced. When nasal bone inclines toward the tip of the nose.

Down in pastern. Weak or faulty pastern joints; a let-down foot.

Drop ear. The leather pendant which is longer than the leather of the button ear.

Dry neck. Taut skin.

Dudley nose. Flesh-colored or light brown pigmentation in the nose.

Elbow. The joint between the upper arm and the forearm.

Elbows out. Turning out or off the body and not held close to the sides.

Ewe neck. Curvature of the top of neck.

Expression. Color, size, and placement of the eyes which give the typical expression associated with a breed.

Faking. Changing the appearance of a dog by artificial means to make it more closely resemble the standard. Using chalk to whiten white fur, etc.

Fall. Hair which hangs over the face.

Feathering. Longer hair fringe on ears, legs, tail, or body.

Feet east and west. Toes turned out.

Femur. The large heavy bone of the thigh.

Fiddle front. Forelegs out at elbows, pasterns close, and feet turned out.

Flag. A long-haired tail.

Flank. The side of the body between the last rib and the hip.

Flare. A blaze that widens as it approaches the topskull.

Flashy. Term used to describe outstanding color-pattern of dog.

Flat bone. When girth of the leg bones is correctly elliptical rather than round.

Flat sided. Ribs insufficiently rounded as they meet the breastbone.

Flews. Upper lips, particularly at inner corners.

Forearm. Bone of the foreleg between the elbow and the pastern.

Foreface. Front part of the head; before the eyes; muzzle.

Fringes. Same as feathering.

Frogface. Usually overshot jaw where nose is extended by the receding jaw.

Front. Forepart of the body as viewed head-on.

Furrow. Slight indentation or median line down center of the skull to the top.

Gay tail. Tail carried above the topline.

Gestation. The period during which a bitch carries her young; normally 63 days.

Goose rump. Too steep or too sloping a croup.

Grizzle. Bluish-gray color.

Guard hairs. The longer, stiffer hairs that protrude through the undercoat.

Gunshy. When a dog fears gunshots.

Hard-mouthed. The dog that bites or leaves tooth marks on the game he retrieves.

Hare foot. A narrow foot.

Harlequin. A color pattern; patched or pied coloration, predominantly black and white.

Haw. A third eyelid or membrane at the inside corner of the eye.

Height. Vertical measurement from the withers to the ground or from shoulders to the ground.

Hock. The tarsus bones of the hind leg that form the joint between the second thigh and the metatarsals.

Hocks well let down. When the distance from hock to ground is close to the ground.

Hound. Dog commonly used for hunting by scent.

Hound-marked. Three-color dogs; white, tan, and black, predominating color mentioned first.

Hucklebones. The top of the hipbones.

Humerus. The bone of the upper arm.

Inbreeding. The mating of closely related dogs of the same breed, usually brother to sister.

Incisors. The cutting teeth found between the fangs in the front of the mouth.

Isabella. Fawn or light bay color.

Kink tail. A tail which is abruptly bent, appearing to be broken.

Knuckling over. An insecurely knit pastern joint often causing irregular motion while dog is standing still.

Layback. Well placed shoulders; also, receding nose accompanied by an undershot jaw.

Leather. The flap of the ear.

Level bite. The front or incisor teeth of the upper and lower jaws meeting exactly.

Line breeding. The mating of dogs of the same breed related to a common ancestor; controlled inbreeding, usually grandmother to grandson, or grandfather to granddaughter.

Lippy. Lips that do not meet perfectly.

Loaded shoulders. When shoulder blades are out of alignment due to overweight or over-development on this particular part of the body.

Loin. The region of the body on either side of the vertebral column between the last ribs and the hindquarters.

Lower thigh. Same as second thigh.

Lumber. Excess fat on a dog.

Lumbering. Awkward gait on a dog.

Mane. Profuse hair on the upper portion of the neck.

Mantle. Dark-shaded portion of the coat or shoulders, back, and sides.

Mask. Shading on the foreface.

Median line. Same as furrow.

Molera. Abnormal ossification of the skull.

Molars. Rear teeth used for actual chewing.

Mongrel. Puppy or dog whose parents are of different breeds.

Monorchid. A male dog with only one testicle apparent.

Muzzle. The head in front of the eyes; includes nose, nostril, and jaws.

Muzzle band. White markings on the muzzle.

Nictitating eyelid. The thin membrane at the inside corner of the eye which is drawn across the eyeball. Sometimes referred to as the third eyelid.

Nose. Scenting ability.

Occipital protuberance. The raised occiput itself.

Occiput. The upper crest or point at the top of the skull.

Occlusion. The meeting or bringing together of the upper and lower teeth.

Olfactory. Pertaining to the sense of smell.

Otter tail. A tail that is thick at the base, with hair parted on under side.

Out at shoulder. Shoulder blades set in such a manner that the joints are too wide, hence jut out from the body.

Outcrossing. The mating of unrelated individuals of the same breed.

Overhang. A very pronounced eyebrow.

Overshot. The front incisor teeth on top overlap the front teeth of the lower jaw. Also called pig jaw.

Pack. Several hounds kept together in one kennel.

Paddling. Moving with the forefeet wide, to encourage a body roll motion.

Pads. The undersides, or soles, of the feet.

Parti-color. Variegated in patches of two or more colors.

Pastern. The collection of bones forming the joint between the radius and ulna, and the metacarpals.

Peak. Same as occiput.

Penciling. Black lines dividing the colored hair on the toes.

Pied. Comparatively large patches of two or more colors. Also called parti-colored or piebald.

Pig jaw. Jaw with overshot bite.

Pigeon breast. A protruding breastbone.

Pile. The soft hair in the undercoat.

Pincer bite. A bite where the incisor teeth meet exactly.

Plume. A feathered tail which is carried over the back.

Points. Color on face, ears, legs, and tail in contrast to the rest of the body color.

Pompon. Rounded tuft of hair left on the end of the tail after clipping.

Prick ear. Carried erect and pointed at tip.

Puppy. Dog under one year of age.

Quality. Refinement; fineness.

Quarters. Hind legs as a pair.

Racy. Tall; of comparatively slight build.

Rat tail. The root thick and covered with soft curls—tip devoid of hair or giving the appearance of having been clipped.

Ring tail. Carried up and around and almost in a circle.

Ringer. A substitute for close resemblance.

Roach back. Convex or upward curvature of back; poor topline.

Roan. A mixture of colored hairs with white hairs. Blue roan, orange roan, etc.

Roman nose. A nose whose bridge has a convex line from forehead to nose tip; ram's nose.

Rose ear. Drop ear which folds over and back, revealing the burr.

Rounding. Cutting or trimming the ends of the ear leather.

Ruff. The longer hair growth around the neck.

Sable. A lacing of black hair in or over a lighter ground color.

Saddle. A marking over the back, like a saddle.

Scapula. The shoulder blade.

Scissors bite. A bite in which the upper teeth just barely overlap the lower teeth.

Screw tail. Naturally short tail twisted in spiral fashion.

Self color. One color with lighter shadings.

Semiprick ears. Carried erect with just the tips folding forward.

Septum. The line extending vertically between the nostrils.

Shelly. A narrow body that lacks the necessary size required by the breed standard.

Sickle tail. Carried out and up in a semicircle.

Slab sides. Insufficient spring of ribs.

Sloping shoulder. The shoulder blade which is set obliquely or "laid back."

Snipey. A pointed nose.

Snowshoe foot. Slightly webbed between the toes.

Soundness. The general good health and appearance of a dog.

Spayed. A female whose ovaries have been removed surgically.

Specialty club. An organization that sponsors and promotes an individual breed.

Specialty show. A dog show devoted to the promotion of a single breed.

Spectacles. Shading or dark markings around the eyes or from eyes to ears.

Splashed. Irregularly patched; color on white, or vice versa.

Splay foot. A flat or open-toed foot.

Spread. The width between the front legs.

Spring of ribs. The degree of rib roundness.

Squirrel tail. Carried up and curving slightly forward.

Stance. Manner of standing.

Staring coat. Dry harsh hair; sometimes curling at the tips.

Station. Comparative height of a dog from the ground—either high or low.

Stern. Tail (or rudder) of a sporting dog or hound.

Sternum. Breastbone.

Stifle. Joint of hind leg between thigh and second thigh; sometimes called the ham.

Stilted. Choppy, up-and-down gait of straight-hocked dog.

Stop. The step-up from nose to skull between the eyes.

Straight-hocked. Without angulation; straight behind.

Substance. Good bone; on a dog in good weight; a well-muscled dog.

Superciliary arches. The prominence of the frontal bone of the skull over the eye.

Swayback. Concave or downward curvature of the back between the withers and the hip-bones. Poor topline.

Team. Three or more (usually four) dogs working in unison.

Thigh. The hindquarter from hip joint to stifle.

Throatiness. Excessive loose skin under the throat.

Thumb marks. Black spots in the tan markings on the pasterns.

Ticked. Small isolated areas of black or colored hairs on another color background.

Timber. Bone, especially of the legs.

Topknot. Tuft of hair on the top of head.

Triangular eye. The eye set in surrounding tissue of triangular shape. A three-cornered eye.

Tri-color. Three colors on a dog; typically white, black, and tan.

Tuck-up. Body depth at the loin.

Tulip ear. Ear carried erect with slight forward curvature along the sides.

Turn up. Uptilted jaw.

Type. The distinguishing characteristics of a dog to measure its worth against the standard for the breed.

Undershot. The front teeth of the lower jaw overlapping or projecting beyond the front teeth of the upper jaw when the mouth is closed.

Upper arm. The humerus bone of the foreleg between the shoulder blade and forearm.

Vent. Area under the tail.

Walleye. A blue eye; also referred to as a fish eye or pearl eye.

Weaving. When the dog is in motion, the forefeet or hind feet cross.

Weedy. A dog too light of bone.

Wheaten. Pale yellow or fawn color.

Wheel back. Back line arched over the loin; roach back.

Whelps. Unweaned puppies.

Whip tail. Carried out stiffly straight and pointed.

Wire-haired. A hard wiry coat.

Withers. The peak of the first dorsal vertebra; highest part of the body just behind the neck.

Wrinkle. Loose, folding skin on the forehead and/or foreface.

PERPETUAL WHELPING CHART

```
Bred—Jan.       1 2 3 4 5  6 7 8  9 10 11 12 13 14 15 16 17 18 19 20 21 22 23 24 25 26 27              28 29 30 31
Due—March       5 6 7 8 9 10 11 12 13 14 15 16 17 18 19 20 21 22 23 24 25 26 27 28 29 30 31   April   1  2  3  4

Bred—Feb.       1 2 3 4 5  6 7 8  9 10 11 12 13 14 15 16 17 18 19 20 21 22 23 24 25 26                    27 28
Due—April       5 6 7 8 9 10 11 12 13 14 15 16 17 18 19 20 21 22 23 24 25 26 27 28 29 30      May      1  2

Bred—Mar.       1 2 3 4 5  6 7 8  9 10 11 12 13 14 15 16 17 18 19 20 21 22 23 24 25 26 27 28 29         30 31
Due—May         3 4 5 6 7  8 9 10 11 12 13 14 15 16 17 18 19 20 21 22 23 24 25 26 27 28 29 30 31 June   1  2

Bred—Apr.       1 2 3 4 5  6 7 8  9 10 11 12 13 14 15 16 17 18 19 20 21 22 23 24 25 26 27 28            29 30
Due—June        3 4 5 6 7  8 9 10 11 12 13 14 15 16 17 18 19 20 21 22 23 24 25 26 27 28 29 30   July   1  2

Bred—May        1 2 3 4 5  6 7 8  9 10 11 12 13 14 15 16 17 18 19 20 21 22 23 24 25 26 27 28 29         30 31
Due—July        3 4 5 6 7  8 9 10 11 12 13 14 15 16 17 18 19 20 21 22 23 24 25 26 27 28 29 30 31 August 1  2

Bred—June       1 2 3 4 5  6 7 8  9 10 11 12 13 14 15 16 17 18 19 20 21 22 23 24 25 26 27 28 29            30
Due—August      3 4 5 6 7  8 9 10 11 12 13 14 15 16 17 18 19 20 21 22 23 24 25 26 27 28 29 30 31 Sept.   1

Bred—July       1 2 3 4 5  6 7 8  9 10 11 12 13 14 15 16 17 18 19 20 21 22 23 24 25 26 27 28 29         30 31
Due—September   2 3 4 5 6  7 8 9 10 11 12 13 14 15 16 17 18 19 20 21 22 23 24 25 26 27 28 29 30 Oct.    1  2

Bred—Aug.       1 2 3 4 5  6 7 8  9 10 11 12 13 14 15 16 17 18 19 20 21 22 23 24 25 26 27 28 29         30 31
Due—October     3 4 5 6 7  8 9 10 11 12 13 14 15 16 17 18 19 20 21 22 23 24 25 26 27 28 29 30 31 Nov.   1  2

Bred—Sept.      1 2 3 4 5  6 7 8  9 10 11 12 13 14 15 16 17 18 19 20 21 22 23 24 25 26 27 28            29 30
Due—November    3 4 5 6 7  8 9 10 11 12 13 14 15 16 17 18 19 20 21 22 23 24 25 26 27 28 29 30   Dec.   1  2

Bred—Oct.       1 2 3 4 5  6 7 8  9 10 11 12 13 14 15 16 17 18 19 20 21 22 23 24 25 26 27 28 29         30 31
Due—December    3 4 5 6 7  8 9 10 11 12 13 14 15 16 17 18 19 20 21 22 23 24 25 26 27 28 29 30 31 Jan.   1  2

Bred—Nov.       1 2 3 4 5  6 7 8  9 10 11 12 13 14 15 16 17 18 19 20 21 22 23 24 25 26 27 28 29            30
Due—January     3 4 5 6 7  8 9 10 11 12 13 14 15 16 17 18 19 20 21 22 23 24 25 26 27 28 29 30 31 Feb.    1

Bred—Dec.       1 2 3 4 5  6 7 8  9 10 11 12 13 14 15 16 17 18 19 20 21 22 23 24 25 26 27              28 29 30 31
Due—February    2 3 4 5 6  7 8 9 10 11 12 13 14 15 16 17 18 19 20 21 22 23 24 25 26 27 28      March   1  2  3  4
```

Ch. Carnaby Rock N Roll is pictured winning Stud Dog Class at a Delaware Valley Yorkshire Terrier Club Specialty. With him are his champion get, Ch. Carnaby Rondeley, Ch. Carnaby Rock Around the Clock, Ch. Carnaby Piece of the Ròck, and Ch. Tiffanys Ravishing Ruby. Handled by Terence Childs.

Everblue's Irish Lass is pictured at three months of age in this Jim Easterday photo. Bred and owned by Arlene Mack of Westlake, Ohio, the sire was Ch. Wolpert's Super Boy ex Everblue's Sheer Delight.

Index

This Index is composed of three sections: a general index for informational matter, an index of persons named in the text, and an index of kennels mentioned.

General Index

Index of People

Index of Kennels

A Prayer for Animals

Hear our humble prayer, O God, for our friends the animals, especially for animals who are suffering; for any that are hunted or lost or deserted or frightened or hungry; for all that must be put to death. We entreat for them all Thy mercy and pity, and for those who deal with them we ask a heart of compassion and gentle hands and kindly words. Make us, ourselves to be true friends to animals and so to share the blessings of the merciful.

Albert Schweitzer